VW Beetle
Specification Guide 1968–1980

VW Beetle
Specification Guide 1968–1980

Richard Copping

The Crowood Press

First published in 2010 by
The Crowood Press Ltd
Ramsbury, Marlborough
Wiltshire SN8 2HR

www.crowood.com

British Library Cataloguing-in-Publication Data
A catalogue record for this book is available from the British Library.

ISBN 978 1 84797 167 8

Typeset by Bookcraft Ltd, Stroud, Gloucestershire

Printed and bound in Malaysia by Times Offset (M) Sdn Bhd

contents

preface

The official view of the period 1968 onwards in Volkswagen's history:

> VW's main competitive advantage – the mass production of one model – now threatened to become an ominous disadvantage. … [Nordhoff had] held firmly onto the Volkswagen Saloon, which during his leadership was perfected into the technically mature Beetle, as well as onto the combination of mass production and the global market orientation, leading the Volkswagenwerk to the pinnacle of the European automobile industry. In order to maintain this position far-reaching changes were necessary after Nordhoff's death, who had been Chairman for 20 years.

Volkswagen AG Group Communications, Corporate History Department, Wolfsburg 2003

Like the *VW Beetle Specification Guide* covering the years 1949 to 1967 before it (The Crowood Press, 2007), when compared to the volumes given over to the VW Transporter in both first- and second-generation guises, this book sets aside more space to the vehicle's history.

Total yearly Beetle production numbers clearly far outweighed those of the second-generation Transporter until such a time that the death knell for German manufacture had been sounded, which might lead to the conclusion that there is more ground to cover, as was the case with respect to the first Beetle volume. However, this is not so, as, with the possible exception of the Latin American market, the car's story headed rapidly into stagnation; even the never-bettered achievement of overtaking the Model T Ford as the single most produced model in the history of the automobile paled into insignificance against the background of earth-shaking changes at Wolfsburg. Instead, it is the Beetle's decline and fall from grace that demands careful study, rather than a glib acceptance of what is still Volkswagen's official line. Could the Beetle have survived unscathed if Nordhoff had lived a further ten years? If his successor Kurt Lotz hadn't been so ineffective during his tenure of office, would Volkswagen's third Director General, the ruthless Rudolf Leiding, still have created the avalanche which swept the Beetle away? These are questions that cannot be summarily dismissed in a simple paragraph and after many intervening years still raise the prospect of heated debate in enthusiast circles.

Against this background of a decided lack of interest in further development of the Beetle at Wolfsburg, and with all Volkswagen's attentions turned on the chrysalis that would become their new bestselling Golf, it came as something of a surprise on completion of this volume to discover that the total word count for year-on-year specification changes for the period 1968 to 1980 (and the end of Cabriolet production), was remarkably similar to that in the volume covering the period 1949 to 1967. There had been an assumption that an inordinate amount of space might easily have had to be devoted to the lengthy series of special edition Beetles produced to combat flagging sales, but this was not to be; not that such vehicles are neglected – far from it.

Another chapter of surprises has to be the one allocated to export and particularly to the satellite operations whose varied fortunes help both to explain the Beetle's decline and to contradict the assumption that it was inevitable. To listen to Kurt Lotz denigrating his predecessor's life achievements, few would have thought the Beetle in at least one country would survive as an eagerly sought-after mode of transport for another thirty years, outliving in the process three successive generations of Golf and the reigns of a further four Director Generals at Wolfsburg, all of whom could have insisted that its time was over.

As with the first *VW Beetle Specification Guide*, writing about the car is always a pleasure, albeit in this instance tinged with a little sadness in appreciation of the fact that not only were the years of massive expansion over, but also that any defence of the vehicle might be viewed at least in official circles as the overreaction of a diehard to the ingress of water. Fortunately compensation comes in the form of sharing with all the results of many years of collecting Beetle sales literature and associated print and the delight when collating the imagery to support the text of finding many a car in either original or restored condition to photograph for posterity.

I trust that, like the preceding Beetle volume, this *Specification Guide* will provide an invaluable comprehensive account of the last years of German production and satellite perseverance.

Richard Copping, 2010

the Beetle's creation, survival and success

1935–1967

ABOVE: The unlikely alliance of brilliant designer and now loathed dictator turned a concept into reality.

The question when summarizing the Beetle's story before 1968 is: where to start?

Should it be with Ferdinand Porsche and the designer's repeated attempts to produce a small car suitable for ordinary Germans; a people's car, a *Volks* auto? Might it be with Adolf Hitler and the Nazis, the regime that for its own reasons made Porsche's dreams of creating such a vehicle come true, before waging war and bringing simple Saloon production to a grinding halt? Could it be with the British and particularly with the man sent to the former KdF-Wagen factory with no other orders than to take control, Yorkshireman Major Ivan Hirst; for it was he that brought the

Beetle back from the grave, satisfying the requirements for much-needed personnel transport in the process? Or ought it to be with Heinz Nordhoff, the former Opel director appointed to take control at Wolfsburg from January 1948 and who in the following twenty years built a vast Volkswagen empire, transforming the humble Beetle from unwanted ugly duckling to the world's most popular car?

The answer is that each of the individuals or organizations highlighted is so crucial to the Beetle's success story that it would be perfectly feasible to start with any of them, while being equally impossible to leave any one of them out.

FERDINAND PORSCHE AND NAZI GERMANY

With Hitler's formidable support, Porsche had what initially appeared to be an open chequebook and all the facilities available to Germany's dictatorial regime at his fingertips. However, by default his hands were also tied when the Beetle finally took shape. Hitler's seemingly unrealistic demands had to be met, particularly so when it came to what was in fact an impossibly low price tag.

In the paper he'd submitted to win the contract to create a people's car for the German nation, Porsche wrote of the *volkswagen* being 'a complete

The first of the W30 series prototypes being wheeled out of the workshop, presumably before an engine was fitted. (Volkswagen AG)

The W30 series prototypes of 1936–8 vintage looked noticeably different from the car that was launched later in the decade. Note the 'suicide' doors and the knuckle-scraping boot lid. (Volkswagen AG)

Instantly recognizable as the Beetle, this is a publicity shot of the pre-war KdF-Wagen, allegedly available ex-works at 990 Reichsmarks.

and fully practical vehicle', rather than a 'small car whose dimensions are reduced at the expense of handling and life expectancy …'. Similarly, he proposed that the *Volksauto* shouldn't be a car 'with limited power at the expense of handling and life expectancy', but instead a 'fully practical vehicle having the necessary power to achieve normal maximum speeds and climbing capabilities'. It should possess a realistic degree of 'comfortable space within the bodywork'; in summary 'a vehicle with as far as possible foolproof equipment', thus 'reducing servicing to an absolute minimum'. Five 'qualities' that Porsche stated were 'demanded' of the *Volksauto* were:

- the best possible suspension and handling
- a maximum speed in the region of 100km/h
- a climbing capability of around 30 per cent
- closed four-seat body to transport driver and passengers
- the lowest possible purchase price and running costs.

To achieve what he had promised, Porsche offered a car with the fortuitous ingredient of a robust air-cooled engine, ensuring that apart from the vehicle neither freezing nor overheating here was a vehicle that could survive the rigours of an outdoor life for many years. To this recipe Porsche added his own patent and technically advanced torsion-bar suspension.

Hitler's unknowing contribution to the long-term success of the Beetle came through his demand that it should sell for just 990 Reichsmarks, a figure well under that of any car, German or otherwise, sold at the time. Porsche had little option but to shave all possible weight from the *volkswagen's* chassis and body, a hard-to-implement but invaluable plus-point for decades to follow. Similarly, that Hitler guaranteed a vehicle which was more thoroughly tested than any product from the stable of a private manufacturer – trialled to the extent of 2.4 million kilometres through his enforced enlistment of 120 SS troops to test it – ensured that all potentially fundamental flaws in the design were removed long before the *volkswagen* had to stand on its own merits.

Despite such a cavalcade of laudable attributes, the Beetle might easily have been seen in later years as nothing more than a fanciful whim of a far from benevolent dictator; something that could be quietly discarded once Hitler no longer existed. However, the resistance, tacit or otherwise, of German car manufacturers to cooperate in the production of the car they saw as a direct threat to their own livelihoods, led the Nazis to requisition land for the purpose of building a factory where their *volkswagen* could be manufactured. The construction of the monolithic structure known after the war as Wolfsburg was an essential factor in the Beetle's survival in an immediate post-war period of general uncertainty. Hitler was dead and his Nazi regime swept away forever, but the now-ownerless factory remained.

It was undoubtedly fortuitous for the Beetle that Ivan Hirst was chosen as the British officer to take control of the war-torn factory buildings and ungoverned workforce. Although in later years he would claim that the successes achieved during the period of British control were the result of teamwork, few would have agreed with him. While politicians argued over the fate of what for a time appeared to be a factory destined for demolition and well-known names in the world's automotive industry visited to reject the Beetle as unworthy of survival, Hirst persisted in his quest of supplying much-needed transport to the occupying forces, often under the most trying of conditions.

IVAN HIRST IMPROVISES AND SAVES THE BEETLE

Hirst's original intention had been to build the military version of the Beetle as developed by Ferdinand Porsche – the so-called *Kübelwagen*. However, by a quirk of fate this proved impossible. In 1938, Ferdinand Porsche had visited the Budd Corporation in the United States and struck a deal whereby he could build Beetle bodies using Budd technology; techniques that ensured the lightweight body he so desired. In return, it was agreed that should a second option on the

Receiving a genuinely enthusiastic response, the VW38 prototypes were paraded far and wide across Germany, indicating the might of the Nazi sales drive. (Volkswagen AG)

Beetle theme become reality, Ambi Budd – the German subsidiary based in Berlin – would build the bodies. That the next variation after the Saloon was not the Cabriolet it had been assumed it would be, but a military version of the Beetle was regarded as unimportant at the time. After the war, not only was the Budd factory more or less reduced to rubble, but also its fate was to fall into the hands of the Russians, it being located in the Soviet sector of conquered Germany. Without an ongoing source of bodies for the versatile *Kübelwagen*, Hirst turned to the Saloon.

After Ferdinand Porsche, British officer Ivan Hirst was the next key player in the Beetle's survival story. (Volkswagen AG)

Against all the odds, a reasonable quantity of Beetles were manufactured by Hirst and his team. That the numbers were as good as they proved to be, indeed that production didn't grind to a shuddering halt on numerous occasions, was entirely due to the ingenuity of Ivan Hirst. Faced with the inevitable shortages of a war-ravaged country, Hirst improvised. Typical was his response when advised that only three weeks' stock of carburettors remained. Stripping one down, he divided the components into those that could be made within the factory and others that couldn't. From there, he enlisted the services of a camera manufacturer in nearby Brunswick to produce the smaller brass parts such as the float and jets.

Despite what to the eyes and ears of serious-minded motor manufacturers must have appeared to be a tale of unmitigated horror, the number of cars produced and Wolfsburg's general contribution to transport issues was sufficient to instigate the first rumblings of a changed attitude to the future of Volkswagen. Realization that British taxpayers were carrying the hefty costs of food imports into the British zone brought forward the decision that German industry must be sufficiently developed to be able to earn enough foreign currency to pay for such items and with it a fundamental reason why Volkswagen should survive. The decision to strengthen the German management team, a move which led

This famous shot portrays a record-breaking Beetle of the era when the British were in control at Wolfsburg. Shortages often resulted in ad hoc supply solutions, as evidenced by the odd-looking headlights on this car. (Volkswagen AG)

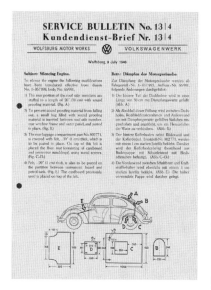

Heinz Nordhoff, Director General of Volkswagen from 1948 to his death in 1968. (Volkswagen AG)

problems, can be summarized in a few short paragraphs.

Speaking some fifteen years after the event, Nordhoff recalled that many in immediate post-war Germany 'were satisfied with any vehicle that would run'. But Nordhoff the engineer, the perfectionist, certainly hadn't been. To him, the Beetle of those days 'had as many faults as a dog has fleas'. However, as he reminded his interviewer, 'you don't kill a dog to get rid of its fleas'. Nordhoff's answer had been to eradicate the faults while

upgrading the presentation so that the car would be of genuine interest to markets other than the relatively fragile home one. This resulted in the introduction of the Export or Deluxe Beetle in the summer of 1949; an altogether superior vehicle with a wider choice of paint colours and a vastly improved finish, a modicum

Major Hirst was anxious to ensure that the Volkswagen wasn't let down by a lack of supportive paperwork and spares. (Volkswagen AG)

to the appointment of ex-Opel man Heinz Nordhoff as general manager, proved to be the next vital move in the Beetle's story.

HEINZ NORDHOFF – A UNIQUE APPROACH

Nordhoff's views relating to both the quality of the Beetles produced by Hirst and the haphazard way in which manufacture was accomplished are well known and, together with the solutions he devised to Volkswagen's

Concerned that production of the Cabriolet would distract Volkswagen from its main goal of ever-increasing numbers of Beetle Saloons, Nordhoff delivered the task of handcrafting the soft-top Beetle to Karmann. This example, which dates from 1949, is located in the Stiftung Museum, Wolfsburg.

of chrome trim and more luxurious interior appointments. Beetle sales spiralled upwards instantly.

Within weeks of joining Volkswagen, Nordhoff had realized the then state of play couldn't continue if the operation was to succeed. Years later he spoke to author Walter Henry Nelson of 'an air of desperation and confusion'. Nordhoff told Nelson how 'seven thousand workers were painfully producing at the rate of a mere 6,000 cars a year – provided it didn't rain too much. Most of the roof and all the windows of the factory had been destroyed. Pools of stagnant water were under foot.' He added that 'no one knew how many man hours it took to build a car, but it must have been 300 or 400'. His answer to the grim prospects at the time had been to address the workforce, advising that 'if we continue in this manner, we shall not continue for long, we must reach one hundred hours per car'. To those assembled the prospect appeared at first hopelessly impossible, but the overall aim that Nordhoff declared was sufficiently

Nordhoff was delighted that Hebmüller opted to build luxury niche-market Beetle coupés while Wolfsburg was engrossed with the mass-market Export or Deluxe model, the Standard Beetle and development of the Transporter.

inspirational that all attending were instantly motivated to follow his lead. 'It is up to us', he said, 'to make this largest of all German motor-car factories a decisive factor for Germany's peacetime economy'.

The third prong to Nordhoff's attack was acknowledged by another key player of the early days, one Otto Höhne, who by 1956 was putting the finishing touches to Volkswagen's new Transporter factory in Hanover. 'One of

Many years of implementing a policy of continual improvement led Nordhoff's Beetle to evolve from a split rear screen, 1948–53, to an oval window, 1953–7, to two sizes of much larger glass, 1957–64, and 1965 onwards.

Essentially Volkswagen's publicity shot demonstrates the changes made during Nordhoff's twenty years as Director General to the rearward appearance of the Beetle – from split panes to large window glass. (Volkswagen AG)

Volkswagen's publicity department excelled itself on the occasion of the arrival of the one-millionth Beetle. The gold-painted, diamanté-encrusted car, now on display in Wolfsburg's Autostadt, was the centrepiece of several days of celebrations.

Nordhoff's Export Beetle, introduced in the summer of 1949, paved the way to spiralling sales both at home and abroad.

The cult of the Beetle and Volkswagen's Director General went hand in hand. A series of specially posed photographs involving the workforce and their leader made perfect sense at the time. (Volkswagen AG)

the first things Nordhoff did', revealed Höhne, 'was to survey world markets and plan a global service organization. No one had even thought that way before!' Nordhoff's demand that service availability be high on the agenda was paralleled by his drive to build an unprecedented sales structure across the world. Despite notable setbacks – both the American and British markets spring to mind initially – in the long term this policy was equally fundamental to Volkswagen's success.

Without doubt, by 1955 and the time of the rightful pageantry surrounding the arrival of the millionth Beetle to be manufactured, Nordhoff's threefold strategy was paying the most handsome of dividends. Production barrier after manufacturing record was set to fall with increasing rapidity and such progress heralded the day when the marketing department's favourite message became a simple statement of worldwide success. 'The Volkswagen is a favourite in 136 countries' resonated against a backdrop of the two-millionth Beetle in December 1957, the three-millionth in August 1959, the four-millionth in November

LEFT: *Throughout the 1950s Volkswagen's products – the Beetle, the Transporter and later the Karmann Ghia – were promoted through the skilful artwork of Bernd Reuters. As with the Cabriolet depicted here, the artist elongated the appearance of the car, streamlined its panels and reduced the size of the occupant in relation to the scale of the vehicle.*

1960 and so on, eventually leading to a new triumph in 1965; the first occasion when more than one million Beetles – 1,090,863 to be precise – were produced in a single twelve-month period.

One further string to Nordhoff's bow guaranteed the Beetle's place at the heart of Volkswagen while he was in charge. In this, the boss of one of the world's largest manufacturing concerns was at odds with at least 95 per cent of the rest of the automobile industry. Speaking on the occasion of the arrival of the five-millionth Beetle in December 1961, Nordhoff summarized the key points in Volkswagen's meteoric rise over the last decade, stressing that 'developing one model of car to its highest technical excellence' was crucial to his strategy. While with others the race to produce new models was paramount, for Nordhoff this was, and always had been, a spurious challenge. Three years earlier when receiving the prestigious Elmer A. Sperry award in November 1958, his philosophy had been unequivocally expressed in an all-embracing address. Nordhoff told the world that he had 'brushed away all temptation to change model and design', for in any basically sound model 'there are almost unlimited possibilities'. He argued that there was 'no sense' in 'starting anew every few years with the same teething troubles, making obsolete almost all the past'. Why were manufacturers,

driven around by a bunch of hysterical stylists trying to sell people something they really do not want to have! … Based on Professor Porsche's original design, the Volkswagen of today looks almost exactly like the prototype model that was produced twenty years ago, but every single part of this car has been refined and improved over the years – these will continue to be our 'model changes'. This policy … has led to success, and there is no greater justification than success.

even in ice and snow

Following the appointment of the Doyle Dane Bernbach advertising agency in America at the end of the 1950s, not only was artwork banished from Volkswagen's publicity, but also the photography that replaced it became increasingly sophisticated when tied to witty, plain-speaking text.

2

the Beetle's decline and fall from grace

1968–1978

ABOVE: The Beetle range that Nordhoff's successor, Kurt Lotz, inherited. The models depicted date from the '70 model year. (Volkswagen AG)

August 1967 and the start of the 1968 model year bore witness to what appeared to be the dawning of a new and even greater age for the Beetle. Changes to the car were of sufficient significance for the marketing department to brand the latest models as '*die neuen Käfer*'. A combination of: vertically set rather than sloping headlamps; larger rear light clusters for all but the 1200 base model; redesigned front and rear wings; changes to the valances, boot, and engine compartment lids; plus visibly more robust boxy U-shaped bumpers (again not extended to the 1200), transformed the appearance of the car, making it appear both more in keeping with the age and more aggressive in stance. Additionally, for the last twelve months

the Beetle had sported an engine option that meant it could keep pace with the rest of the crowd, an engine of sufficient potency for some to refer to the 1500 model as the 'hot Beetle', while for others it was at last regarded as a real driver's car. Together with a similarly new Transporter, a revamped larger Saloon, estate and Fastback in the form of the VW 1600, plus the prospect of an even bigger family car not too far distant, Volkswagen's Beetle-based path for the future was fully mapped out.

NORDHOFF'S FAREWELL

Come January 1968 and the customary gathering of distributors and dealers to celebrate the New Year and by

coincidence Heinz Nordhoff's birthday, the Director General reasserted his faith in the Beetle as Volkswagen's future; not that anyone doubted where his loyalties lay. 'The star of the Beetle is still shining with undiminished brightness', Nordhoff told his audience, 'and you see for yourself what vitality there is hidden in this car which has been pronounced dead more often than all those designs of which hardly a memory remains ...'. 'I am completely certain', he concluded, 'that our Beetle will be built for a very long time to come.'

Although Nordhoff's prediction proved accurate, the Beetle's evolution and its role within Volkswagen proved to be very different from the one he had envisaged. Drastic changes were imminent, a revolution brought about by the death of the man who had been at the helm for the last twenty years. Those who had seen the by then sixty-nine-year-old Nordhoff had been shocked by the change in him. Recent illness had taken a heavy toll: most realized that this gathering was to be his valedictory. Determined as ever, Nordhoff overexerted himself once too often shortly afterwards. Admitted to the hospital in Wolfsburg, he died there on Good Friday, 12 April 1968.

While the departure of the Beetle's mentor for the past twenty years did not inevitably mean that its position as the mainstay of the company was jeopardized, circumstances relating to recent years determined its fate. However, before summarizing the Beetle's fall from grace it is worth sparing a moment to reflect on the glories that were still to come. Key amongst these were: the 1970 figure for new Beetle registrations in West Germany, a number which proved to be one of the best in the car's history; the best-ever export figure to the United States, an occurrence relating to the calendar year 1968; the highest annual production figure, a staggering 1,291,612 Beetles produced in 1971; and then the most remarkable achievement of all, the arrival of *Der Weltmeister*, the World Champion Beetle on 17 February 1972, and the point at which, at 15,007,034 units of production, the Beetle overtook the legendary Ford Model T.

Throughout the 1960s and even earlier, Nordhoff had been plagued by a small but vociferous band of critics who repeatedly demanded the Beetle's replacement with a more modern design. His response ranged from the sage, with 'as long as our product sells as well as it does at present, it is wiser and more economical to go on developing it', to the dismissive, as was the case when questioned about the lack of a new model for the 1959 Motor Show. 'My answer in brief … because demand for this vehicle is so great, because not a single manufacturer in Europe can point to anything like three million satisfied owners of a single type … that is all I have to say on the matter.' Whether sanguine or bullish, Nordhoff remained consistent.

An official publicity shot designed to illustrate the new and more purposeful stance of the '68 model year Beetle. (Volkswagen AG)

Throughout the 1950s and for the first five years of the 1960s, Germany had experienced a prolonged period of growth; unbridled economic prosperity epitomized by Volkswagen's fortunes. However, as 1966 dawned the thunderclouds of recession were gathering, not just in West Germany but throughout Europe. By early 1967 Nordhoff was left with little option but to retrench, in common with both Ford and Opel, Volkswagen's two main rivals. To his dismay, the Coalition Government that had come into office late in 1966 did little to help the auto industry, instead making it more difficult for the average West German to buy a Beetle or any other car. In addition to raising the tax on petrol, Bonn cut the allowance enjoyed by German workers who drove their cars to and from work by 50 per cent. Nordhoff felt he had little option but to openly criticize the Government for what he considered its short-sighted, if not blatantly damaging policies. Nordhoff urged that consideration should be given to the cancellation of all vehicle ownership taxes.

The Government's retort to Nordhoff's suggestions, voiced through Finance Minister, Franz Josef Strauss, was swift and all-embracing. Apart from a haughty rejection of his proposals, Strauss openly attacked Volkswagen, and by implication Nordhoff, as having 'produced too many cars and too few ideas'. Adopting the views of Nordhoff's critics of old, he accused Volkswagen of 'hoarding up vast financial reserves over many years', instead of developing new models appropriate to counter the effects of recession. Rounding on the Beetle, he declared that 'two glorious initials on the bonnet of the car don't make up for a lack of comfort', while demanding to know why only 30 per cent of total production found its way onto the German market. 'What happens', he asked, 'when the Americans stop being amused by the Beetle?', conveniently forgetting that the USA certainly didn't account for the remaining 70 per cent.

It was against this background that plans were accelerated to ease Nordhoff into retirement. No one should forget that Volkswagen was partly owned by the Government and the danger therein of such arrangements. Clearly all recognized that Nordhoff couldn't go on forever and, despite his reluctance to let go of the reins, even he had planned to retire at the beginning of 1969, just a few days

A Royal Red 1300 with sunroof manufactured during the course of the 1968 model year.

Two images of what enthusiasts might describe as an early example of an 'upright headlamp' model. The car would have been built at Wolfsburg just a few months after Nordhoff's death in April 1968. This 1300 model is finished in Savannah Beige.

Die neuen Käfer.

More than thirty years before the New Beetle – the water-cooled, Golf-based, front-wheel-drive car – made its debut, Volkswagen was sufficiently confident in the radical nature of the upgrades made for the '68 model year that they branded the original cars 'Die neuen Käfer', or 'The New Beetles', in their publicity material.

before his seventieth birthday. Previously, his proviso had always been that a suitable successor be found. Now the succession was to be taken out of his hands. Josef Rust, an industrialist, but more importantly a one-time aide to Strauss, had been chairman of the Volkswagenwerk AG Supervisory Board since 1966. His task was to find a successor that suited his political masters; a task he accomplished with ease in the appointment of Kurt Lotz, a former Managing Director of a Swiss-owned engineering and electrical firm, but an outsider not only in terms of his lack of any form of association with Nordhoff's Volkswagenwerk, but also in his background, which was devoid of involvement with the automobile industry in any shape.

A LACK OF CLARITY – THE LOTZ YEARS

This seemingly lengthy story serves to illustrate why the Beetle's fortunes changed so rapidly despite a story of ongoing success. When Lotz took over the reins following Nordhoff's death, the short-lived recession was already little more than a distant memory, production figures had climbed rapidly, while profitability – never in doubt even in the darkest days of 1967 – was set to increase to a level over and above that of 1965.

However, within a very short time Lotz could be heard to criticize his predecessor. 'It was bitter to discover that too little had been invested in the future during a period of high profits', he said on one occasion, while he told *The Autocar* in 1969 that Volkswagen had been 'a monolithic firm under the presidency of a sovereign'. Crucially, he decreed that 'Wolfsburg will never see the twenty million mark [in Beetle production] … we won't repeat Ford's mistake.'

The problem facing Lotz was not that he wished to rid Volkswagen of Nordhoff's strategy of improving one model of car to as near perfection as possible, but that he had nothing with which to replace the Beetle. What attempts he made to rectify the situation only resulted in tarnishing Volkswagen's reputation and reducing profitability, while giving the general air of a company adrift since Nordhoff's departure. The purchase of the German car and motorcycle manufacturer NSU in 1969 gave Lotz what he craved in the form of a water-cooled three-box Saloon, designated the

K70. However, the model was fundamentally flawed in that its unfriendly shape led to high fuel consumption, while a plague of manufacturing faults ensured that production costs were and remained uneconomical. Inextricably linked to this last issue was the reality that Lotz couldn't charge more for the car than he already was doing, as it was in direct competition with another Volkswagen model, Nordhoff's planned-for 411 – a larger family Saloon and estate car. Ridiculously, Lotz made as little as just DM33 per car, while Volkswagen's reputation for longevity was tarnished as premature rusting was in evidence with its newest model.

Perhaps Lotz would have ridden the brewing storm if he had been able to demonstrate sound model policy, but his attempts to find a Beetle successor foundered as he failed to identify a practical, stylish, and above all economical model. Bearing in mind the vast quantities of Beetles being produced, not to mention the success of Nordhoff's second-generation Transporter, decline rather than growth in profits seemed inexcusable and not surprisingly when his first contract of four years' duration was due for renewal the decision was made to replace him.

THE 1302 BEETLE

Despite his desire to rid Volkswagen of the Beetle, Lotz, the all-time master of befuddled thinking, was responsible for a new generation of models; cars that were sold as the Super Bug in America and as the 1302 range in Europe. By a strange quirk of fate, even the official designation left people wondering. The logic behind the number 1302 was that the car was a development of the traditional Beetle, thereby warranting its own identifying digits. Unfortunately, Simca had beaten Volkswagen in the use of the term 1301, so rather than think of a different route the mismanaged giant accepted second best with 1302.

While the marketing men struggled to emphasize the dynamics of the new Beetle, with headlines such as 'the most powerful, most exciting and most comfortable Beetle ever', the accountants found it nigh on impossible to justify

the expense involved. Lotz assumedly regarded the 1302 model as a stopgap in his quest to change direction, but he failed to realize that if such a radical 'improvement' to the Beetle was genuinely necessary, Nordhoff would have instigated such changes years earlier.

Of primary significance was the decision to abandon Ferdinand Porsche's beloved and much praised torsion bars and replace them with MacPherson struts, a device adopted by many other manufacturers in their more recent designs of the time. As the brochure copywriters put it, the 1302 had a 'completely new front axle. A so-called transverse link axle with suspension struts. Wider track. Long suspension travel. Optimum suspension balance. All adding up to outstanding road-holding, precise cornering and maximum lateral stability.'

A genuine improvement came in the form of the decision to adopt what had previously been exclusive to US-bound Beetles and the relatively recently introduced semi-automatic models. Thus the 1302 benefited from revised rear swing axles, which were double-jointed and no longer contained within tubes. The result was that under hard cornering conditions the car was less likely to tuck under a rear wheel, an altogether safer system, but also one that allowed the more enthusiastic drivers to attack bends at much greater speeds.

Although the 1302 Beetle was a bigger car than its siblings, its turning circle was smaller, while due to the MacPherson strut arrangement the boot was considerably larger; an increase calculated to be in the region of 85 per cent thanks to the spare wheel now being laid horizontally below the main loading area. Additionally, the new arrangements allowed for the petrol tank to be placed further back.

The net result of the changes in front suspension and boot size was that the bonnet, front valance and wings had to be modified and it was here where the problems for Volkswagen began. While the buying public might have countenanced the new look, the motoring press derided the 1302's appearance mercilessly, with the terms 'pregnant-looking' and 'bloated' riding high amongst the considered opinions.

Kurt Lotz – Nordhoff's successor and architect of the decline in the Beetle's fortunes. (Volkswagen AG)

The 1302 Beetle was launched during Kurt Lotz's thankfully brief tenure of office to a somewhat mixed reception. Although this publicity shot for press usage doesn't illustrate the car's bulbous frontal appearance to the full, its elongated boot lid and somewhat disproportionate lines are clear to see. (Volkswagen GB)

The bloated or pregnant stance of the 1302 range is apparent in this full frontal photograph.

Nothing fundamental had been achieved as a result of Lotz's decision to create a new stopgap Beetle, while one further concern was to be added to the 1302's tale of woe. New engines were offered, a twin-port 1600 to replace the much admired 1500 and a 1300 with the similarly revised cylinder heads with two inlet ports per head. The argument in both cases was that the engine could breathe more easily, with the 1300's power output being boosted from 40PS to 44PS. The 1600 unit, with its increased bore of 85.5mm, 2.5mm up on the old 1500, delivered 50PS. The problem with both engines was that each was notorious for dreadful flat spots and, worse still, cracked cylinder heads. For once, Lotz couldn't be blamed directly for such a problem; or could he? The demand for additional power had been a constant one for a good number of years at Volkswagen. Nordhoff had introduced the 1300 engine in the summer of 1965 and the 1500 twelve months later. What he wouldn't have sanctioned was the move to simply bore an additional hole in each head, in order to avoid the expense of designing a completely new engine.

The Cabriolet in 1302 guise – somehow the hood appeared out of proportion against the flat screen and bulbous boot lid.

Although the image of the 1302S Beetle on the cover of the launch brochure appeared to have been subjected to a curious tinting process, it nevertheless illustrated that the top model in the Beetle range had a changed appearance.

**The Super Beetle.
We've made so many improvements
they're beginning to show.**

Perhaps because the 1302S Beetle, or Super Beetle, was designed primarily with the American market in mind, the way in which it was promoted was much more blatant.

LEIDING CARVES THE WAY TO A NEW TYPE OF VOLKSWAGEN

Lotz's successor was Rudolf Leiding, a Volkswagen man through and through. His career had begun in the early days of the Nordhoff era and he had worked his way through the ranks of the service department to the top position. In 1958, as a reward for his diligence, Nordhoff made Leiding head of the Kassel plant, while seven years later he was transferred to the newly acquired Auto Union, where his brief was to bring the operation up to speed. From there he moved to Brazil, on that occasion to restore Volkswagen's 80 per cent market share from its decline of recent years to just 66 per cent. The job done, Leiding went back to Audi, now intertwined with NSU, where his job as the man in charge was to resolve a critical issue of unit cost. This potted history of Leiding's rise serves to demonstrate his suitability to take a firm grip on the situation at Wolfsburg and resolve the dalliances of Lotz's vagaries forthwith. Leiding might have chosen to restore the Beetle to its position as keyholder to Volkswagen's future success. His respect for the car was well known, but the reality of four wasted years forced him down a different route.

On the occasion of the ceremony heralding the Beetle's achievement as the most produced single model of all time, Leiding was asked both when it was likely that it would be superseded and if there would be a thirty-millionth example. He carefully avoided a direct answer to the first issue, but answered the second fairly and squarely and in so doing gave the strongest of hints regarding the Beetle's longer-term future. 'If you had asked, will there be a twenty-millionth Beetle I would definitely answer in the affirmative,' Leiding replied, 'but the thirty-millionth? We will have to wait and see!'

Rudolf Leiding presided over the ceremonies held to mark the Beetle becoming the most produced single model of all time. However, Leiding saw no route back to Beetle supremacy at Volkswagen – his task was to originate a worthy successor. (Volkswagen AG)

Preserved for posterity in the Stiftung Museum, Wolfsburg – a 1974 1303LS finished in Marathon Metallic.

Although not too widely accepted even in Volkswagen circles, it is Leiding who should be credited with the transformation of Volkswagen from a one-time enormously successful Beetle manufacturing and world-conquering machine to a company producing a series of ground-breaking front-wheel-drive models spearheaded by the world's first hatchback, the Golf. Make no mistake about it Leiding would have axed the Beetle from German production if he had remained in office past the date of his so-called retirement in January 1975. Renowned for his ruthlessness, it was Leiding who banished the Beetle from Wolfsburg to Emden to make way for the Golf, and there is little doubt that it would have been his decision rather than that of his successor, Toni Schmücker, to reduce the Beetle range to little more than the basic 1200 and a deluxe version known as the 1200L for the start of the 1976 model year.

Leiding's only definitive positive action regarding the Beetle was to sanction the planned progression of the 1302 range of cars into the curved-screen, plastic dash and far from traditional 1303, a product of the 1973 model year dating from August 1972. Proposed American Government legislation had suggested that the Beetle could well fall short of the desired standard, in that the windscreen of the enormously costly 1302, and for that matter the rest of the range as well, was too close to the driver. Lotz and those working for him should have thought of this; belatedly and undoubtedly in a state of panic, while again at considerable expense, they set about rectifying the problem. Their solution, the most un-Beetle-like of all the Beetles, met with, to say the least, a mixed reception. While the car's curved screen did little damage to its profile, indeed some went as far as to say that it actually improved

the looks of the Cabriolet when the hood was up, the faceless vinyl dashboard, an attempt at a contemporary look without the instrumentation and trimmings to match, won few admirers. The irony of the matter was that America's proposed standard never went into effect.

Leiding was acutely aware of the need to boost sales during difficult financial times and countenanced a series of special edition Beetles to this effect. Costing Volkswagen only the equipment loaded into the given model, in reality often little more than a special paint finish and less than a handful of trinkets, a slight drop in margin in exchange for augmented volume was an appropriate stopgap measure in advance of new models.

Leiding's fall is accounted for purely in financial terms and should never be associated with any hint of failure to take decisive action. From the first days of his tenure in office Leiding struggled, for not only did he inherit a company that was far less financially secure than it had been four years previously, but also within months of his ascendancy the Nixon Administration in America floated the dollar against other world currencies. The resultant increase in the value of the Deutsche Mark, one of the strongest currencies at the time, had the unfortunate effect of imposing a price increase on would-be Beetle buyers in America, the last thing Leiding wanted, particularly as Volkswagen reaped no benefit whatsoever. From such a starting point, Leiding's situation grew rapidly worse as the world came to struggle with recurrent oil crises and rampant inflation, with the result that he faced truly staggering development costs to keep Volkswagen afloat. Such was the enormity of the crisis, that nothing less than a price increase for the Beetle of 20 per cent in a single year was demanded, admittedly in part to combat the excesses of spiralling material costs, but also to contribute a percentage of the finance necessary to progress its replacement. From the modest DM86 million Volkswagen made in 1972, and the slightly more respectable DM109 million amassed in 1973, a truly staggering loss of DM555 million was experienced in 1974, a pattern that would continue into 1975,

A restored Marina Blue 1303 on display at a gathering of Volkswagen enthusiasts.

ABOVE: *The curved screen of the 1303 blended well with the hood of the Cabriolet. Unlike the Saloon, which was axed from the range at the end of July 1975, the 1303 Cabriolet survived until January 1980.*

RIGHT: *In comparison to sales literature of earlier days, Beetle brochures of the 1303 era were distinctly dull, if clinically informative. As the text serves to indicate, the image reproduced here is part of a double-page spread lacking the power to draw the browser to the page. Similarly off-putting, the car is shown in a colour not available to the market for which the pitch was intended.*

1303LS Convertible or Saloon.

The convertible top is unhooked in a jiffy, and folded back. You get all the sunshine and fresh air you want. When up, it keeps draughts and rain outside where they belong.

This top is a master-piece in plastic and fabric: three layers stitched together by hand, fitted by hand for a perfect fit.

The chic of the Convertible appeals to the young at heart. It's gay and breezy. And as handy as a car should be for sporty driving. Altogether a little dearer but a lot more fun.

when a further DM145 million loss was experienced.

1972, the year when the Beetle eclipsed all others in terms of total production numbers for a single model, saw a slight fall from the record of the previous year to 1,220,686 cars. Nevertheless, this was still better than any of the annual totals of the Nordhoff era and this would be the case again in 1973, when 1,206,018 cars were produced. Production of the Golf started during the course of 1974 and when coupled to the precarious situation of the economy, Beetle numbers of 791,053 were quite remarkable. However, in 1975 the Golf accounted for 419,620 units sold, with a further 74,810 examples of the new Polo again eating into Beetle sales figures. A creditable 441,116 Beetles were sold that year and, despite the severe rationalization of the range, both 1976 and 1977 saw Beetle sales in excess of a quarter of a million units.

THE END OF GERMAN BEETLE PRODUCTION

Former Ford executive, and the third Director General after Nordhoff's lengthy reign, Toni Schmücker decreed that German production of the Beetle should cease in

the first days of 1978. When the last Beetle rolled off the assembly line on 19 January, 16,255,500 such cars had been produced in Germany, while manufacture worldwide stood at 19,300,000 units. Production of the Saloon would continue for a further twenty-five years, primarily in Brazil, but also in Mexico – a country which not only had the unusual honour of

supplying diehard Germans with the car until the last months of 1985, but also of returning to the principles of the Nordhoff era and a policy of continual improvement throughout the remainder of the twentieth century.

The somewhat peripheral Cabriolet lingered on after the demise of the Saloon, still nurtured in the hands of the Karmann operation based in

US sales literature retained a degree of life even towards the end of the Beetle's production, as the centre spread of a brochure dating from 1977 and relating solely to the Cabriolet serves to illustrate.

The final Beetle Saloon to be produced on German soil in January 1978 was a straightforward, no-frills 1200. Today it resides in Wolfsburg's Stiftung Museum.

It is against this backdrop of an era where the primary intention was to replace the Beetle that this *Specification Guide* is set. From model years demonstrating numerous changes the decline is such that by the end of the German production there is little, if anything, to recall. An enduring pattern of decline will emerge as each page is turned, but enthusiasts should not despair. Not only was there another lengthy chapter in the Beetle's history ahead of those dismal days, but also after a period when the cars, including Cabriolets, dating from the years 1968 to 1980 were looked down upon by many, a revival in their fortunes is evident, as a demand for this title suggests.

A NEW DAWN FOR THE BEETLE

Osnabrück. Indeed, in its final years its popularity increased and particularly so in America. Nevertheless, its fate was sealed not only by the obsolescence of the 1303 on which it was modelled, but also by Volkswagen's wish to present its customers with an up-to-date interpretation of fresh-air motoring. Always based on the top-of-the-range Saloon, with effect from August 1972 the Cabriolet had become a derivative of the curved-screen 1303, a model that was discontinued in the summer of 1975, as already noted. Clearly, the Beetle Cabriolet in this form could not go on forever, as one day parts would cease to be available, but development of a Golf Cabriolet was the determining factor in its demise. The last example trickled off the Osnabrück production line on 10 January 1980, making its way the short distance to the Karmann Motor Collection, its place in motoring history assured.

The final words are granted to Beetle axeman Rudolf Leiding, demonstrating, in case anyone should think otherwise, that there was plenty of life left in the old master in 1978. 'It is undeniable that for Mexico the Beetle was the ideal automobile. In this country, where the paved roads ended and other models failed, the Beetle kept right on going towards its goal … in this market the Beetle had displaced its competitors.'

A reasonable percentage of the last 300 Beetles produced for the British market survive. All were 1200L models and finished in Diamond Silver, the onus being on the VW dealerships to supply a dashboard plaque indicating the car's status and its unique number in the final roll-call.

production survey

ABOVE: *Wolfsburg, Volkswagen's headquarters and key Beetle manufacturing factory until 1974. (Volkswagen AG)*

1) TYPE AND MODEL DESIGNATIONS

Before August 1968 and the 1969 model year, model designations were expressed as shown in the table overleaf.

With effect from August 1968 all Beetles carried a six-figure identification number. The first digit referred to the 'type' and therefore remains constant at (1). The second digit referenced the specific model, or series of models.[1] The third digit denoted whether the vehicle was a left-hand- or right-hand-drive model.[2] The fourth digit served to illustrate the trim level, specifically 'L' for European models and 'Custom' for US-bound cars.[3] The fifth digit indicated the engine and its output[4] and the sixth one determined whether transmission was via a manual four-speed box, or semi-automatic.[5]

Using the model year 1973 – and the introduction of the 1303 – further explanatory notes are required to determine the nature of the example given below (*see* reference points in the text above).

[1]Second digit – Models 1973
  1 1200/1200L
  2 not used
  3 1303
  4 Karmann Ghia (coupé and Cabriolet)
  5 Cabriolet
  6 General purpose vehicle (USA – The Thing)

[2]Third digit – Left-hand drive 1, 3, 5
            Right-hand drive 2, 4, 6

[3]Fourth digit – 1 = L, or Deluxe specification

7/8 = Custom specification or model for USA

[4]Fifth digit – engines 1973
  1 1200 (34PS)
  2 1300 (44PS)
  3 1600 (50PS)
  4 Not in use
  5 1600 (48PS)
  6 1600 (48PS)

[5]Sixth digit
  1 = 4-speed manual transmission
  2 = semi-automatic

2) PRODUCTION DETAILS: CHASSIS NUMBERS

All chassis numbers relate to the last day of the month. (Additional 1303- and Cabriolet-related information is included overleaf.)

Type	Description	With equipment variations	Official designation
111	VW 1200 LHD		11
112	VW 1200 RHD		11
115	VW 1200 LHD with steel sunroof		11
116	VW 1200 RHD with steel sunroof		11
113	VW 1300 LHD		11
114	VW 1300 RHD		11
117	VW 1300 LHD with steel sunroof		11
118	VW 1300 RHD with steel sunroof		11
113/4	VW 1300 with 34PS engine	M88	11
113	VW 1500 LHD	M157 (44PS engine)	11
114	VW 1500 RHD	M157 (44PS engine)	11
151	VW 1500 Cabriolet LHD	M157 (44PS engine)	11
152	VW 1500 Cabriolet RHD	M157 (44PS engine)	11

1967/68 1968 model year		1968/69 1969 model year		1969/70 1970 model year	
August	118 077 888	August	119 102 259	August	110 2 092 844
September	118 160 490	September	119 201 925	September	110 2 191 729
October	118 258 722	October	119 307 792	October	110 2 300 599
November	118 351 958	November	119 397 734	November	110 2 395 272
December	118 431 603	December	119 474 780	December	110 2 473 153
January	118 520 744	January	119 565 362	January	110 2 562 429
February	118 613 634	February	119 653 984	February	110 2 656 704
March	118 706 923	March	119 753 726	March	110 2 749 553
April	118 799 672	April	119 852 530	April	110 2 855 740
May	118 895 641	May	119 942 556	May	110 2 949 762
June	118 1003 667	June	119 1 040 194	June	110 3 050 707
July	118 1016 098	July	119 1 093 704	July	110 3 097 089

1970/71 1971 model year		1971/72 1972 model year		1972/73 1973 model year	
August	111 2 082 956	August	112 2 067 069	August	113 2 115 694
September	111 2 177 986	September	112 2 124 590	September	113 2 199 639
October	111 2 273 792	October	112 2 299 678	October	113 2 287 110
November	111 2 345 460	November	112 2 356 908	November	113 2 372 878
December	111 2 427 591	December	112 2 427 792	December	113 2 438 833
January	111 2 518 856	January	112 2 482 841	January	113 2 524 536
February	111 2 669 687	February	112 2 583 722	February	113 2 606 864
March	111 2 730 614	March	112 2 679 613	March	113 2 705 303
April	111 2 832 863	April	112 2 772 211	April	113 2 787 815
May	111 2 932 741	May	112 2 859 409	May	113 2 883 926
June	111 3 034 569	June	112 2 951 706	June	113 2 978 660
July	111 3 143 119	July	112 2 961 362	July	113 3 021 911

1973/74 1974 model year		1974/75 1975 model year		1975/76 1976 model year	
August	114 2 135 126	August	115 2 020 343	August	116 2 004 793
September	114 2 175 197	September	115 2 028 299	September	116 2 041 746
October	114 2 264 932	October	115 2 049 312	October	116 2 047 072
November	114 2 356 316	November	115 2 120 504	November	116 2 060 534
December	114 2 423 795	December	115 2 143 743	December	116 2 071 467
January	114 2 489 587	January	115 2 171 603	January	116 2 082 265
February	114 2 565 673	February	115 2 187 424	February	116 2 097 865
March	114 2 646 530	March	115 2 204 329	March	116 2 114 297
April	114 2 663 304	April	115 2 231 771	April	116 2 131 217
May	114 2 772 768	May	115 2 248 549	May	116 2 146 453
June	114 2 818 457	June	115 2 259 792	June	116 2 162 096
July	114 2 818 457	July	115 2 266 092	July	116 2 176 287

1976/77 1977 model year		1977/78 1978 model year	
August	117 2 006 331	August	118 2 007 084
September	117 2 033 696	September	118 2 008 911
October	117 2 048 703	October	118 2 016 615
November	117 2 057 509	November	118 2 019 775
December	117 2 063 700	December	118 2 026 312
January	117 2 069 049	19 January	118 2 034 030
February	117 2 070 620		
March	117 2 071 675		
April	117 2 081 654		
May	117 2 087 283		
June	117 2 094 861		
July	117 2 096 890		

Selected chassis numbers 1303 models including Cabriolet.

		1 August	31 December	31 July
1973 model year	Aug 1972–July 1973	133 2000 001	133 2438 833	133 3200 000
1974 model year	Aug 1973–July 1974	134 2000 001	134 2423 795	134 2999 000
1975 model year	Aug 1974–July 1975	135 2000 001	135 2143 743	135 2600 000
1976 model year	Cabriolet	156 2000 001	156 2071 467	156 2200 000
1977 model year	Cabriolet	157 2000 001	157 2063 700	157 2200 000
1978 model year	Cabriolet	158 2000 001	158 2028 542	158 2100 000
1979 model year	Cabriolet	159 2000 001	159 2018 069	159 2036 062
1980 model year	Aug 1979 – Jan 1980	159 2000 001	159 2018 069	10 Jan 1980 159 2044 140

3) PRODUCTION DETAILS: ENGINE NUMBERS (SELECTED)

Model year 1968 (August 1967–July 1968)	1 August 1967 Engine no.	31 December 1967 Engine no.	31 July 1968 Engine no.
1200 34PS	D 0234015	D 0297008	D 0382979
1300 37PS	E 0014001	E 0014311	E 0015981
1300 40PS	F 1237507	F 1296298	F 1462598
1500 40PS	L 0019337	L 0020200	L 0021115
1500 44PS	H 0874200	H 0915221	H 1003255
1500 44PS (M157)	H 5000001	H 5173897	H 5414585

Model year 1969 (August 1968–July 1969)	1 August 1968 Engine no.	31 December 1968 Engine no.	31 July 1969 Engine no.
1200 34PS	D 0382980	D 0438824	D 0525049
1300 37PS	E 0015982	E 0018367	E 0020021
1300 40PS	F 1462599	F 1592024	F 1778163
1500 40PS	L 0021116	L 0021903	L 0024106
1500 44PS	H 1003256	H 1057844	H 1124668
1500 44PS (M157)	H 5414586	H 5648888	H 5900000

Model year 1970 (August 1969–July 1970)	1 August 1969 Engine no.	31 December 1969 Engine no.	31 July 1970 Engine No.
1200 34PS	D 0525050	D 0592445	D 0674999
1300 37PS	E 0020022	E 0020937	E 0022000*
1300 40PS	F 1778 164	F 932 908	F 2200000*
1500 40PS	L 0024107	L 0024788	L 0026500*
1500 44PS	H 1124669	H1187829	H 1350000*
1600 47PS	B 6000001	B 6192532	B 6600000*

* = Final number in series

Model year 1971 (August 1970–July 1971)

	1 August 1970 Engine no.	31 December 1970 Engine no.	31 July 1971 Engine no.
1200 34PS	D 0675000	D 0719487	D 0835006
1300 40PS	AC 0000001	AC 0000706	AC 0003239
1300 44PS	AB 0000001	AB 0141591	AB 0350000
1600 46PS	AF 0000001	AF 0000247	AF 0000444
1600 50PS	AD 0000001	AD 0139549	AD 0360022
1600 50PS (M157)	AE 0000001	AE 0218430	AE 0558000

Model year 1972 (August 1971–July 1972)

	1 August 1971 Engine no.	31 December 1971 Engine no.	31 July 1972 Engine no.
1200 34PS	D 0835007	D 0881604	D 1000000
1300 40PS	AC 0003240	AC 0005192	AC 0006700
1300 44PS	AB 0350001	AB 0447700	AB 0699001
1600 46PS	AF 0000445	AF 0000654	AF 0000801
1600 48PS (M157)	AH 0000001	AH 0002731	AH 0005900
1600 50PS	AD 0360023	AD 0363001	AD 0598001

Model year 1973 (August 1972–July 1973)

	1 August 1972 Engine no.	31 December 1972 Engine no.	31 July 1973 Engine no.
1200 34PS	D 1000001	D 1039792	D 1115873
1300 40PS	AC 0006701	AC 0007219	AC 0008195
1300 44PS	AB 0699002	AB 0820427	AB 0990000
1600 46PS	AF 0000802	AF 0034850	AF 0036768
1600 48PS	AE 0917264	1 Oct AK 0000001	
(M27 from 1 Oct)	1 Oct AE 1000000	31 Dec AK 0060039	AK 0239364
1600 50PS	AH 0005901	AH 0056 934	AD 0114418
	AD 0598002	AD 0749789	AD 0990000

Model year 1974 (August 1973–July 1974)

	1 Aug 1973 Engine no.	31 Dec 1973 Engine no.	31 July 1974 Engine no.
1200 34PS	D 1115874	D 1204346	D 1284226
1300 44PS	AR 000001	AR 081514	AR 121271
1600 50PS	AS 000001	AS 109138	AS 171566

Model year 1975 (August 1974–July 1975)

	1 August 1974 Engine no.	31 December 1974 Engine no.	31 July 1975 Engine no.
1200 34PS	D 1284227	D 1309681	D 1347142
1300 44PS	AR 121272	AR 132045	AR 150000
1600 50PS	AS 171567	AS 243557	AS 269030
1600 50PS	AJ 0000001	AJ 0012142	AJ 0012405

Model year 1976 (August 1975–July 1976)

	1 August 1975 Engine no.	31 December 1975 Engine no.	31 July 1976 Engine no.
1200 34PS	D 1347143	D 1368488	D 1393631
1600 50PS	AS 269031	AS 332893	AS 401299
1600 50PS	AJ 0012406	AJ 0012504	AJ 0095935

Model year 1977 (August 1976–July 1977)

	1 August 1976 Engine no.	31 December 1976 Engine no.	31 July 1977 Engine no.
1200 34PS	D 1393632	D 1410177	D 1415740
1600 50PS	AS 401300	AS 468053	AS 526948
1600 50PS	AJ 0095936	AJ 0110696	AJ 0119687

Model year 1978 (August 1977–January 1978)			
	1 August 1977	**31 December 1977**	**1 January 1978**
	Engine no.	**Engine no.**	**Engine no.**
1200 34PS	D 1415741	D 1430280	D 1430281
1600 50PS	AS 526949	AS 563435	AS 563435
1600 50PS	AJ 0119688	AJ 0126171	—

4) PRODUCTION NUMBERS

The chart below serves to indicate total Beetle production on a year-by-year basis, together with comparative figures for other selected models, as well as total manufacturing figures for both Volkswagen AG and the worldwide Volkswagen Group. Figures for 1967 are included, as the new Beetle for 1968 went into production in August of that year. Production in 1978 for the Beetle more or less relates to Brazil and its satellites, plus Mexican cars.

Golf production has never equalled that of the Beetle in a single twelve-month period, the best ever figure being recorded in 1992 when 927,286 cars were sold.

Year	Beetle	Transporter	VW 1600	Golf	Polo	Volkswagen GMBH/AG	Volkswagen Group
1967	925,787	162,741	201,800			1,162,258	1.339,823
1968	1,186,134	253,919	244,427			1,548,933	1,777,320
1969	1,219,314	273,134	267,358			1,639,630	2,094,438
1970	1,196,099	288,011	272,031			1,621,197	2,214,937
1971	1,291,612	277,503	234,224			1,715,905	2,353,829
1972	1,220,686	294,932	157,932			1,483,350	2.192,524
1973	1,206,018	289,022	**Passat** 114,139			1,524,029	2,335,169
1974	791,053	222,233	340,589			1,239,698	2,067,980
1975	441,116	221,351	258,953	419,620	74,180	1,121,937	1,948,939
1976	383,277	234,912	288,018	527,074	144,677	1,316,039	2,165,627
1977	258,634	211,024	274,992	553,989	112,274	1,371,453	2,218,880
1978	271,673	207,625	340,884	714,947	112,456	1,349,048	2,384,563

This Turquoise 1302L dates from 1971, the calendar year when Beetle production and sales reached a peak of 1,291,612 cars manufactured in a twelve-month period.

Production numbers Beetle Cabriolet

From three prototypes in 1948 and 364 vehicles sold in 1949, the Cabriolet slowly but surely edged its way upwards. The best year of the Nordhoff era was 1961, when Karmann produced 12,005 examples of the top-of-the-range model, but this figure was to be dwarfed by the annual totals of the early to mid-1970s. Curiously, following the demise of German production of the Beetle Saloon, Cabriolet figures leapt upwards, the majority of production destined for the United States. A grand total of 331,850 Cabriolets were built by Karmann.

Year	Total Cabriolet production	Cabriolet production as a percentage of Saloon production
1967	7,583	0.8
1968	13,368	1.1
1969	15,802	1.3
1970	18,008	1.5
1971	24,371	1.9
1972	14,865	1.2
1973	17,685	1.5
1974	12,694	1.6
1975	5,327	1.2
1976	11,081	2.9
1977	14,218	5.5
1978	18,511	
1979	19,569	
1980	544	

Sales figures – West Germany and USA, Saloon and Cabriolet

Year	Beetle – home market	Beetle – USA	Cabriolet – home market	Cabriolet – USA
1968	259,276	390,079	2,174	9,595
1969	311,323	367,307	3,013	10,025
1970	323,513	366,790	5,202	11,432
1971	285,432	318,990	5,880	12,201
1972	252,436	335,646	5,306	8,471
1973	232,055	342,790	4,253	7,567
1974	118,915	220,368	2,596	5,730
1975	41,070	78,412	2,075	3,618
1976	15,914	23,313	3,207	3,581
1977	6,524	12,090	4,000	7,155
1978	10,876 (includes Mexican imports)		5,450	9,932
1979			6,276	10,681
1980			324	4,572

Notable production and general dates

August 1967	Production of '*Die neuen Käfer*' began.
1967	Volkswagen do Brasil assembled its 500,000th Volkswagen.
12 April 1968	Death of Heinz Nordhoff (6 January 1899–12 April 1968).
1 May 1968	Kurt Lotz succeeded Nordhoff as Director General.
29 November 1968	Fifteen-millionth Volkswagen of any type since the end of the war was produced.
1 August 1969	US-spec Beetles and Cabriolets fitted with the 1600 engine (47PS) from the Transporter.
8 July 1970	The millionth Brazilian-built Volkswagen left the factory in São Bernardo do Campo.
1 August 1970	Introduction of the 1302 Beetle (Super Bug), available with either a twin-port 1300 or a 1600 engine for many markets.
27 August 1971	Five-millionth Volkswagen was shipped to the United States of America.
1 October 1971	Rudolf Leiding succeeded Lotz as Director General.
17 February 1972	VW Beetle number 15,007,034 left the assembly line, breaking the production record previously held by the Model T Ford.
1 August 1972	The 1303 Beetle, sometimes referred to as the 'Panorama' Beetle due to its curved windscreen, replaced the 1302 range.

15 December 1972	300,000th Beetle since 1953 arrived in Britain. Celebratory limited edition GT Beetle produced; 2,500 examples.
January 1974	Production of the Golf began at Wolfsburg.
1 July 1974	The last Beetle to be produced at Wolfsburg rolled off the assembly line at 11.19am. A total of 11,916,519 Beetles had been built at Wolfsburg since 1945.
July 1974	VW do Brasil built its one-and-a-half-millionth Beetle since 1959.
4 October 1974	The eighteen-millionth Beetle to be produced worldwide left the Emden plant.
10 February 1975	Toni Schmücker replaced Leiding as Director General.
March 1975	Production of the Polo began at Wolfsburg.
1 August 1975	The Beetle range was reduced to three variations on the basic torsion-bar Beetle theme. A 1200 was available in base model form and as a Deluxe. The latter model could be specified with a 1600 engine and disc brakes for some markets
27 October 1976	The one-millionth Golf rolled off the assembly line.
19 January 1978	The final Beetle to be built on European soil left the Emden factory. Total production stood at 19,300,000, with 16,255,500 of this number having been built in Germany.
February 1979	Karmann started production of the Golf Cabriolet.
10 January 1980	The last Karmann Cabriolet Beetle left the assembly line. 331,850 cars had been built since the prototypes of 1948.

Steel sheets ran straight from the roll into the massive presses which produced the panels for each section of the Beetle.

Carousel assembly of the Beetle's rear section involved in excess of 250 spot welds per vehicle at a rate of 210 revolutions per hour.

Close on 3,000 bare bodies moved along the assembly line each day in the early 1970s.

Roof panels were mated to the already melded front and rear sections of each Beetle.

After each shell had been washed for twenty-five minutes and dried for a further eight, it was painted with primer, then with a second layer of undercoat and finally with a finishing coat, before being baked at a high temperature.

The trim lines involved a greater degree of manual labour, which saw items such as cables, chrome strips, linings and bulbs being fitted by hand.

LEFT: With engines brought in from Hanover, transmissions from Kassel and front axles from Brunswick, final assembly saw the body and chassis bolted together automatically, before the fuel tank, steering gear and wheels were added. The car's seats were the last addition before fuelling took place.

specification detail changes model year by model year

August 1967–January 1980

The following survey endeavours to capture all the important detail changes made to the Beetle Saloon or Sedan and the Karmann Cabriolet from the watershed point of August 1967 to the end of German Saloon production on 19 January 1978 and soft-top manufacture on 10 January 1980.

Such were the modifications brought into effect in August 1967 (for the '68 model year) that Volkswagen's marketing department was deemed entirely vindicated in its description of the company's bestselling product as 'Die neuen Käfer' – 'The New Beetles'. The concurrent launch of a brand-new, second-generation Transporter should have guaranteed a rosy future for Volkswagen, but following the death in April 1968 of the Beetle's mentor of many years, Heinz Nord-hoff, increasingly difficult times lay ahead. The emergence of the Passat, Polo and, most importantly, the Golf, vehicles that marked the change from traditional air-cooling to mainstream water-cooled engines would eventually safeguard Volkswagen's future prosperity. Once production of these cars had begun in earnest, Volkswagen in Germany virtually abandoned the Beetle, with changes in its specification dwindling rapidly into insignificance. However, before this occurred in the mid-1970s not inconsiderable sums were spent on the development of a new range of 'Super Beetles' – the MacPherson strut cars with larger boots and in the case of the final model revision, the 1303, a 'modern' moulded plastic dashboard coupled to a pronouncedly curved windscreen. These vehicles, which were produced in parallel to the traditional torsion-bar Beetles between August 1970 and their demise at the end of July 1975, are covered to the same level of detail as the cars they temporarily supplanted as the flagship models in the Beetle range.

Note should also be taken that in the tradition that had evolved in the 1960s, when first the 1300 and then the 1500 Beetle topped the Saloon range, the core of the Cabriolet's specification lay with the highest specification model, including engine size. Hence between the '68 model year and the end of production for most markets the Cabriolet on offer was successively based on the 1500 Saloon, the 1302S Super Beetle and the curved-screen 1303. However, despite the axing of this last-mentioned vehicle from the range in 1975, as previously mentioned the Cabriolet continued in this mode up to and including the final vehicles built at the Karmann works.

BACKGROUND INFORMATION RELATING TO LATER MODEL SPECIFICATIONS

Volkswagen's model year policy

With effect from August 1955 VW adopted the practice (originally favoured by American manufacturers) of disregarding the start of a calendar year in favour of a mid-summer factory holiday and model year to bring about the most significant of specification changes. Thus a 1954 model Beetle would be rightly described as a vehicle manufactured between January and the end of December that year, while a 1956 model year car was one produced on or after 1 August 1955 and theoretically up to and including 31 July 1956. Putting this into the context

of the years covered in this book, a '68 model year Beetle would have left the assembly line between 1 August 1967 and 31 July 1968 inclusive, while a 1978 Beetle Saloon – the last such cars to have been manufactured on German soil – would have been built between 1 August 1977 and the day the final Beetle rattled off the Emden production line in January 1978.

The essentials and evolution of the Beetle's specification

The essentials of the Beetle concept designed by Ferdinand Porsche in the 1930s survived throughout the years of German production and beyond, yet very few of the individual parts remained the same. For a detailed outline of the basic principles of the Beetle's construction see the sister volume to this title, *VW Beetle Specification Guide 1949–1967* (The Crowood Press, 2007). The task here is to summarize the essentials of the pre-'68 Beetle, while adding details of the evolutionary process affecting the car's appearance primarily, but not exclusively, in the 1960s as the foundation on which the '68 model year Beetle was based.

- All-steel body bolted to lightweight platform chassis with central backbone and seal between the two.
- The rolling chassis consisted of two ribbed floorpans welded to a central tunnel and at the rear forming a fork to which the gearbox was mounted. This was originally split both vertically and horizontally and lacked any form of synchronization. Modifications inevitably occurred, the most significant for this book being at the start of the '61 model year, when Deluxe-specification cars gained synchromesh all-forward gears – previously not on first – while the redesigned box had a one-piece casing similar to that fitted to the Porsche 356. (The base model struggled on with a 'crash box' until October 1964.)
- Independent suspension by means of transversely mounted torsion bars at both the front and rear of the car remained a feature of the Beetle from concept to the end of

production, the exception being the 1302 and 1303 series. From the start of the '66 model year the rear track of the 1300 Beetle and the base model 1200 increased from 1,250mm to 1,349mm. The new 1500 Beetle had a rear track of 1,350mm. All Beetles at this point were fitted at the rear with what is usually referred to as an anti-roll bar, but which more correctly should be known as an equalizer spring. The objective of eliminating the car's tendency to oversteer was successfully achieved.

- Originally fitted with cable brakes, hydraulic brakes became part of the specification for all cars except the base or Standard model as early as April 1950. Drums all round were the norm until the '67 model year, when the top of the range 1500 model acquired 277mm discs and callipers with pistons of 40mm diameter. Cars destined for America retained drums despite being fitted with the 44PS 1500 engine and would continue to do so until the end of exports of both the Saloon and Cabriolet towards the end of the 1970s.
- From the earliest days up to the end of the '66 model year all Beetles had a 6V electrical system. Cars for the American market adopted a 12V system with the advent of the '67 model year. (Coincidentally, such cars had a revised style of front wing with headlamps set vertically into the metal.) The battery was always located on the right-hand side of the floorpan under the rear seat.
- The Beetle conceived by Ferdinand Porsche was powered by a 985cc, four-cylinder, air-cooled, overhead flat-four engine. With a bore of 70mm, stroke of 64mm and a compression ratio of 5.8:1, it developed a maximum of 23.5PS at 3,000rpm. All subsequent engines for the Beetle, and in reality for the Transporter and other air-cooled models, were in effect enhanced versions of this original unit. Porsche's intentions had been to build and develop an engine that demonstrated longevity, a reasonable degree of frugality and a power unit that neither boiled

The 1200 Beetles

ABOVE: *From the start of the period covered by this book to July 1973 the 1200 Beetle's appearance was similar to cars produced in the earlier years of the 1960s, vertically set headlights being the main exception to this.*

ABOVE: *From the start of the '74 model year the 1200 benefited from the box-style Euro bumpers, the latest style of rear light cluster and other features which brought it into line with its larger brothers. Note the use of paint rather than chrome and with the later Marino Yellow car the lack of hubcaps and soundproofing in the engine compartment.*

Following the demise of the 1303 range in the summer of 1975 and the departure of the 1300 Beetle at the same time, the 1200L became the standard-bearer of the Beetle range. As befitted an L specification, the car was adorned with chrome, a full headlining and even such items as rubber bumper inserts.

The 1500 and 1300 Beetles

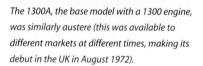

The 1300A Beetle.
It looks like a 1200. It goes like a 1300.

The 1300A, the base model with a 1300 engine, was similarly austere (this was available to different markets at different times, making its debut in the UK in August 1972).

From August 1967 to July 1970 the 1500 Beetle and its smaller-engined brother, the 1300, represented the Deluxe models in the range. The rear light clusters never filtered down to the 1200. For the '70 model year, the 1500 was endowed with two sets of cooling louvres in the engine lid, while US-market cars were upgraded to a 1600 engine in advance of all other markets. (The black and white press shot depicts the 1970 US 1600 – note the reflectors on the rear lights and the large wing-mounted indicators – Volkswagen of America.)

The 1302 Range

RIGHT AND BELOW: The 1302S replaced the 1500 Beetle (1600 in America) in August 1970 for the '71 model year. 1300 models continued in production but were joined by the 1302. Although varying in many respects from the torsion-bar cars, the MacPherson strut models only exhibited significant variations on the tried and trusted theme at the front of the car. Reshaped front wings and a humped wider bonnet led to some calling this car the 'pregnant Super Beetle'.

The 1303 Range

ABOVE AND RIGHT: The 1303 range took the 1302's place in the summer of 1972 for the '73 model year. Its curved screen distinguished it externally from its predecessor, while inside a 'modern' plastic moulded dashboard replaced what was essentially the flat panel in use since 1957. In Saloon guise the 1303 ran until the end of the '75 model year, while in Cabriolet form there was no reversion to earlier times and production continued unabated until January 1980.

The Beetle Sedan (USA)

ABOVE AND RIGHT: Throughout the production run of the 1302 and 1303 Super Beetles, American buyers could still opt to buy a torsion-bar car endowed with a 1600 engine. Variously referred to as the Sedan 111 Beetle, the Basic Beetle and, after the demise of the 1303, simply as the Sedan, trim levels were generally more basic than those of the Super Beetles, but nowhere near as austere as the 1200 cars in Europe. The engine lid badge initially read Volkswagen, but later carried the words Fuel Injection.

Engine Lid Badges – all models except 1200 1968 onwards

VW1300.

VW1300L.

VW1500.

VW Automatic.

VW1302.

VW1302L.

VW1302S.

VW1302LS.

VW1303.

VW1303S.

VW1303LS.

Volkswagen – US market.

Fuel Injection – US market.

With the exception of the 1200 and 1200L, all Beetles carried an identifying badge on the engine lid.

RIGHT: *Boot lid VW badge, August 1967–July 1972; not 1200 models*

over in hot conditions nor froze solid in winter when the vehicle wasn't garaged. At least until the '68 model year Volkswagen's philosophy remained the same; the engine's development was evolutionary rather than revolutionary. During the war the 1131cc engine favoured in the military version of the Beetle – the so-called *Kübelwagen* – was adopted as the power plant for the Saloon. With a bore of 75mm and an unaltered stroke of 64mm, this engine, which developed a maximum of 25PS at 3,300rpm, was used until the last days of December 1953. The 30PS engine that replaced it had a top speed of 110km/h (68mph) compared to 102km/h (63mph) for the older power plant. This was achieved by a further increase in the bore, this time to 77mm (stroke remained constant once more at 64mm), while the inlet valves were increased in diameter from 28.6mm to 30mm. There was also an increase in the compression ratio – at first from 5.8:1 to 6.1:1, but to 6.6:1 from August 1954. In August 1960 the 30PS engine was replaced with a 34PS unit, which was still an essential part of the engine line-up for the '68 model year and the period covered by this book (for further details *see* Chapter 5). The 34PS engine, plus the 1300 and 1500 power plants, new for the '66 and '67 model years respectively, are similarly outlined in Chapter 5.

- The bodyshell was made from a number of panels welded together and included: roof; front and rear valance; front and rear cross-member (both of which were bolted to and sat on the floorpan); rear luggage compartment; front luggage compartment floor: floor and back of well for spare wheel; two rear quarter panels (including window cut-outs); inner wings, front and rear (the former joined by the front valance); sills (designed to accommodate the movement of warm air from the engine directed through exhaust heat exchangers to the interior of the car via screen plus front and rear footwell outlets at both sides of the car); and a large panel forming the dashboard and the inner sections of the windscreen pillars.
- The Beetle's bonnet was curved and strengthened by a convex centre pressing and edges achieved in the pressing process. The lid was hinged internally and released by a pull mechanism under the left-hand side of the dashboard. From

the '61 model the lid was supported when open by two sprung rods.
- The Beetle's engine lid, like so many other parts, was modified over the years but throughout retained convex edge pressings to assist with rigidity. For the '67 model year the engine lid became shorter in the lower section, while to satisfy the demands of American market legislation the pressing designed to 'hold' the number plate became noticeably closer to vertical.
- Bumpers were of chrome – excepting the painted specification offered for most markets that sold the base or Standard model – and demonstrated a relatively broad profile that was curved in 'section'. Overriders were standard. (American-specification cars featured an additional rail supported by extended overriders as standard from the mid-1950s.)
- Sloping headlamp lenses were surrounded by chrome trim on all Deluxe models, while front indicators were positioned on the

The all-metal wind-back sunroof manufactured by Golde could be specified when ordering a Beetle, although one or two special edition models came with one as standard.

With effect from 1 August 1971 the overall height of the rear window was increased by 40mm (left), compared to those fitted to cars built between 3 August 1964 and 31 July 1971 (right).

Licence plate light cover – as introduced 1 August 1966 – 31 July 1974 – metal.

Licence plate light cover – 1 August 1974 – moulded black plastic, ribbed on top and painted.

Licence plate light.

top of the wings from the '61 model year as far as the European market was concerned. From the start of the '64 model year the slender, elegant teardrop indicator became both larger and broader in design. At the rear of the car with effect from May 1961 the tail lights became noticeably larger and dual section in nature.

■ Door quarter lights made their debut in the autumn of 1952 and remained a part of the Beetle's specification up to and beyond the end of German production. Window glass sizes increased over the years – most noticeably in the 1950s at the rear of the vehicle. For the '65 model year the size of the windscreen was increased through a 28mm encroachment into the roof panel. The rear window was 20mm higher and 10mm wider, while the side windows were made larger by slimming down the pillars (windscreen 11 per cent, rear window 20 per cent, rear quarter windows 18 per cent, door windows 6 per cent larger).

■ Sunroof models were fitted with a canvas fold-back roof until the end of the '63 model year in the case of the Export/Deluxe model and to the start of the '68 model year and the beginning of the period covered by this volume in the instance of the base model. After these dates, a crank-operated steel sunroof smaller in size than the cloth version became standard.

■ The Beetle's wings were bolted to the rest of the bodyshell. Hinges (at the front of the doors) were exposed. Metal running boards were fitted under the doors and rear quarter panels and were covered with ribbed rubber invariably, but not exclusively, black in colour. Deluxe models included an anodized aluminium trim strip on the lower edge of the running board.

■ Hubcaps, domed for many years, became flat for the '66 model year in the style of those fitted to the VW 1500 (Type 3). At the same time, the Beetle's five-stud wheels were ventilated by means of ten elongated oval perforations in the steel disc wheels. This resulted in

ABOVE: Boot of torsion-bar Beetle – capacity 140ltr.

RIGHT: Two-tier boot of 1302 and 1303 models with spare wheel concealed under lower level 'floor' – capacity 260ltr.

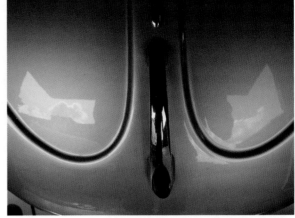

The wider nature of the boot lid panel on the 1302 and 1303 series of cars (left) compared to the classic look of the torsion-bar Beetles (right).

slightly better cooling for the drum brakes, while reducing the vehicle's unsprung weight. Five-stud wheels were replaced on the 1500 Beetle of '67 vintage with four studs. This became universal the following year.

■ Inside the car, the style of dashboard adopted in August 1957 for the '58 model year would remain essentially the same throughout the remaining years of German production and to the end of Beetle production in 2003. (The short-lived curved-screen 1303 being the exception.) A long-awaited fuel gauge fitted adjacent to the car's only other dial made its debut at the start of the '62 model year. (Base models retained the previous system of a reserve fuel tap.) Steering wheel design had changed many times over the years. From August 1965 onwards the pattern of the steering wheel was two-spoke and featured a semicircular horn ring. The popular ivory finish of old was dispensed with, in favour of black. For the '67 model year ivory-coloured control knobs were replaced by flatter, softer and more safety-conscious plastic fittings finished in black, thus also avoiding unwanted reflections in the screen glass. Again from August 1965 the front seats of the Cabriolet and Deluxe models were fitted with a locking device designed to prevent them from unintentionally folding forwards. A backrest catch followed for the '67 model year, while interior door handles became recessed again for reasons of improved safety. The doors could be locked by a button at the rear corner of the window frame, while the armrest on the driver's door was redesigned so that it could be used to pull the door shut. For the start of the '63 model year a perforated plastic headlining replaced the prone-to-rot woollen material headlining. The rotating heater control was replaced for the '65 model year with two pull-up/push-down levers. The right lever operated the heater, while the left one controlled the flaps, varying the amount of warm air that circulated in the rear footwells.

All cars had a flat rear valance until the end of the '74 model on 31 July 1974.

All cars were fitted with a curved, or humped, rear valance from the start of the '75 model year on 1 August 1974.

European-market cars with carburettors retained twin tailpipes and lacked a catalyst, throwing into question the need to change the valance.

Specification detail changes month by month

1968 – Beetles built between 1 August 1967 and 31 July 1968

The '68 model year Beetle was branded as 'The New Beetle', such were the number of changes in its appearance. Realistically, some of these were forced upon Volkswagen by the demands of increasingly stringent US legislation, although it can be convincingly argued that the modifications were the company's way of meeting the challenge from a rapidly emerging host of small economy cars from Japan.

Date	Chassis no.	Change
Body		
1 Aug	118 000 001	Headlights mounted vertically on all models for all markets (previously with effect for the '67 model year US cars only). Resultant modifications to design of front wings. Horn grille and matching dummy grille discontinued on all cars with the exception of the 1200.
1 Aug	118 000 001	Larger front wing-mounted indicators with side marking reflectors built in (cars for US market only).
1 Aug	118 000 001	Larger rear light clusters both in terms of pods and lenses (not base model). Lenses nearer rectangular in shape compared to the elongated oval of old. Reversing lights available as an optional extra – if fitted clear lens lowest section of light, otherwise three-fold function of: stop, rear light, indicator (US version – reversing lights standard and reflectors built into the outer side of the lens housing; indicator section red compared to European standard of orange).
1 Aug	118 000 001	Bumpers of beefier appearance with distinctive U profile (same basic design as the new Transporter). Chrome with decorative black tape trim fixed to central recessed area. Bumper brackets strengthened considerably with new 'double prong', or Y-shaped arrangement. Fixed higher on the body of the car (conforming to US automobile bumper height), overriders no longer part of the standard package for any market (base model retained previous style bumpers, but was no longer fitted with overriders). New body mounting plates with three 8mm bolts per bracket instead of two.
1 Aug	118 000 001	New bumper design and position necessitated shortening of both the boot and engine lids, giving the car a less gentle, more outwardly aggressive and generally chunkier stance. Front and rear valances similarly amended, becoming longer to suit the modified boot and engine lids. Front valance no longer incorporated slots to accommodate the bumper brackets. Bumper brackets fed through the area towards the inner edges of the new front wings and mounted on the outside of the inner wings instead of the inside as previously (within the spare wheel well).
1 Aug	118 000 001	Exhaust tailpipes – chromed as previously – now 249mm long rather than 276mm in length, a consequence of the redesign of the rear valance.
1 Aug	118 000 001	Boot lid – nineteen vents/louvres cut into the lid above the VW symbol and closer to the windscreen. Vents directed air into a plastic box fitted centrally behind the dashboard on the boot side of the car. Two flexible pipes took air from the box to dash-mounted vents, which were regulated by flat-topped, soft plastic, rotating knobs.
1 Aug	118 000 001	New handle for boot lid with push button and additional catch hook operated by soft plastic pull knob below dashboard on left-hand side of car (Cabriolet control operated by lever in lockable glove compartment).
1 Aug	118 000 001	Engine lid – new lock and handle fitted with additional catch hook with push-button release.
1 Aug	118 000 001	Filler neck for fuel tank accessible via flap in right-hand front quarter panel (no longer necessary to open the boot when filling up with fuel at a garage). Neither fuel cap nor flap lockable. Flap opened with the aid of a 'finger cut-out' in front of the flap. Rubber bumper plug fitted for the filler flap to close upon.
1 Aug	118 000 001	New larger external mirror – driver's side only as standard – attached to door; previously fixed to external door hinge.
1 Aug	118 000 001	Horn location changed – now lower down on the body and partially under the wing.
1 Aug	118 000 001	Door handles redesigned with trigger release behind the main body of the handle – previously less secure push-button style handle.
1 Aug	118 000 001	Base model joins other models with crank-operated steel sunroof; previously folding canvas roof.
1 Aug	118 000 007	US-spec cars – windscreen double thickness laminated plastic between the two glass layers necessitating modified windscreen rubber with trim strip.
Interior		
1 Aug	118 000 001	Gear lever moved 78mm backwards; as a result handbrake lever shortened. Gear lever now straight – previously cranked.
1 Aug	118 000 001	To accommodate three-point seat belts, suitable securing points added.
1 Aug	118 000 001	Dashboard – thermo-electric fuel gauge incorporated into single combination instrument. Two additional air outlets added (fed from plastic box/louvres as described in Body section above). Air outlets controlled by individual rotary knobs positioned below radio blanking panel. All dashboard controls are flatter and broader in design – marked with appropriate function symbols. US models fitted with dashboard brake warning light (between wiper and headlamp switches).

RIGHT: European-market front-wing-mounted indicator – all models except 1200 – October 1963 to end of July 1974; chromed casing.

FAR RIGHT: European-market front-wing-mounted indicator – 1200 base models at the start of the period covered by this volume were fitted with painted casings for the indicators. For most markets the 1200 was subsequently fitted with chromed covers as per Deluxe models.

RIGHT: With effect from August 1967, the size of the US-specification front indicator was increased dramatically. The larger indicators remained the norm until the end of production.

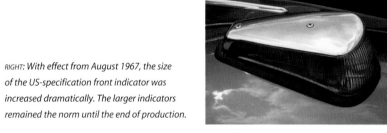

Rear light cluster, 1 August 1972 to end of production – 1303 range from 1 August 1972 to end of production. 1300 and 1200 from 1 August 1973 to end of production – Special Edition GT Beetle.

Rear light cluster 1200 Beetle to 31 July 1974.

Rear light cluster, European specification as per image above, but with lower section changed to clear to accommodate reversing lights (normally reserved for L-specification models, but also available as an extra cost option). (See also the black and white press shot on page 33 depicting a 1970 US-specification 1600 – note the reflectors on the rear lights.)

Rear light cluster, 1 August 1972 to end of production – without clear lens for reversing lights. Theoretically allocated to 1200 or 1300A basic models, but in reality many UK-specification basic 1200 models came with clear lens lower section – but no reversing lights, while some fully fledged 1303 models carried the kind of cluster pictured here.

Rear light cluster, European specification 1 August 1967–31 July 1973: 1500 Beetle to the end of production; 1300 Beetle to date stated; 1302 range throughout lifespan.

From the start of the '75 model year, European-specification Beetle front bumpers were altered to house the indicators (not applicable to USA, Canada or Japan markets).

Date	Chassis no.	Change
1 Aug	118 000 001	Ignition switch repositioned from dashboard location next to ashtray to more convenient location on the steering column.
		Ashtray now detached itself when pulled out and pressure applied from above; also had spring-loaded smoke deflector guard.
		Initially an optional extra on European-specification cars – but standard for safety reasons on US models – black plastic padding for dashboard (would become standard on late L-specification models – all markets). Initially glovebox lid and grilles to side of single instrument painted in body colour of the car – later Silk Black.
1 Aug	118 000 001	Interior rear-view mirror increased in size; coated in plastic and incorporated a safety release mechanism if struck in an accident.
1 Aug	118 000 001	Quarter-light catch design changed – now incorporated a deformable twist knob similar in appearance to dashboard control knobs.
1 Aug	118 000 001	Backrests on front seats now locked on both sides – released by cable control (lift upwards) positioned on the outer side of each front seat (US seat backs included a wide integral headrest).
1 Aug	118 000 001	Armrest on door now horizontal rather than angled.

Technical, mechanical and electrical changes

Date	Chassis no.	Change
1 Aug	118 000 001	Electrics now universally 12V (1500 and 1300 models only including Cabriolet) (1967 model 12V US and associated markets only); previously 6V. Battery: 12V 36AL, formerly 6V 66AL. Entire system uprated: light bulbs; coil; dynamo; starter motor.
		'12V' sticker – silver with red lettering – stuck on bodywork below the A-post on left side of the vehicle.
1 Aug	118 000 001	Four × 14mm diameter by 1.5mm thread bolts replaced five 12mm diameter × 1.5mm bolts securing the wheels on 1300 and 1200 models. The newly introduced 1500 Beetle of '67 model year vintage – not US examples – had been fitted with four-stud wheels, but previously not any other members of the Beetle family.
		New hubcaps fitted over four raised bumps on the steel wheel rather than sitting in the hub, as had been the case since the introduction of 'flat' rather than 'domed' hubcaps for the '66 model year.
		New trim rings designed to fit new wheels – eight slots instead of ten. Fitted as standard on Cabriolet and optional on Saloon.
1 Aug	118 000 001	Interior light – bulb now spring-loaded.

Crescent-shaped through-flow vents – introduced on all models except 1200 1 August 1970; note the brightwork trim.

Later crescent-shaped through vents lacked brightwork trim. The change took place at the start of August 1972.

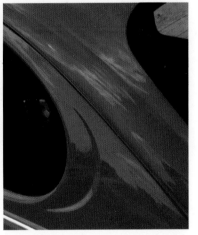

Basic 1200 models manufactured after 1 August 1970 exhibited a crescent-shaped indentation in the metal, which was previously plain.

FAR LEFT: From 1 August 1967 all Beetles except the 1200 carried fresh-air intake slots in the boot lid. When the 1200L was introduced this also had the air intake slots.

LEFT: The curved windscreen of the 1303 demanded a redesign of the boot lid and the air intake slots.

LEFT: Headlamp trim rings included three screws until late September 1973: one to hold the trim ring to the body at 6 o'clock; two others at 1 o'clock (vertical aim) and 7 o'clock (lateral aim) respectively to adjust the beam setting.

RIGHT: Post-September 1973 headlamp trim rings following bonding of reflector and lens. Single screw to hold trim to body of car. Trim rings initially metal-chromed, latterly plastic.

Before the '70 model year the only cars to include cooling louvres in the engine lid specification were the Cabriolets.

From 1 August 1969 the number of cooling louvres in the Cabrio's engine lid was increased to twenty-eight, set in four equal banks of seven louvres.

From 1 August 1969 1500 Saloons were fitted with ten horizontal engine lid cooling louvres. Twelve months later, the 1300 was similarly attired.

On 1 August 1971, the start of the '72 model year, the number of cooling louvres in the engine lid was standardized at twenty-six, in four banks – outer banks seven louvres, inner banks six. At the same time the engine lid was slightly recontoured.

A metal water collection tray sat behind the engine lid cooling louvres. The drainage pipes are clearly visible.

The collection tray and drainage pipes were discontinued when the number of cooling louvres increased to twenty-six.

Date	Chassis no.	Change
1 Aug	118 000 001	1500 engine 30 PICT-2 carburettor – enlarged float chamber.
1 Aug	118 000 001	Steering column – new safety steering column with crushable lattice section, which in an accident collapsed if the driver hit the steering wheel.
1 Aug	118 000 001	Brake show width on rear brake drums increased to 40mm from 30mm. 17.46mm diameter rear brake cylinder.
1 Aug	118 000 001	Dual-circuit brakes replaced older single-circuit system on all but the 1200 or base model.
1 Aug	118 000 001	Plastic brake fluid reservoir relocated to front luggage compartment inner wing on left-hand side close to rear of compartment.
1 Aug	118 000 001	Windscreen washer bottle new location. Secured by two plastic pins to inside of spare wheel in wheel well. Compressed air taken from spare wheel; previously fitted to wheel well cross panel.
1 Aug	118 000 001	Wiper shaft spigot increased from 5mm to 7mm diameter.
1 Aug	118 000 001	Repositioned longer windscreen wipers and blades.
1 Aug	118 000 007	US models: brake warning light positioned between wiper and headlamp switches. If problem with brakes, lamp lit immediately.

Changes later in the model year

Date	Chassis no.	Change
14 Aug	118 054 329	Oil strainer – new funnel-shaped pick-up and spring-loaded valve.
1 Sept	118 071 448	Primarily designed for the American market, a semi-automatic version of the 1500 Beetle launched; badged 'VW automatic' and from 118 431 604 US market only as 'Automatic Stickshift' on engine lid (known as the stickshift Beetle in some circles). Three-speed gearbox – ratios correspond to second, third and fourth on manual car. Conventional clutch with torque converter. Not fully automatic, as necessary to use gear lever to change gear either up or down. Pneumatic operation of the clutch – vacuum control valve on left-hand side of the engine bay operated by a solenoid engaging a switch at base of gear lever – dispensed with need for clutch. Performance and fuel consumption figures poor in comparison to manual box.

(Brochures show top speed of VW 1500 manual as 78mph and automatic at a respectable 75mph, but lack reference to the time taken to achieve this feat. Fuel consumption variances – 32mpg VW 1500, 30mpg automatic. Many an owner would not have achieved such economy!)

Gear range selector had to be set in '0' (neutral) position to start vehicle. '0' located between speeds 2 and 3. Lowest 'gear' only used when starting with a full load or for climbing steep hills. Middle gear – normal starting 'gear' and ideal for around town use. Might also be used on hills and if more power required for overtaking. The highest gear was inordinately slow. Reverse could only be engaged when the car was stationary – lever had to be pushed down (like manual car) before gear would engage.

Semi-automatic Beetle fitted with completely new, technically sophisticated, double-jointed rear swing-axles no longer contained within tubes. Offered uniform road-holding characteristics whatever the load – vastly reduced the tendency of the Beetle to tuck under wheels when cornering hard.

Left and right diagonal trailing arms connected to spring plates at one end, pivoted in bushings on brackets added to rear torsion-bar cross-tube on the other.

The only cars to feature a grille in the wing, intended to improve the audibility of the horn after August 1967, was the 1200 (discontinued August 1973).

RIGHT: *US cars fitted with fuel injection and a catalytic converter had one single tailpipe (from 1 August 1974).*

From August 1968, the 1200 had a dummy grille on the offside front wing to match the horn grille on the nearside wing (discontinued August 1973).

The horn was located under the nearside wing.

The basic 1200 lacked brightwork inserts in the rubbers surrounding the windows. Note the marking on the glass in this shot – 'Be', indicating that the car was built at Volkswagen's factory in Belgium.

Date	Chassis no.	Change
1 Sept	118 071 448	New rear axle half shafts. New type of universal joint clipped onto each end of both axles – Constant Velocity (CV) joints.
		New shock absorbers attached to the diagonal trailing arms. New 22mm diameter, 676mm long torsion bars (Standard 21mm × 522mm). Equalizer spring assembly dropped.
	118 096 786	USA and Canadian markets – new three-point lap and shoulder harness style seat belt (M185).
10 Oct	118 227 175	Hump rim on pressed steel wheel.
13 Oct	118 233 162	Thermostat regulated intake air preheating. Bowden cable now 800mm, previously 650mm. Incorporates conduit and spring from Transporter.
10 Nov	118 328 519	Oil pressure switch fitted horizontally (from 1 August 1967 had been positioned vertically).
22 Nov	118 431 164	Breather pipe relating to new petrol tank filler etc. introduced in August '67 was external – running more or less on top of tank from left-hand side of car to filler neck. Now replaced by internal breather on Saloons only. 2 January 1968 158 398 840 new tank with internal breather also fitted to Cabriolet.
Jan 1968	118 345 661	Corrosion prevention for engine studs – clear varnish coating on parts of cylinder heads.
3 Jan	118 443 379	Hazard warning lights introduced for 1500 and 1300 Beetles. Pull-out switch to right of ashtray – centre section red with 'warning' triangle. When in use, red light flashed on and off in time with the car's indicators (US market already had emergency flashers).
Jan	118 516 995	Anti-corrosion agent in fuel put in cars at factory.
20 Feb	118 582 000	Carburettor 30 PICT-2 carburettor on 1.3-litre engine with enlarged float chamber.
29 Feb	118 613 500	Carburettor 30 PICT-2 – upper section of housing modified.
1 Mar	118 618 635	Carburettor 30 PICT-2 power section and seal modified.
27 Mar	118 701 827	Window lifting mechanism – now one-track rather than two-track design. Window crank handle had plastic covering.
3 Apr		High-performance ignition coil replaced normal coil.
18 Apr	118 778 781	Engine fuel pipe – zinc plated; previously copper plated.
25 Apr	118 739 438	Sunroof sealing material – now 67 per cent Trevira, 33 per cent cotton velvet.
6 May	118 857 240	Front axle track end spigot increased from 12mm to 14mm. Steering knuckle – inner taper roller bearing seat increased to 29mm; previously 27mm.
May	118 799 673	Sticker on fan housing indicating ignition/timing setting. Battery text now in English and French as well as German. Rocker cover gaskets now made of cork – previously Flexolit.
29 May	118 899 936	Clutch 200mm diameter – new torsion sprung clutch disc with single springs.
7 Jun	118 953 664	Fused terminal blocks now with push-on plug terminals; previously screw terminals.
21 Jun	118 980 404	New safety armrest without decorative trim (fitted to US cars from 1 August 1967).
1 July	118 1003668	Petrol tank filler hose linked by pipe necessitating additional clips; previously one pipe hose.

Petrol filler flap with finger release on 1303 Beetle. Note additional side trim on these models.

Petrol filler flap 'pull' opener, August 1968–July 1972.

ABOVE: From August 1967 the petrol tank filler neck and cap was located in the right-hand-side front quarter panel (previously necessary to open the boot to refuel). Flap opened by recess for finger from August 1967–July 1968 and again from August 1972 to end of production. BELOW: Petrol filler flap without finger release – opened by 'pull' inside the car; August 1968–July 1972.

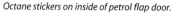

Octane stickers on inside of petrol flap door.

1969 – Beetles built between 1 August 1968 and 31 July 1969

Following the introduction of the 'New Beetle' for the '68 model year and the addition of a semi-automatic version of the car, as might be anticipated changes for the '69 model year were mostly restricted to detail.

Date	Chassis no.	Change
Body, interior modifications		
1 Aug	119 000 001	VW 1200 – decorative grille added to right-hand-side wing. Matching grille on left-hand-side wing as per 1500/1300 models of pre-August '67 vintage.
1 Aug	119 000 001	Lockable petrol filler flap operated by cable pull with ring located under the dashboard on the driver's side of the car. Flap sprung open when cable pulled; when closed by driver after refuelling would lock automatically (discontinued July 1972).
1 Aug	119 000 001	Front heater vents – now made of heat-resistant plastic - moved backwards to a position beneath the car's doors and opposite the seat slide rails. Open/close flaps operated by cables (encased in carpet) on the footwell sides; previously vents opened/closed with sliding vent mechanism.
1 Aug	119 000 001	Diameter of heating pipe larger. Rear outlet flaps now additionally sealed with silicone with gaskets of silicone-rubber.
1 Aug	119 000 001	Fresh-air outlets connected to heating air ducts on 1500 and 1300 Beetles (1200 not fitted with fresh-air outlets).
1 Aug	119 000 001	Right-hand-side guide rail of seat frame now had 'stop'. Left-hand-side fitted with spring strip.
1 Aug	119 000 001	Release mechanism for boot relocated to glovebox with metal, plastic knobbed pull-down handle fixed to metal bracket on side of glovebox closest to centre of car.
1 Aug	119 000 001	Engine lid water catch tray amended on Cabriolet – made necessary by new oil-bath air filter.

Bumper brackets as fitted to 1500 and 1300 models from August 1967: the 1302 from its introduction; the 1303 from its launch; and the 1200 from August 1973. Replaced in August 1974.

More than reminiscent of earlier days, the bumper bracket associated with the 1200 Beetle produced between August 1967 and July 1973.

Towing eye on bracket August 1967 to end of July 1973.

Bumper bracket on all Beetles from August 1974 with slot for towrope.

Telescopic dampers/shock absorbers associated with the meatier US bumpers, from 1 August 1973.

ABOVE: 1303-style seal between front wing and bumper bracket. LEFT: Seal associated with European model Europa bumper.

US-style seal associated with telescopic damper 'brackets', on rear of car.

specification detail changes model year by model year August 1967–January 1980

Date	Chassis no.	Change
1 Aug	119 000 001	Engine compartment sealing now moulded foam rubber; previously lip seal (two-piece).
1 Aug	119 000 007	Transfer on ashtray added indicating the position of each gear.
1 Aug	119 000 007	Anti-dazzle interior rear-view mirror standard for all US Beetles (M206).
15 Sept	119 150 000	Front seat backrests – retaining bolts and springs added to inner adjusting cams.

Technical, mechanical and electrical changes

Date	Chassis no.	Change
1 Aug	119 000 001	Hazard warning light system fitted to indicators.
1 Aug	119 000 001	Switch buttons identified by symbols (this extended to all 'switches', e.g. glovebox latch control – anti-clockwise arrow in white).
1 Aug	119 000 001	Speedometer face – new design with numbers vertical instead of radial placing. International symbols now adopted, e.g. oil light red – formerly green. Other 'symbols' relocated, e.g. full beam, blue light, now 'over' 20mph.
1 Aug	119 000 001	Earth leads fitted to all electrical fittings.
1 Aug	119 000 001	Tyre valve diameter changed from 19.5mm to 15.2mm diameter. Wheel valve hole diameter changed from 16mm to 11.5mm.
1 Aug	119 000 002/9	Weighted regulating flap in intake manifold – oil-bath air filter. Air filters for all Saloons and the Cabriolet (1500) – now only one intake pipe with warm air regulating. Flap and regulator flap for crankcase. 1300 automatic – Bowden cable-controlled warm air flap in filter intake pipe. Clip and eye fastening of wire cable to warm air flap lever. Cable previously 800mm, casing 700mm – now cable 850mm and casing 750mm.
1 Aug	119 000 007	US market models fitted with heated rear window, M102. (Switch to right of steering column under the dash, with green indicator light within speedometer – above 15mph – as a reminder that the 'heater' was switched on.)
22 Aug	119 058 113	83mm diameter piston – nature of oval shape changed

Other modifications

Date	Chassis no.	Change
1 Aug	119 000 002	VW 1300 available with front disc brakes (M80).
1 Aug	119 000 008	VW 1300 available as semi-automatic (M9).
1 Aug	119 000 007	Electrophoretical body priming. Electric charge guaranteed both even and full coating of the body.
1 Aug		US option only – manual gearbox change coupled to double-jointed rear suspension; previously automatic only.

From August 1967 1500 and 1300 Beetles were fitted with box-section-style bumpers front and rear. European models retained this style until the end of production.

The 1200 retained the curved style of bumper until the end of the '73 model year in July 1973.

From August 1973 basic 1200 Beetles were fitted with black painted versions of the box-section bumper – the so-called Europa bumper.

L models were supplied with a rubber trim strip on both front and rear bumpers.

From 1 August 1973 US cars were fitted with more substantial bumpers, which, in conjunction with revised brackets, were capable of withstanding impacts at speeds of 8km/h (5mph) or less.

The heftier US bumper had black plastic end caps.

1970 – Beetles built between 1 August 1969 and 31 July 1970

The Beetle range became more complex with the introduction of an L version of both the 1500 and 1300 cars, while the base model 1200 could be specified with both a 1300 engine and automatic box. The 1300 in turn was available with a 1200 engine and front disc brakes! The external appearance of the 1500 in both Saloon and Cabriolet form made recognition of the latest models easy – the former had engine lid louvres for the first time, while the number allocated to the soft-top model increased dramatically. For the first time the chassis number extended to ten digits; previously nine.

Date	Chassis no.	Change
Body and interior		
1 Aug	110 2 000 003	Engine lid – ten horizontal louvres in two banks of five on 1500 Saloon, while Cabrio (which had always had louvres) now had twenty-eight horizontal louvres in four banks of seven. The introduction or addition to the number of louvres was dictated by the introduction of the 1600 Transporter engine (47PS) for US Beetles, replacing the previous 1500 engine (M157).
1 Aug	110 2 000 001	Wheels – painted silver; formerly cream outer, black inner.
1 Aug	110 2 000 001	Passenger sun visor no longer swivelled to the side.
1 Aug	110 2 000 001	Boot lining – one-piece covering floor of boot and back of instrument panel; formerly two piece.
1 Aug	110 2 000 001	Dashboard trim strip (1500 and 1300) discontinued.
1 Aug	110 2 000 001	Speedometer surround casing matt/brushed silver finish; formerly chromed.
1 Aug	110 2 000 001	Front sill warm outlets – now with lever to operate open/close flaps; previously remote cables.
1 Aug	110 2 000 001	Black plastic covers for window winder cranks smaller diameter than previously. Cover designed to snap off in case of an accident.
1 Aug	110 2 000 001	Drillings for indicators modified on front wings.
1 Aug	110 2 000 001	1500 and 1300 models available with a luxury L package – identified by L addition to engine lid script, as in 'VW 1500 L'. L package consisted of: two reversing lights (included within rear light cluster); chromed bumpers with moulded rubber insert; black padded dashboard with glovebox lid and corresponding grilles around speedometer finished in matt black paint (LD43); anti-dazzle interior rear-view mirror; lockable glove compartment; vanity mirror inset in passenger sun visor; pocket in passenger door to match standard one in driver's door; additional ashtray in rear of car; luxury loop pile carpet. (US versions of the Beetle were in essence based on the L model.)
Technical, mechanical and electrical changes		
1 Aug	110 2 000 001	Oil circulation (crankcase) amended on 1.6- and 1.2-litre engines.
1 Aug	110 2 000 001	Two oil pressure valves, diameter of oil channels increased and hub of crankshaft pulley lengthened. Drilling for cylinder studs – 1200 engine – now 90mm, formerly 87mm.
1 Aug	110 2 000 005	Distributor – double-action vacuum regulation.
1 Aug	110 2 000 001	Preheating of carburettor by hot air taken from right-hand cylinder head.
1 Aug	110 2 000 001	Carburettor 28 PICT-2 – adjusting screw, slimmer cone, finer thread. Set in cast housing, sealed plastic cap.
1 Aug	110 2 000 001	Air filter from 1.3 automatic fitted to both 1300 cars with manual box and 1200 models. Intake preheating with thermostat controlled warm air flap.
1 Aug	110 2 000 002	Carburettor 30 PICT-2 – two mixture adjustment screws, formerly one.
1 Aug	110 2 000 004	Export models for California – activated carbon-filtered system in fuel tank.
1 Aug	110 2 000 001	1200 models now fitted with dual-circuit brake system.
1 Aug	110 2 000 001	New diffusing lenses with new approval marks in headlights.
1 Aug	110 2 000 001	Both indicator and rear lights amended to conform with US and European import regulations.
1 Aug	110 2 000 001	Interior light – switch now incorporated into lens.
1 Aug	110 2 000 001	Spline cone and cap nut secured wiper system.
1 Aug	110 2 000 001	US models: ignition with alarm key device – driver's door contact switch, additional contact for buzzer.
1 Aug	110 2 000 007	US models: larger wraparound-style front indicator housings.
1 Aug	110 2 000 007	US models: tail light housing – reflectors no longer on rear, but fixed to outer side of each housing.
1 Aug	110 2 000 007	US models: 1970 model year only – small rectangular reflectors fitted to the top of both rear bumper brackets.
Later modifications		
12 Aug	110 2 059 477	New sealing ring between front wings and headlights.
13 Aug	110 2 061 659	Anodized upper surface of bearing bush for clutch shaft; previously untreated.
13 Aug	110 2 163 149	Clutch – new guide shell for return spring spin coated in polyamide.
15 Aug	110 2 159 161	Door hinges revised – hinge pin with oil chamber replaced by hinge pin with two spiral-shaped lubrication grooves designed for multipurpose grease.
19 Sept	110 2 358 175	Interior door release handles – opener and escutcheon now made of black plastic, replacing 'chromed' type.
15 Dec	110 2 459 522	Front indicators – side area lengthened by 1.5mm.
2 Jan 1970	110 2 473 154	Brass idling cut-off valve replaced by steel casing.
2 Jan	110 2 473 154	Steel dowel pin replaces steel grooved pin on stop for stepped cam of automatic choke.

specification detail changes model year by model year August 1967–January 1980

Date	Chassis no.	Change
13 Jan	110 2 528 697	Petrol tank held in place with clamp plates with rounded-off corners.
	150 2 572520	A percentage of late model year Cabriolets fitted with heated rear window.

1971 – Beetles built between 1 August 1970 and 31 July 1971

For the first time there were two distinct breeds of Beetle. The classic torsion-bar model, which continued principally as a VW 1300 or VW 1200, was supplemented rather than replaced by a Beetle with MacPherson strut front suspension, semi-trailing arm rear suspension and what was quickly referred to as a pregnant-looking boot. With a 1600 engine the new Beetle was known as the 1302S, but for some markets it was also available with the 1300 engine, or in one or two cases the 34PS 1200 engine, when it became simply the 1302. That the Cabriolet from this point was based on the new body shape indicated that Volkswagen regarded the 1302 as the flagship of the Beetle family. In America the 1302 shape was marketed as the Super Beetle, while the torsion-bar model was branded as the custom. Both the new 1600 engine and the now redesigned 1300 unit featured double inlet ports.

Date	Chassis no.	Change
New model 1302, 1302S – Super Beetle		
1 Aug	111 2 000 011 – 1302	1302 and 1302S (Super Beetle) launched to run in tandem with the classic torsion-bar models.
	111 2 000 012 – 1302S	Main distinguishing features: MacPherson struts with integral damper and coil spring sited in turret built into redesigned inner front wing; linked at base with steering ball joint and anti-roll bar attached to redesigned, flatter, frame head; strut, frame head and radius arm made up a triangular construction of considerable strength; frame head – flatter T-shaped design and construction; steering with control arms – increased radial elasticity – tie rod ends.
		Clutch and brake pedals both positioned closer to vertical and width between the two reduced from the 80mm of the torsion-bar models to 60mm.
		Redesigned front wings – generally rounder in shape; wider front valance and larger wider bonnet (car's general appearance more bulbous).
		Boot capacity increased by 85 per cent (140ltr/4.9cu.ft to 260ltr/9.2cu.ft). Spare wheel now lay flat in specially recessed all-metal floor. Spare wheel concealed by fibreboard cover. Boot space stepped onto two levels – upper level (closest to windscreen) concealed fuel tank (fuel tank capacity 42ltr (9.2 Imp gal), torsion-bar models 40ltr (8.8 Imp gal)).
		New washer bottle of elongated design secured to body by bracket on right-hand side of the boot; appeared to be larger (capacity '1.6ltr (2.8 Imp pints)', compared to torsion-bar models '1.6 ltr (3.0 Imp pints)'; both sets of figures taken from VW handbooks: note 1.6ltr does not equate to 3.00 Imp pints!) (Also note: both designs of windscreen washer bottle – compressed air-feed pipe from spare wheel – were originally exclusive to VW 411 model.)
		Effect of new boot, bonnet and suspension arrangements was to extend the front of the car by 74mm.
		Double-jointed rear axle – previously only available on the semi-automatic Beetle and US market Sedans standard to the 1302 range.
		Enlarged drum brakes (248mm diameter) and increased shoe width, now 45mm, on 1302 model – disc brakes on the 1302S (not US market) – discs optional extra on European 1302 model. (Shape changed of disc brake with backplate resulting in improved cooling.)
		Warm air outlets modified due to increase in length of front end of the car.
		Other distinguishing features for the model year 1971 were shared with 1300 torsion-bar Beetle (and in some instances base model VW 1200) and are listed under general modifications.
General range development		
1 Aug		Home market – semi-automatic transmission and double-jointed rear axle available for all models including basic 1200 level of body trim, but not in conjunction with 34PS engine.
		L package – two-speed fresh-air fan included.
		US range – in addition to the Super Beetle, there was the Custom Beetle – 1600 engine, torsion-bar style bodywork, double-jointed rear axle and drum brakes. Specification detailed as M108. (Also sometimes known as Basic Beetle or Price Leader.)
		Full US range therefore: Custom – manual, stick-shift; Custom sunroof – manual, stick-shift; Super Beetle – manual, stick-shift; Super Beetle sunroof – manual, stick-shift; Super Beetle convertible.
		Note Super Beetle based on European L models: 'Door-to-door carpeting, flow-through ventilation with a two-speed blower, bucket seats, telescopic steering column, dual braking system, built-in headrests, day/night rear-view mirror, ignition steering lock, rubber strips on bumpers … electric rear-window defogger.'
		Standard UK model range by comparison: VW 1200; VW 1300; VW 1302S – the 1600cc Super Beetle.
		Special order only: VW 1302; VW 1302 LS Convertible; Sliding roof; Heated rear window; L package.

Door handle style August 1967 to end of production, although note longer trigger coupled to bigger finger recess from August 1971.

Boot lid handle with push button opener in chrome (August 1967–July 1973).

LEFT: Some special edition models (for example the Jeans Beetle) and utilitarian versions of the car were furnished with matt black painted door handles.

Boot lid handle with black plastic button opener ('74 models to end of production).

Engine lid catch with lock in chrome – note configuration of metal on engine lid on this early example.

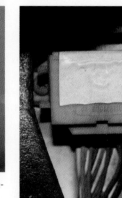

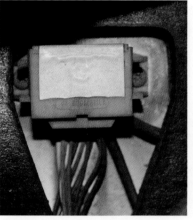

Electronic diagnosis socket in the engine bay introduced in August 1971; no longer fitted by August 1975 when Beetle range simplified.

Engine lid catch with lock in chrome – compare configuration of metal on engine lid on this late example with an earlier model.

Engine lid catch post July 1973 with non-lockable black plastic button.

Quarter-light frame sprayed silver on basic 1200 models (early examples were painted).

The jack was located in the corner of the spare wheel well until July 1970. With the advent of the 1302 and its different-shaped boot, all jacks were relocated to a position under the rear seat.

1971 – Beetles built between 1 August 1970 and 31 July 1971

Date	Chassis no.	Change

Body and interior

1 Aug	111 2 000 001	Engine lid redesigned – more sharply curved, due to increased height of new 1600 and 1300 twinport engines. (1600 models – water drainage tray behind engine lid discontinued.)
1 Aug	111 2 000 001	Engine lid louvres (Sedan – ten in two horizontal sets of five; previously restricted to VW 1500) now extended to all models other than VW 1200 with 34PS engine.
1 Aug	111 2 000 001	Two additional air louvres in the dashboard – positioned below existing vents above glovebox and speedometer respectively.
1 Aug	111 2 000 001	Crescent-shaped ventilation vents to facilitate through-flow ventilation behind rear-side windows. Plastic trim with horizontal louvres and brightwork surround. (Excluding 1200, which had blank indentations.) Inside plastic fittings either side of rear window with two elongated 'slots' through which air could exit – interior arrangement one year only.
1 Aug	111 2 000 001	Two-speed fresh-air blower fitted as standard to VW Cabriolet – option M121 on rest of range.
1 Aug	111 2 000 001	Towing hook fitted to left-hand bumper bracket and on 1302 models to frame-head right.
1 Aug	111 2 000 001	Sheet metal thickness of bumpers – more robust at 1.75mm, previously 1.5mm.
1 Aug	111 2 000 001	Locking pin replaced locking hook on tank filler flap.
1 Aug	111 2 000 001	Front seats – backrest sides more substantial (wider). U-section guide rails attached to floorpan for seats now T section; previously U section. Similarly redesigned on seat frame for compatibility.
1 Aug	111 2 000 001	Jack relocated on all models to position behind battery under rear seat (held by retaining clip).
1 Aug	111 2 000 008	US models: tail light – new enlarged light lenses and bigger reflector inserts.

Technical, mechanical and electrical changes

1 Aug	111 2 000 001	Twin port cylinder heads on 1600 and 1300 engines – better breathing at higher rpm, better fuel burning and more power (*see* Chapter 5 for more details).
1 Aug	111 2 000 001	Relay board for fuse box (1302 models fitted on left of steering column – LHD models).
1 Aug	111 2 000 001	30, 31 and 34 PICT-3 carburettors – new – bypass mixture cut-off valve and bypass drilling, now without electromagnetic cut-off valve.
1 Aug	111 2 000 001 (1200) 111 2 000 002 (1300)	Steering column and attendant bolting modified. Switch mounted on steering column shortened.
1 Aug	111 2 000 002	Fuel filler cap – screw cap replaced bayonet cap.
1 Aug	111 2 000 002	New breather with trap valve on fuel system.
1 Aug	111 2 000 002	New axially guided release bearing on clutch – clutch lacked release ring and torsion spring redesigned.
1 Aug	111 2 000 002	Fan belt – now stretch-resistant.
1 Aug	111 2 000 002	Thermostat on oil-bath air filter; previously Bowden cable.

ABOVE: Tool kit – late models; plastic bag to be stored in boot.

LEFT: Windscreen washer bottle – 1302 and 1303 series cars.

Windscreen washer held by lugs to spare wheel; note sticker indicating required tyre pressure of spare wheel to operate washer bottle.

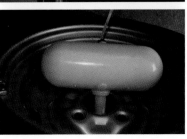

LEFT: Windscreen washer bottle attached to spare wheel – torsion-bar car, late model.

Windscreen washer bottle, circa 1969.

Vehicle identification plate located within spare wheel well on torsion-bar cars.

Vehicle identification plate located on metal-work close to the boot lock within the boot of 1302 and 1303 ranges.

Seat belt anchorage conforms to British Standards sticker – 1302 and 1303 cars – in boot near boot lock.

Paint colour sticker – spare wheel well torsion-bar cars.

Seat belt anchorage conforms to British Standards sticker – torsion-bar cars, spare wheel well.

Paint colour sticker – in boot on side of tower for MacPherson strut, 1302 and 1303 Beetles.

Emissions conformity sticker for US fuel-injected cars, on underside of engine lid.

Recommended setting stickers – 1300 engine 1969.

LEFT: 12V sticker on doorpost applicable to 1500 and 1300 Beetles from August 1967. 1200 Beetles retained 6V electrics, but by August 1970 UK market cars had moved over to 12V and warranted a sticker.

The Beetles:

More safety:
Larger rear window, safety steering wheel with special impact-absorbing element, stalk switch for windshield wiper/washer operation. Non-dazzle speedometer surround. Safety rear-view mirror for VW 1200. An even stronger door locking mechanism and a screw-threaded fuel tank filler cap give extra protection in collisions.

More reliability:
Air-cooling slits doubled in number Six different shielded plugs and other devices to prevent water and condensation from affecting operation of electrical components such as the distributor, generator and spark plugs; they make the water drain plate superfluous. Improved pre-heating of the intake air and the incoming mixture gives better cold running and improves the behaviour of the engine on acceleration. Baffle plates in the fuel tank eliminate swishing.

More comfort:
Bigger recesses and longer triggers for the outside door handles: the doors will be easier to open. Practical lid for stowage compartment behind rear seat. Rear air extraction slots to have retractable flaps to prevent draughts from the rear Special sound damping for wheel arches and transmission mounting to reduce interior noise.

More economy:
Modifications designed to facilitate and improve diagnosis. Larger disc brake pads for longer service life. These are the most important changes to the basic models. Any variations on individual models are indicated in the Table of Modifications. In addition there are some new M options such as halogen headlamps, an intermittent operation setting for the wipers, a bad weather package and a new radio. They are listed in the table at the end of the brochure.

LEFT: Dealers were supplied with literature detailing the 'arguments with which you can convince your customers that changes on Volkswagens are improvements'. This is the 1972 model year version.

1971 – Beetles built between 1 August 1970 and 31 July 1971

Date	Chassis no.	Change
1 Aug	111 2 000 003	Single spring plates – previously double spring plates – on semi-trailing arm suspension.
1 Aug	111 2 000 003	Material used in manufacture of crankcase halves of better quality and more heat-resistant.
1 Aug	111 2 000 009	1600 and 1300 engines available with a compression ratio of 6.6:1 where petrol was of a low octane level.
1 Aug	111 2 000 011	1302 models – sender for fuel gauge transmitter – two float arms of differing lengths; previously on torsion-bar cars – one float arm.

Later modifications

Date	Chassis no.	Change
1 Sept	111 2 082 957	Retaining lugs added to rocker covers for gaskets.
12 Sept	111 2 148 684	1600 engine – distributor and coil – rubber protective caps modified.
17 Sept	111 2 156 331	Carburettor 31 PICT-3 – main jet × 145, idle jet 60oz, idle air jet 120 and air correction jet 170oz.
17 Sept	111 2 158 703	M157 – engines with exhaust fume purification system. Manual Beetles – new throttle valve with closing damper.
29 Sept	111 2 026 187	Thread length of filler cap increased to 41mm; previously 37mm.
30 Sept	111 2 174 804	19mm opening bore on gasket for left-hand preheating pipe; previously 6mm.
6 Oct	111 2 186 917	1600 engine – new washers on terminals – protective rubber caps on cable eyes.
16 Nov	111 2 325 213	Towing eye added to front axle beam.
25 Nov	111 2 339 482	Sheet metal cover for upper carbon brush window – dynamo.
26 Nov	111 2 342 211	1600 engine – upper carbon brush window on dynamo now covered.
12 Feb 1971	111 2 580 353	New marking for TDC on pulley.
2 Feb	111 2 526 082	1302 models – new lip seal for fuel tank filler cap; previously 'O' ring.
1 Mar	111 2 669 688	Champion L88A spark plugs; previously L88.
1 Mar	111 2 669 689	Stepped cam on 31 PICT-3 carburettor marked with code 37; previously 47.
9 Mar	111 2 688 024	Two combination sizes – pistons and cylinders; previously three.
20 Apr	111 2 810 528	1302 models – 7.5 mm securing flange of shock absorbers upgraded to 9.5mm.
28 Apr	111 2 823 698	Oil pump – gear wheels changed from 21mm wide to 26mm – necessary oil level increased accordingly (camshaft modified to revised pump specification).
15 Jun	111 2 920 875	Retard take-off for ignition timing on carburettor discontinued – 30, 31, 34 PICT-3 (excluding US and Canadian models).
15 Jun	111 2 920 875	Single vacuum take-off for distributor replaced double vacuum.

1972 – Beetles built between 1 August 1971 and 31 July 1972

After the momentous introduction of a new breed of Beetles at the start of the previous model year, 1972 saw comparatively little in the way of changes. The Director General who had replaced Nordhoff in April 1968 was unceremoniously ousted part-way through the model year. While Kurt Lotz had decreed that the Beetle would be replaced as the mainstay of Volkswagen's fortunes, he had done precious little about it. His successor, Rudolf Leiding, was a far more determined individual and, with the exception of a major revision to the Super Beetle – in reality sanctioned by Lotz – at the start of the 1973 model year, the process of modifying and improving the Beetle spiralled downwards as new models came on-stream.

During the course of the 1972 model year total worldwide Beetle production exceeded that of the legendary Model T Ford (*see* Chapter 9 for further details).

Date	Chassis no.	Change
Bodywork and interior		
1 Aug	112 2 000 001	Height of rear window increased by 40mm. This was the final increase in glass size of the rear window while the Beetle was manufactured in Germany (previous increase in size was 1965). VW in Mexico and other satellite operations didn't follow suit and when German production ended cars imported from the Puebla factory exhibited rear window glass consistent with that of German Beetles manufactured in the 1971 model year and before.
1 Aug	112 2 000 001	Engine compartment lid – four sets of horizontal cooling louvres with outer banks numbering seven each and inner ones six each, totalling twenty-six overall; previously ten louvres in two horizontal sets of five. Applicable to 1302 range and 1300 torsion-bar models, but not to 34PS 1200 model. Water drainage tray discontinued on 1300 model; previously already discontinued on larger engine model (good aftermarket business generated in protective plastic cowls).
1 Aug	112 2 000 001	Interior ventilation – somewhat brittle plastic fittings either side of rear window with two elongated 'slots' through which air could exit replaced with much neater arrangement of three separate ventilation slots. Also fitted with one-way flap to avoid draughts when windows open and to stop water ingress from external vents to the interior of the car (not 1200 models).

Dashboard and two-spoke steering wheel 1200, circa 1968.

Dashboard and steering wheel with horn ring - 1300 or 1500, circa 1969.

Stalk for indicators and on/off full beam head-lamps.

Speedometer calibrated to 90mph on UK models until the start of the '72 model year (from August 1967 fuel gauge housed in main dial, previously separate).

Speedometer calibrated to 100mph from August 1972 onwards – surround black; late models, UK market, sometimes also show kilometres.

Hazard warning light switch – pull out to activate; all cars from January 1968. From August 1968 decal on dashboard ashtray illustrated gear-change pattern.

LEFT: 1969 model year cars and after – boot lid release in glovebox.

Switch for lights – pull out one notch for 'sidelights' and rear lights, two notches for headlamps.

All models with the exception of the 1200 were endowed with a dash-mounted passenger grab handle until the end of July 1972. New glovebox knob – flatter, broader, 'softer'; introduced in August 1967 would remain on all torsion-bar Beetles to end of production.

LEFT: Wiper switch; two-speed all models except 1200 (push centre to wash screen). On Deluxe models replaced in August 1971 by wiper stalk.

Pre-August 1968 cars – 'pull' under left-hand side of dashboard to open boot.

Late torsion-bar cars – two speed air-circulation fan and handbrake warning light above radio, or radio blanking panel on dashboard.

With effect for the '70 model year the central trim strip on the dashboard was deleted on the 1500 and 1300, while a Deluxe padded version was offered as part of the package for the 1300L, 1500L and Cabriolet.

Plastic moulded dashboard of the curved-screen 1303.

Left-hand-drive version of 1303 dashboard.

Padded dashboard 1200L (Last Edition).

Mock wood trim on selected special edition 1303 saloons and cabriolets.

LEFT ABOVE: *Steering wheel pre-August 1971 – two-spoke with Wolfsburg crest centre boss and chromed horn ring.*

ABOVE: *Safety-style steering wheel with large centre pad – introduced August 1971 on all cars except the 1200.*

LEFT BELOW: *Deluxe version of safety-style steering wheel with padded rim, and so on; note plastic wood inserts on dash – common on later US-specification Super Beetles.*

Clock on 1303 dashboard, rocker switch for lights and knurled disc to regulate brightness of instrument lights. Out of focus – handbrake warning light.

Compartmentalized 1303 glovebox, also showing boot release catch.

Glovebox lid 1303, with August 1973 onwards push button lock; previously rotary knob.

Date	Chassis no.	Change
1 Aug	112 2 000 001	Carpet-covered luggage shelf for rear luggage compartment; attached to backrest – dropped down as and when required. While being a useful asset in itself, the shelf also had the effect of deadening sound (not 1200 models).
1 Aug	112 2 000 001	Rear wheel arches – inside car – sound-deadening material fitted (including 1200).
1 Aug	112 2 000 001	Rear seat held in place with catch hook on seat frame, plus when folded forward to increase luggage-carrying capacity strap attached to luggage compartment floor.
1 Aug	112 2 000 001	Longer trigger on external door handles, necessitating deeper recess in door panel bodywork.
1 Aug	112 2 000 001	Fixing support – body to frame – on rear side panel modified.
1 Aug	112 2 000 001	New style of four-spoke steering wheel with large centre horn pad engraved with Wolfsburg crest. Designed to reduce the risk of chest injuries to the driver in the event of a collision.
1 Aug	112 2 000 001	Stalk to right-hand side of steering wheel to operate two-speed wipers (upwards once slow wipe, upwards twice faster wipe) and supply of water from washer bottle (pull towards); previously button on dashboard – turn once, twice and push centre (not 1200 models, which retained one-speed dashboard button).

Technical, mechanical and electrical changes

Date	Chassis no.	Change
1 Aug	112 2 000 001	VW Diagnosis – plug-in socket fitted top left of engine bay. Extract from VW marketing brochure: 'Every VW comes fully equipped for Computer Diagnosis – a unique concept in automatic servicing. We plug in our Computer and ask your car up to 77 questions. Your car gives the answers … On an automatically printed condition report form you will see that everything has been checked accurately, and you'll know just what needs attention …'
1 Aug	112 2 000 001	Speedometer adjusted with higher end of scale increased. Face revised with red section on fuel gauge indicating reserve.
1 Aug	112 2 000 002	Single vacuum distributor; previously double vacuum. Retard take-off for ignition no longer applicable to Solex 30, 31 and 34 PICT/3 carburettors.
1 Aug	112 2 000 002	Intake manifold preheating at exhaust – previously right to left – now left to right.
1 Aug	112 2 000 002	1300 models – primarily due to discontinuation of tray behind engine lid louvres – distributor and ignition coil, modifications to rubber protection caps. New washers under terminals of generator. Protection of cable eyes with rubber protection caps, upper carbon brush window covered.
1 Aug	112 2 000 002	Fuel tank baffle.
1 Aug	112 2 000 008	US market – distributor and ignition timing adjusted to meet additional exhaust emission regulations.
1 Aug	112 2 000 008	Compression now 7.3:1 – previously 7.5:1 – as a result of modifications to pistons and cylinder heads (engines for the US market).
1 Aug	112 2 000 009	Californian cars: recirculation of exhaust gases – emission control system to meet the Sacramento legislature's new stricter emission requirements.

Later modifications

Date	Chassis no.	Change
1 Sept	112 2 073 652	Clutch release spindle 20mm diameter, previously 16mm diameter.
1 Sept	112 2 073 652	Longer clutch lever; operation of clutch modified, resulting in improved performance of clutch disengagement.
3 Sept	112 2 076 199	Three-point location for gear change and lateral guide for stop plate; previously four-point system.
12 Oct	112 2 206 303	Positioner on throttle deleted.
12 Nov	112 2 266 171	Revised rear guide for window glass lifting mechanism.
6 Dec	112 2 389 435	Rubber insert between top of boot lock and boot; previously not part of specification.
10 Jan 1972	112 2 429 477	Ends of accelerator guide tube closed up with plugs. Clutch pedal now with stop.
24 Jan– 4 Feb	112 2 471 100	
	112 2 497 034	Pressed steel wheels – 4½J × 15 with 34mm offset; previously 4J × 15 with 40mm offset. Tyres consequently now 6.00 × 15, previously 5.60 × 15 (restricted to specified US models, or in conjunction with other packages).
8 Feb	112 2 540 929	Fuel pipe outlet moved to right side of frame head; previously outlet above.
23 Feb	112 2 509 832	Repositioned stop on steering gear.
1 Mar	112 2 581 695	Built in cut-off valve – fuel pump with pressed casing; previously cut-off valve separate from fuel pump.
6 Mar	112 2 636	Dual control replaced single control – temperature control for air filter.
24 Mar	112 2 670 583	Clutch release bearing centrally carried; previously carbon release ring.
27 Apr	112 2 767 602	Constant velocity joints – protection boots enclosed in protective caps; previously held with hose clips.
15 May	112 2 837 179	Residual pressure valve deleted from brake master cylinder specification.
16 Jun	112 2 927 493	Crankshaft pulley cover piece discontinued.
20 Jun	112 2 933 968	Drain plug and washer deleted from oil strainer cap.
30 Jun	112 2 857 574	Temperature warning device – switch discontinued.

1973 – Beetles built between 1 August 1972 and 31 July 1973

The 1973 model year saw the Super Beetle modified to incorporate a prominent curved windscreen and a radically different style of dashboard, the car now being branded as the 1303 to denote this progression. Developed out of fear that US safety legislation would shortly demand a greater distance between the driver/front seat passenger and the windscreen than the 1302 range afforded, the expense involved in the advance was in vain, as any such plans were aborted by the American authorities. Although the modernistic dashboard of the 1303 was frowned on by many Beetle owners and not just diehards, the curved screen was undoubtedly suited to the Cabriolet – the hood seeming to meld into the screen, something not achieved previously.

Date	Chassis no.	Change

Facelift model 1303, 1303S – Super Beetle

1 Aug	133 2 000 004	The 1303 retained the MacPherson struts, wider bonnet shape, rounder front wings, larger two-tier boot with spare wheel lying flat and double-jointed rear axles of the 1302 series. The facelift involved the following items.

Windscreen sharply curved, increasing overall size by 42 per cent – improving both forward vision and the aerodynamics of the vehicle (known by some as the 'Panorama' Beetle).

Revised shape of the windscreen resulted in a shorter boot lid and elongated roof panel. Modified windscreen wipers and blades were required to ensure the sweep was adequate with the larger area.

Panel below window and before boot lid redesigned to accommodate curved screen – included nineteen louvres (for fresh-air intake system). Middle three louvres shorter than the rest to make room for windscreen washer nozzle.

'Chrome' VW emblem deleted from boot lid – although early press release images of the new car show the badge as still being in place.

Black plastic push button on boot lid handle (press release and launch brochure images show chromed push button).

Additional short strip of grooved anodized trim above traditional strip at top of front quarter panel.

Rear wings reshaped – more rounded/bulging – to accommodate much larger and rounder tail-light clusters (soon known by enthusiasts as 'elephant foot' tail lights). New three-section lens cluster: top (orange) indicator; middle (red) rear light, brake function and reflector; and bottom (clear) reversing light where fitted, meld straight with wing – i.e. lack metalwork of previous tail lights. (Note dealer model year preview which states rear lights were 'ready glazed for the addition of reversing lights'.)

Forty-two louvres below rear window compared to fifty on flat-screen Beetles.

Interior dominated by totally redesigned dashboard made possible by the design and shape of the new windscreen. Unlike previous cars either with metal dash or padded covering of classic shape, the 1303 dash was a plastic moulded affair capable of deforming on impact. Although still austere in comparison to the dashboard of many a contemporary vehicle, the 1303 dashboard more closely mirrored the appearance of the products of other manufacturers. Fresh-air vents with directional flaps sat into a raised moulded section which ran around the perimeter of the top section of the dashboard closest to the windscreen. In similar but even more pronounced vein, the moulded shroud for the speedometer stood proud of the rest of the top section of the dash, with the single gauge being fully visible over the steering wheel for the driver. Behind the raised section of the upper part of the dash and following the contour of the windscreen was a heat and fresh-air channel comprising forty-two air louvres (providing faster, more efficient demisting etc. than the vents that were part of the flat-screen models). Below the section of the dashboard described was a flat-fronted section, with a width corresponding to that of a radio and an extra on all models. This section housed rocker switches to switch on lights, emergency hazard warning lights (previously pull knobs), heated rear screen (optional extra) etc., in easy reach of the driver, plus for selected models a handbrake warning light and rectangular clock. The gear-change pattern, illustrated on the ashtray of the flat-screen models, was included on a slightly raised and 'shiny' piece of plastic within this section and almost immediately below the speedometer. A blanking panel for a radio formed the central part of this area (above the central tunnel and in line with the gear lever) and part of the glovebox lid (in front of the passenger.) Finished in black as standard for some Special Edition models this section was overlaid with a mock wood trim. The glovebox was opened by a rotary-type catch, as per the flat-screen cars. The lower section of the dash was angled away from the car's occupants and towards the bulkhead. The central section included an ashtray and two turn knobs (in the style of those used on the flat-screen Beetles, including blue directional arrows on the flat centre section), to control the fresh-air flow, while the area in front of the passenger seat was a continuation of the glovebox lid. A fuse box of amended design was fixed to the underneath of the boot section – i.e., below the dashboard and above the frame tunnel within the car.

Glovebox divided into three separate compartments – full length in top section, unequal division lower section. Although easier to keep tidy than the single space glovebox of the flat-screen Beetles, the compartments had the effect of reducing overall storage capacity. 1303 glovebox lid didn't open flat, denying use as a 'picnic' feature to carry a cup.

Door furniture – late.

Push button to lock door from inside – all cars throughout period covered.

Recessed interior door handle – 1200 early.

Recessed interior door handle – 'chromed' finish all but 1200, early.

Recessed interior door handle – all models late.

Basic 1200 door pull.

Door pull late – all but basic 1200; door pulls doubled as an armrest.

1200 window winder.

Window winder late for all but basic 1200.

Basic 1200 headlining. Other models extended to areas around the windows.

Detachable headrests became the norm for all cars which included such items in their specification in the Beetle's later years.

LEFT: Pedal cluster; also illustrates inclusion of metal sheets between floorpan and bulkhead and extensive usage of rubber matting.

US-specification seats with integral headrests – early cars.

US specification – fasten seat belts warning and handbrake warning lights on Super Beetle.

1303 fuse box mounted below dash.

Large brake pedal and lack of clutch pedal indicate that this is a semi-automatic car.

Date	Chassis no.	Change
Range availability UK and US market		
1 Aug	133 2 000 004	UK range available without special order:
		1200
		1300A (basic trim as per 1200, but with 1285cc engine.)
		1300
		1303
		1303S
		US range:
		Custom – with or without sunroof, manual or semi-automatic
		Super Beetle – with or without sunroof, manual or semi-automatic
		Super Beetle convertible – manual or semi-automatic
		Sport Bug – based on Super Beetle, manual only.
General modifications		
1 Aug	113 2 000 001	Gear lever moved back towards driver by 40mm – lever shortened accordingly and position of handbrake similarly adjusted.
1 Aug	113 2 000 001	Front seats mounted on pyramid-style structures for safety reasons and to facilitate greater seat adjustment. Rear legs of seats travelled in new slot type tracks. Backwards/forwards movement controlled by 'handles' fixed to the frame tunnel. Described in dealer preview literature thus:
		• 'Luxury new front seats.
		• Contoured backrest for greater support when cornering. When the backrest is folded down, it is held down automatically, which makes it easy to reach through to the rear seat.
		• Additional lumber support for more comfort.
		• Easily adjusted to 84 different positions.
		• Strengthened floor positions for safety.'
1 Aug	113 2 000 002	Ashtray in rear of car (where fitted) – now finished in black plastic, previously chrome.
1 Aug	113 2 000 002	New style of air filter for all engines except 34PS. Large near-oblong plastic box containing conventional paper filter allowing easy change without mess; previously oil-bath filter.
1 Aug	113 2 000 002	Vent pipe from oil filler with rubber valve discontinued (crankcase ventilation).
1 Aug	113 2 000 003	Diaphragm spring clutch, formerly coil spring clutch.
1 Aug	113 2 075 826	1200 model – sealing plugs, lubrication holes and tapped holes deleted from specification.
1 Aug	113 2 031 720	Emden-built cars – noise suppression on warm air hose between heat exchanger and body (previously flexible metal tube).
Later modifications		
25 Sept	113 2 196 230	31 PICT-4 carburettor – new thermostat for accelerator pump.
7 Nov	113 2 297 983	Gear ratios amended, previous ratio shown in brackets:
		4th 0.931 (0.883)
		1st 3.78 (3.80)
		Reverse 3.79 (3.80).
10 Nov	113 2 302 030	Oil deflector ring discontinued on exhaust valve.
21 Nov	113 2 360 845	Brake cable – twelve wire strands, previously nineteen.
23 Nov	113 2 362 151	Foam float – 30 PICT-3 carburettor, previously hollow.
4 Dec	113 2 380 035	Four lead terminals – previously five – dual-circuit brake warning light.
5 Dec	113 2 376 816	Ductile studs on cylinder head; previously tensile stud.
4 Jan 1973	133 2 445 273	US models: alternator with voltage regulator replaced DC generator with control box.
11 Jan	113 2 452 529	Semi-automatic – parking 'brake'.
22 Jan	113 2 509 096	Lower joint protector discontinued on joint steering shaft.

Date	Chassis no.	Change
29 Jan	133 2 518 621	WB3 distributor introduced (US models: twin vacuum advance discontinued – not California cars).
1 Feb	113 2 522 922	Galvanized pulley for engine and generator 'V' belt; previously painted black.
7 Feb	113 2 529 939	Tandem brake master cylinder – one brake light switch, previously two.
5 Mar	153 2 541 768	Cabriolet rear window positioned 30mm higher up on canvas roof.
23 Mar	113 2 687 765	New twin preheater tubes – inlet manifold and exhaust box; previously single tube. Tailpipes altered in both length and diameter.
8 May	113 2 797 156	Heater flap regulator with springs on floor vent ducts – heat exchangers; previously spiral springs on lever mountings.
10 May	133 2 802 561	Fuel tank with full-flow filter in fuel line – drainer discontinued; previously strainer in fuel tank.
12 Jul	113 2 986 992	Spark plugs – gap now 0.6mm, previously 0.7mm.

1974 – Beetles built between 1 August 1973 and 31 July 1974

With the launch of the Passat taking place just a couple of months before the start of the 1974 model year and work proceeding at fever pitch to bring the Golf into production, noteworthy changes to the Beetle's specification tended to be restricted to trim packages and the advent of a series of special limited edition models during the model year. The launch of the Scirocco in February/March of 1974 – essentially the Golf with a sporty body – and the press launch of the Golf in May both detracted from the Beetle's long-lived supremacy, while cessation of Beetle manufacture at Wolfsburg in July 1974 in favour of the Golf confirmed that Volkswagen's direction for the future had fundamentally changed.

Date	Chassis no.	Change

Range adjustments and modifications

Date	Chassis no.	Change
1 Aug	114 2 000 001 134 2 000 005	Note: some models not available for selected markets. Range adjustments listings refer primarily to the home market.

VW 1200

Revamped for the new model year; key changes were as follows.

Large 'elephant foot' tail light; previously style replaced for the '68 model on 1500 and 1300 cars. Rear wing shape adjusted accordingly.

Euro-shape bumpers finished in matt black with silver tape stuck to central section; previously blade-style bumpers (but without overriders) of the type fitted to Deluxe Beetles up to and including the '67 model year. Boot handle and engine lid catch also finished in matt black.

Decorative grilles on front wings discontinued.

VW 1200L

Fully chromed bumpers, external trim as per Deluxe models of earlier years, through ventilation (crescent-shaped air vents behind rear side windows, air intake louvres in boot lid etc., but note not fan-assisted), two-speed wipers with auto park and reversing lights.

Interior trim included pocket on driver's door, rear parcel shelf. Available with both 34PS engine and 44PS (1300) engine (with 44PS engine marketed as VW 1300 in, for example, Britain).

VW 1303

Continuation of 1303 with standard and Deluxe, or L specification, plus larger 1600 engine S model, again with standard and Deluxe specification. Cabriolet offered as an LS model only. New to the range is the VW 1303A – effectively an economy version with the 34PS engine, black bumpers and minimal trim.

Bodywork and interior

Date	Chassis no.	Change
1 Aug	114 2 000 001	Sills strengthened in region of jacking point.
1 Aug	134 2 000 005	1303 windscreen ventilation amended – distinct and separate outlet louvres to right and left; previously full width arrangement with forty-two louvres.
1 Aug	134 2 000 005	Glovebox catch now required use of finger and thumb to pinch the sides of a near rectangular catch; previously rotary latch.
1 Aug	134 2 000 005	US models only. New, larger, sturdier reinforced bumpers with telescopic dampers/shock absorbers capable of resisting accident damage at speeds of 5mph or less (to comply with latest US state requirements). Reinforced panels and redesigned brackets for new style bumper mounts.

Technical, mechanical and electrical changes

Date	Chassis no.	Change
1 Aug	134 2 000 001	1303 based models – self-stabilizing steering, achieved by modification of MacPherson strut suspension to give negative rather than positive steering roll radius.
1 Aug	114 2 000 001	Alternator with voltage regulator replaced DC generator with control box (European market; US cars had alternator from 4 Jan 1973).
1 Aug	114 2 007 917	31 PICT-4 carburettor – replaceable thermostat; previously non-replicable.

Later modifications

Date	Chassis no.	Change
11 Sept	114 2 147 150	Accelerator pump now with vent-hole on 31 PICT-4 carburettor; previously without.
24 Sept	114 2 153 057	Headlight reflector and lens bonded; previously separate.
24 Sept	114 2 165 704	Catch for backrest on forward folding backrest discontinued.

19 Oct	114 2 248 672	Lubrication holes and plugs discontinued on track rod joints.
21 Jan 1974	114 2 458 359	Cover for oil pressure switch.
29 Jan	114 2 487 143	Captive nuts welded onto stabilizer bar mounting to underside of frame; previously threaded sockets.
1 Feb	114 2 489 588	Wash-wipe simultaneous with intermittent wipe relay where fitted.
19 Feb	114 2 509 962	Rear drain tube for steel sunroof ran to side of engine compartment; previously ran to rear quarter panel above running board.
11 Apr	114 2 683 124	Redesign of front seat backrest – similar in style to that of the VW Passat.
12 Jun	114 2 802 587	Vacuum advance retard only replaced by combined centrifugal and vacuum advance retard on 34PS distributor.

1975 – Beetles built between 1 August 1974 and 31 July 1975

As the Golf went into series production, *en masse* modifications improvements to the Beetle's specification were significantly reduced. That having been said, one change for the European market at least made the latest models instantly identifiable, while US cars benefited from fuel injection.

Date	Chassis no.	Change
1 Aug	115 2 000 001	Front bumper of all cars except those destined for North America and Japan altered to accept indicators; previously indicators located on top of wings.
1 Aug	115 2 000 001	Bumper brackets front and rear of car redesigned and strengthened as single bracket, also now incorporated slot for tow rope; previously Y-shaped bracket with welded on towing eye (European market).
1 Aug	115 2 000 001	Rear valance now humped single sheet metal; previously double-skinned metal flat in appearance (European market).
1 Aug	115 2 000 001	Licence plate cover containing bulb to illuminate plate at night now made of plastic rather than metal as previously; can be identified by nineteen corrugations on upper surface.
1 Aug	115 2 000 001	Tailpipes on 1200 model black; previously chromed. Chromed hubcaps deleted from 1200 specification and replaced by plastic caps to cover the wheel centres and nuts. Door and side panelling simplified (little more than a hardboard sheet). Glovebox lid discontinued on home market models but not all export destinations (e.g., UK).
1 Aug	115 2 000 001	Clutch cable rerouted to reduce effort required to operate pedal.
1 Aug	115 2 000 001	Electronic voltage regulator; previously mechanical.
1 Aug	135 2 000 001	1303 range now with rack and pinion steering; previously worm and roller. Steering damper discontinued as a result on these models.
1 Aug	135 2 000 001	1303 range no longer adorned with either L or S suffixes on the badge at the rear of the car.
1 Aug	135 2 000 005	Cars destined for the North American market and Japan fitted with 50PS Bosch L-Jetronic fuel-injected engine, exhaust pump and, at least for California, catalytic converter. Designed to meet California's stringent emission regulations and to pre-empt the inevitable extension to other US states. Single-skin valance humped as per European models (for the specific purpose of housing the catalytic converter). Single tailpipe on exhaust exits from right-hand end of valance. US cars therefore now ran exclusively on unleaded fuel. Petrol filler neck amended to suit unleaded fuel nozzles. (The words 'Fuel injection' replaced 'Volkswagen' on all engine compartment lids.)

Later modifications

16 Jan 1975	115 2 160 733	Screen wash washer bottle fitted with strainer.

1976 – Beetles built between 1 August 1975 and 31 July 1976; 1977 – Beetles built between 1 August 1976 and 31 July 1977; 1978 – Beetles built between 1 August 1977 and 19 January 1978*

*The Cabriolet continued in production until 10 January 1980, the only significant change of its final years occurring in 1977, when horsehair used in the make-up of the hood was replaced by modern foam material.

The 1976 model year saw the Beetle Saloon range reduced to just two models, both of which were based on the trailing arm, swing axle, torsion-bar 1200. Offered as a basic model and with a full package of L trimmings, the car was generally available with the 34PS engine, although some markets were offered the 50PS engine in addition to, or instead of, the smaller unit. Cabriolets continued to be based on the MacPherson strut, curved-screen 1303.

The oil-bath air cleaner was finally replaced on the 1200 model with the now familiar dry paper cleaner, with plastic housing and paper cleaner. Inlet air preheating was now thermostatically controlled.

The VW 1200L with 50PS engine was fitted with both a compensating spring on the rear axle and front disc brakes. The US Custom model was upgraded in trim specification to match the 1200L and continued to come with the 50PS fuel-injected engine and its attendant attributes, plus double-joint rear axle and drum brakes all round; the last two features remained throughout a characteristic of such cars.

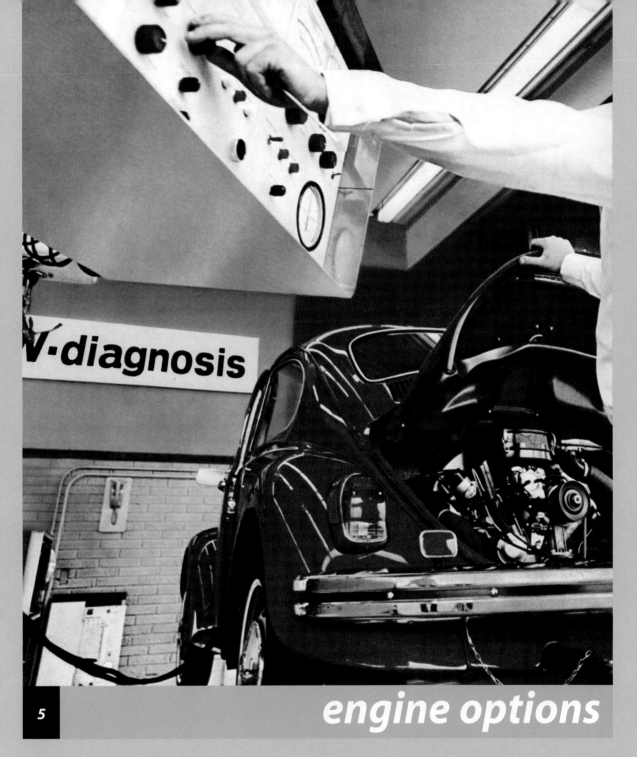

engine options

ABOVE: In 1967 engine options consisted of the old trusty but leisurely 34PS 1200, the 40PS 1300 and the 44PS 1500. While the 1500 would be replaced by a 50PS 1600 unit and the 1300 would be upgraded to 44PS, not to mention the arrival of fuel injection on American cars, nevertheless the general criticism was that the air-cooled units weren't keeping pace with the times.

INTRODUCTION

The Beetles produced for the 1968 model year were powered by what was essentially the same engine as the 985cc, four-cylinder, air-cooled, flat-four devised by Ferdinand Porsche for the original Volkswagen, the so-called KdF-Wagen, or Strength-through-Joy car of 1930s vintage. Porsche's engine had a bore of 70mm and a stroke of 64mm. Compression stood at 5.8:1 and the engine developed a maximum of 23.5PS at 3,000rpm. Top speed for the vehicle was an estimated 95km/h (59mph).

By the end of the war period, the KdF-Wagen's engine had been upgraded to 1131cc, the bore now being 75mm. A maximum of 25PS was achieved at 3,300rpm. The more powerful engine had been devised specifically for the military version of the KdF-Wagen, the *Kübelwagen*, as the smaller engine was not only deemed underpowered, but also didn't comply with the prescribed minimum for any German army vehicle.

Beetle engine production at Hanover circa 1971.

THE 34PS ENGINE

The 34PS engine, albeit modified over the years, endured throughout the period covered by this book, essentially but not exclusively powering the base model of the Beetle range, and proved to be the mainstay of the Beetle's final years of German production.

In 1960 the essential differences between the 30PS and 34PS engine were that the latter featured: a more robust crankcase; a stronger crankshaft; a removable dynamo pedestal; a modified fuel pump drive; and greater spacing of the cylinder barrels. The design of the cylinder head had also changed, use being made of wedge-shaped combustion chambers, with valves positioned at a slant. A larger dynamo pulley and a smaller crankshaft pulley resulted in reduced speed for the cooling fan, with resultant reduced noise levels.

During the Nordhoff era covering the years 1948 to 1968, the Beetle gradually acquired more powerful engines. At the end of 1953 the first increase occurred with the arrival of an 1192cc, 30PS unit to replace the 25PS engine. This endured until the summer of 1960, when it was replaced by a 34PS engine on all but the basic, or Standard, model of Beetle.

The bore and stroke of the 34PS engine at 77mm × 64mm was the same as that of the 30PS, as was the cubic capacity of 1192. However, the increased compression ratio, up from 6.6:1 to 7.0:1, had the desired effect of increasing usable power significantly. A new Solex carburettor – 28PICT with automatic choke – was fitted, not necessarily to universal approval. This was replaced in 1963 by a Solex 28PICT/1, which continued in use to July 1970.

The appearance of the 34PS engine changed in December 1962 with the revision of the Beetle's heating system to include heat exchangers. The result was the addition of air hoses, one to the right and the other to the left of the engine, feeding from the fan housing to the exchangers that were out of sight under the engine's tinware.

34PS 1200 engine circa 1968.

As the Golf, Passat and Polo took the ascendancy, a promotional shot of the 34PS 1200 engine in a brochure was relegated to a position accompanying the petrol cap and a wheel.

The 40PS 1300 engine, circa 1968.

The near ubiquitous oil-bath air filter, from time immemorial to November 1972 and later on the basic 1200 Beetle.

The 44PS engine was the flagship of the range between August 1966 and its demise in July 1970 and to many is still regarded as the best Beetle power plant.

THE 40PS ENGINE

With effect from August 1965 for the 1966 model year a more powerful engine was produced to propel the Deluxe and Cabriolet, which were now branded as the VW 1300. Although the basic design was retained, an additional 6PS was achieved through the adoption of the crankshaft from the larger VW Saloon, notchback and estate, the VW 1500. This lengthened the stroke from 64mm to 69mm, giving an overall capacity of 1285cc. The compression ratio stood at 7.3:1 compared to the smaller engine's 7.0:1. Some had argued that a more powerful engine should feature twin-port inlets, but Nordhoff preferred to ensure that the 1300 remained under-stressed like its smaller brother.

The 1300 engine as introduced in 1965 was carried forward to the 1968 model year and beyond.

THE 44PS ENGINE

Twelve months after the launch of the 1300 engine and just a year away from the period covered by this volume, Volkswagen added a still more powerful engine to the range. The 1493cc 1500 engine powered the top-of-the-range Saloon and the Cabriolet, while the 1300 engine remained an option with the former. The 1300 engine was also optional on the base model.

Although the 1500's stroke remained the same as that of the 1300 at 69mm, the bore was enlarged to 83mm, while the compression ratio was increased once more, this time to 7.5:1. Maximum torque of 78lb.ft occurred at 2,600rpm. The Beetle endowed with a 1500 engine was capable of a top speed of 78mph, but it was thanks to the noticeable boost in power right across the range, despite an increase of just 4PS to 44PS over the 1300, that

the 1500 came to be regarded as a real driver's car.

The 1500 engine can be readily distinguished from the 1200 and 1300 by a twin-pronged air filter – a necessary modification due to the intake preheating air being taken from both cylinder heads through two narrow flexible hoses to its destination.

As might be expected, the 1500 flagship engine was carried forward to the '68 model year and beyond.

TECHNICAL DATA
1968 MODEL YEAR

Compared to brochure information of earlier years, Volkswagen wasn't particularly forthcoming in its description of the engines offered with the 'new' Beetle of August 1967. The following text pertains to the 1200. Note the use of the American bhp (SAE) despite the brochure being offered to a British

44PS 1300 twin-port engine, circa 1972.

50PS 1600 engine, circa 1977.

audience (PS from German brochure added in brackets).

Engine:

Four-cylinder, four-stroke, horizontally opposed, rear-mounted. Air cooling, special oil cooler, low maximum revs: can cruise for hours at top speed. Automatic choke: flick-of-the-switch starting no matter what the temperature, full power at once. Capacity – 1.2 litres. Output – 41.5 bhp (SAE) [DIN 34PS]. Electrical system – 6V.

Performance:

Maximum speed in mph	71
Consumption*	37.5
(regular fuel) in miles	
per imperial gallon	

*With half permissible payload at steady ¾ of maximum speed on level roads plus 10 per cent

The text to describe the VW1300/VW1500 is almost a copy of that written for the 1200. PS details have been added from an equivalent German brochure as before.

Engine:

Four-cylinder, four-stroke, horizontally opposed, rear-mounted. Air cooling, special oil cooler, low maximum revs: can cruise for hours at top speed. Automatic choke: flick-of-the-switch starting no matter what the temperature, full power at once. Capacity/Output:

VW 1300	1.3 litres/50bhp
	(SAE) [40PS]
VW 1500	1.5 litres/53bhp
	(SAE) [44PS]

Performance:

Maximum speeds in mph:

VW 1300	75
VW 1500	78

Consumption* (regular fuel) in miles per imperial gallon

VW 1300	33.0
VW 1500	32.0

*With half permissible payload at steady [3/4] of maximum speed on level roads plus 10 per cent.

NEW ENGINE FOR AMERICAN MARKET ONLY – AUGUST 1969 (1970 MODEL YEAR)

The following release was issued by the PR Manager of Volkswagen America on 9 October 1969: 'Volkswagen's 1970 Beetle Sedan features a slightly larger engine giving it greater response and more rapid acceleration in the lower ranges of its four-speed synchromesh transmission …'.

The only visible sign of the change was the introduction of ten horizontal louvres in two banks of five each in the engine lid. The Cabriolet, which had always featured ten engine lid louvres, now had four banks of louvres totalling twenty-eight in number. An increase in ventilation was required for the new American-only engine,

but Volkswagen decided to apply the change to European-specification 1500 models as well.

The 1600 engine was the single port unit as fitted to the second-generation Transporter from the point of the vehicle's launch in August 1967. With a bore and stroke of 85.5mm × 69.0mm, this engine produced a maximum of 47PS. Careful analysis of the finer detail reveals that officially this engine (as it was fitted with an exhaust gas-purification system) came under the optional extra code of M157.

CHANGES TAKING EFFECT IN AUGUST 1970 (FOR THE 1971 MODEL YEAR)

A 1584cc engine replaced the 1500 engine with effect from August 1970. The change was relevant to all markets including the USA, as this engine was not the same as the one fitted twelve months previously to top-of-the-range American Beetles. A revised 1300 engine was introduced.

Both engines had modified cylinder heads with two inlet ports per head intended to facilitate more efficient 'breathing'. The inlet manifold now had two separate pipes at each end. The new 1300 engine developed a

Specification – twin-port engines		
Cubic Capacity	1285cc (1300)	1584cc (1600)
Bore and Stroke	77 × 69mm	85.5 × 69mm
Compression Ratio	7.5:1	7.5:1
Carburettor	Solex 31 PICT4	Solex 34 PICT3
Maximum Power	44PS at 4,100rpm	50PS at 4,000rpm

With a more powerful engine.

The new VW 1302 S has a 1600 cc engine with an output of 60 bhp (SAE). It accelerates from 0 to 50 mph in 12.5 seconds and has a maximum and cruising speed of 80 mph plus.

Now some companies would have produced the extra horsepower at the expense of engine life. But this was never our policy.

The new 1600 cc Super Beetle pro-duces its output at comfortably low revs.

And although we've made various other important changes to the engine, it's still rear-mounted, still horizontally opposed.

And still air-cooled.

Because what would even a brand spanking new Beetle be without a good old, traditional Volkswagen engine.

With a more powerful engine.

The new VW Super Beetle has a 1600 cc engine with an output of 60 bhp (SAE). It accelerates from 0 to 50 mph in 12.5 seconds and has a maximum and cruising speed of 80 mph plus.

Now some companies would have produced the extra horsepower at the expense of engine life. But this was never our policy.

The new Beetle produces its output

at comfortably low revs.

And although we've made various other important changes to the engine, it's still rear-mounted, still horizontally opposed — and still air-cooled.

Because what would even a brand spanking new Beetle be without a good old, traditional Volkswagen engine.

Und er ist sicherer, als es der Gesetzgeber vorschreibt.

ABOVE AND RIGHT: As these pages taken from contemporary literature illustrate, Volkswagen's publicity department went into overdrive on the launch of the 1302S Beetle with its more powerful 1600 engine.

maximum of 44PS, up 4PS on the old unit, and the same as the now dis-placed 1500 engine. The new 1600 offered 50PS, mainly thanks to an increase of 2.5mm to 85.5mm in bore over that of the 1500.

These changes coincided with the introduction of the 1302 range, but are coincidental to the appearance of these cars. (As proof positive, the 1300 torsion-bar car also received the new twin-port engine.)

The following extracts indicate what copywriters preparing brochures for the British and American markets had to say:

The Beetles, brochure dated 8/70, UK market.

With a more powerful engine.

The new 1302S has a 1600cc engine

with an output of 60bhp (SAE). It accel-erates from 0 to 50mph in 12.5 seconds and has a maximum and cruising speed of 80mph plus. Now some com-panies would have produced the extra horsepower at the expense of engine life. But this was never our policy. The new 1600cc Super Beetle produces its output at comfortably low revs. And although we've made various other important changes to the engine, it's still rear-mounted, still horizontally opposed. And still air-cooled. Because what would even a brand spanking new Beetle be without a good, old, traditional Volkswagen engine.

The Super Beetle. We've made so many improvements they're beginning to show. Brochure dated 8/70, American market.

And to make our Super Beetle go, we put in an even longer lasting engine. It's the strongest engine we ever offered in the Beetle. It's made out of the same stuff Porsche uses to make its race car engines: lightweight mag-nesium alloy. And it also has 3 more hp than the '70 Beetle. So it doesn't have to work as hard to get from one place to the other. Any automobile engineer will tell you that that will make it last even longer.

A FINAL CHANGE FOR AMERICAN-SPECIFICATION BEETLES

The replacement of the 1302 and 1302S with the curved-screen 1303 range brought no changes to engine size or performance. However, there

ABOVE AND RIGHT: *US-specification fuel-injected 1600 engines.*

When the 1302 series evolved into the 1303 with its curved screen there was no change in the range of engines offered. Volkswagen's publicity department therefore resorted to the following line when illustrating the new car's engine: 'Drive the 1303 Beetle. With the engine of a World Champion.'

were problems looming on the horizon for the American market.

New and tougher Californian emissions regulations which would soon be extended to other states demanded that US cars be fitted with fuel injection. Bosch's design was relatively simple with a fuel loop that supplied the injectors with fuel at constant pressure. The injectors were activated by contact points in the distributor. Although effective, Bosch fuel injection had little effect on performance or fuel economy. A catalytic converter was added to California-bound cars from August 1974 and in the case of all other US-specification Beetles at the start of the 1977 model year.

American-specification 1977 model specification – Sedan and Cabriolet

Engine

No. of cylinders	Four opposed
Bore	3.37in (85.5mm)
Stroke	2.72in (69mm)
Displacement	96.66cu.in (1584cc)
Compression ratio	7.3:1
Horsepower (SAE net)	48@4,200
Engine block	Magnesium alloy
Cylinder heads	Aluminium alloy
Cooling system	Air-cooled, belt-driven blower through alternator; oil cleaner
Fuel/air supply	Bosch Electronic fuel injection (AFC)

Selected performance information					
	Engine	Year	0–50km/h[1]	0–80km/h[1]	0–100km/h[1]
VW 1200L	1192cc 34PS	1977	7.0	18.0	37.0
VW 1200L	1584cc 50PS	1977	5.0	12.0	19.5
VW 1300	1285cc 40PS	1970	6.0	14.0	26.0
VW 1300	1285cc 44PS	1973	6.5	14.0	24.0
VW 1500	1493cc 44PS	1970	6.0	13.0	23.0
VW 1302	1285cc 44PS	1971	6.5	16.5	32.0
VW 1302S	1584cc 50PS	1971	5.5	12.5	22.5
VW 1303	1285cc 44PS	1973	6.5	15.0	25.5
VW 1303S	1584cc 50PS	1973	5.5	13.0	20.5

[1] = half load in seconds.

factory-fitted optional equipment

ABOVE: M14 Volkswagen script badge.

Whether it was to meet the rules and regulations pertinent to the market to which a car was to be exported, to cater for the demands of individual customers, or to create a special model out of a standard package, many Beetles leaving Wolfsburg and other factories did so with factory-fitted optional equipment.

The German equivalent for the English word 'equipment' is *Ausstattung*, while 'extra' translates as *mehr*. Each item of factory-fitted optional equipment was given a number, which was preceded by the letter 'M' – short for *Mehrausstattung*.

On occasion, an M item might become a standard part of the Beetle's make-up. In such instances it was not unusual for the M number to be reissued to an entirely different option. Where feasible, the items listed are solely pertinent to models produced during and after the 1968 model year. As applicable, those models, and in certain cases countries, to which the M code applied are listed.

M no.	Description	Country or excluded markets	Years	Model/s
M1	Torsion-bar front and swing axle rear – instead of suspension struts and dual suspension struts		1971 and 1972	1300
M4	Double-joint rear axle	USA/Canada	1969 and 1970	1500 Cabriolet
M4	Double-joint rear axle	USA/Canada	1969–77	1200
M6	Heavy duty chassis in vicinity of front axle and strengthened torsion bars on rear		1970	Cabriolet

factory-fitted optional equipment

M no.	Description	Country or excluded markets	Years	Model/s
M6	Heavy duty chassis in vicinity of front axle and strengthened torsion bars on rear		1970–77	Saloons excluding 1302 and 1303 series and 1200 Beetle
M9	Semi-automatic gearbox		1968 onwards	All
M12	Exhaust control	USA/Canada	1975–9	All
M14	'Volkswagen' script badge	Selected export markets	(1967) 1968–79	All except 1200 (1974 only)
M19	No headlight flasher		(1966) 1968–69	1300, 1500 and Cabriolet ('69 only 1200)
M20	Speedometer calculated in miles rather than kilometres	Selected export markets	To the end of production	All
M22	Sealed beam headlamps	Not USA or Canada	1968–9	All
M22	Sealed beam headlamps and reversing lights		1970 onwards	All at some point in the period
M23	Electrical specifications	USA and Canada	1968–79	All
M26	Fuel evaporate emission	USA, Canada, Australia & Japan	1970–79	All
M27	Compliance with exhaust regulations	Japan, USA west coast, California	Start Japan 1976 Start USA 1972	All
M30	Headlight flasher coupled to simultaneous number plate illumination	Austria	(1967) 1968–72	All
M32	Lockable petrol cap		1973–9	All
M34	Lighting arrangements (clear lenses, side repeaters, absence of hazard warning lights)	Italy	1968 (and before) to end of production	All
M36	Energy-absorbing bumpers	European countries	1974	All
M37	Minus hazard warning light system	Italy and France	To 1974	All
M39	Minus rear seat		1975–7	1200
M40	Fuel gauge added to speedometer		1970–7	1200
M46	Side repeater indicators	Denmark, Israel, Italy, Norway	To 1974	All
M47	Reversing lights on bumper	European countries	To 1973	1200
M48	Front seat of special design for *Bundespost* and West German police	Germany	1976–8	1200
M50	Dual-circuit brakes and handbrake		1968 onwards	
M52	Compensating spring allied to low and regular octane engines of varying capacities	Not USA market	Varying – some start 1968; last finishes 1975	1200
M53	Cloth to replace leatherette upholstery		1969–73	1200
M54	Lockable glovebox	Most markets – USA Custom Beetle from 1975–7	1968–77	All – USA Custom model only
M55	Steering wheel lock with ignition starter switch	Not German market as already standard	To 1969	All
M55	Thermostatically controlled flap in rear engine lid	USA only	1974	All

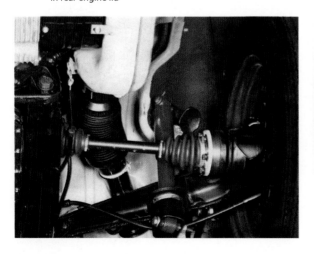

ABOVE: *M9 semi-automatic option.*

LEFT: *M4 double-joint rear axle.*

M no.	Description	Country or excluded markets	Years	Model/s
M58	Bumper overriders	European markets	1970–74	1300, 1302 and 1303
M59	Thermostatically controlled preheat for carburettor	Export markets but not USA	1968–70	All
M60	Eberspächer petrol-fuelled stationary heater		To end of production	All
M62	Washer reservoir with reduced air space plus additional air take-off pipe	Sweden	1961–70	All
M62	Additional exterior convex rear view mirror		To end of imports	All
M67	Larger 77 Ah 6V battery and cover	Export markets	To 1975	Basic 1200
M74	Rear mudflaps		To end of production	All
M78	Leatherette instead of cloth upholstery		1976 to end of production	1200
M79	Leatherette instead of cloth upholstery		1974–5	1200
M80	Discs instead of drum brakes (note: M87 1302, M88 1302, M87 1303, inc Cabrio, M88 1303)	Excluding USA	1967–73	All excluding 1200
M82	First-aid kit and mounts		1971–5	All
M86	Self-adjusting drum brakes	Sweden	1973–4	All
M89	Laminated windscreen		To end of production	All
M93	Opening, hinged rear side windows		To end of production	All
M94	Lockable engine lid		To end of production	All
M102	Heated rear window		To end of production	All
M103	Heavy duty or reinforced bumpers		To end of production	All
M105	Harder rubber or metal bearings for transmission mountings		(1961) 1968–72	All
M106	Heavy duty cloth upholstery for West German Police and Post Office usage	Home market	To end of production	All excluding Cabriolet
M107	Bumper overriders and additional rails		1968–70	Basic 1200
M108	'Custom' model with torsion bar instead of MacPherson struts – linked with: M4, M9, M20, M23, M89, M137, M185, M227, M228, M617	USA	1971–5	1200 North America
M110	'Custom' model – torsion-bar front axle included M20, M23, M60, M88, M89, M227 and variations … 'rubber' matting instead of carpet, no equalizer spring, minus rear ashtray and lacked fresh-air system	Canada	1968–71	1200
M110	'Custom' model torsion-bar front axle included M167	Canada	1972 to end of production	1200

RIGHT: M58 bumper overriders.

FAR RIGHT: M74 rear mudflaps.

factory-fitted optional equipment

LEFT: M93 opening hinged rear side windows.
BELOW: M162 rubber strip on bumper.

M no.	Description	Country or excluded markets	Years	Model/s
M113	Safety-belt warning system	Canada	1975 to end of production	All
M121	Air blower for ventilation		1971 to end of production	All 02/03 series
M121	Air blower for ventilation	USA	1976 to end of production	1200
M123	Special remote interference suppression equipment	France	(1961) 1968 to end of production	All
M124	Amber headlamps and safety rear-view mirror	France	(1956) 1968 to end of production	All
M139	Dual-circuit drum brakes	Canada, Norway, Sweden, Finland	(1967) 1968–9	All
M149	Painted replacing chrome parts		1968 to end of production	1200
M153	Double oil-bath filter system		(1966) to end of production	All
M157	Variety of engines with exhaust gas-purification systems	Mainly USA, Canada, but includes Japan	From 1968 1976 to end of production	All
M162	Rubber strips on bumpers		1968 to end of production with variations in design	All
M167	Grab handle and coat hooks		1973 to end of production	1200 basic
M179	Locking devices for front seat backrests		1969–72	1200 basic
M183	Lap belt for rear seat	West Germany		1303 Cabriolets
M184	Three-point safety belt for front seats	USA	1972–9	1200
M185	Three-point safety belt for front seats and automatic lap belts for rear seat	USA	1972–77	Sedan
M186	Lap belt for back seat	USA	1968–72	Sedan and Cabriolet
M186	Automatic lap belt for back seat	All markets except USA	1972 to end of production	1200, 1200L
M187	Headlamp for RHD cars		1968 to end of production	All models
M190	Improved door security	USA	1973 to end of 1974	All US models
M193	Exhaust and electrical equipment law compliance	Japan	1974 to end of production	All models exported to Japan
M194	External convex rear mirrors	West German *Bundespost*		RHD 1200
M206	Anti-dazzle rear view mirror		1969 Deluxe 1971 1200	All – see dates for start
M208	Electrics for towing trailer		1972–5	All models
M218	Wheel trim rings		1967–9	1300
M220	Locking differential		To end of production	All models
M227	High-backed front seats		1968 to end of production	All models

M no.	Description	Country or excluded markets	Years	Model/s
M228	Padded dashboard covering		1969 to end of production	All torsion-bar models
M233	Basic version of 1303 Beetle		1972 to end of 1975	
M240	Dished pistons to accommodate lower octane fuel		1966 to end of production	
M248	Ignition/starter switch minus steering wheel lock	All export markets	1970 to end of 1975	
M258	Adjustable headrests	Export markets	1973 to end of production; 1200 from 1977	1300, 1303, 1200
M261	External rear-view mirror to right as well as left		1968 to end of production	Cabriolet
M277	Engine lid without air vents	Switzerland	1973 1300 and 1303 to end of production; 1975 1200 to end of production	
M282	Sun visor for front seat passenger		1971 to end of production	1200 basic
M288	Headlamp washers		1974 to end of 1975	1300 and 1303
M289	Steering column fastening – screw capable of shearing	Denmark	1970–74	
M307	Model 110 – basic torsion-bar Beetle	United States, Canada	1970 onwards	
M335	1.6-litre 50PS engine – in conjunction with M599	Austria	1976 to end of production	1200 Beetle 1303 Cabriolet
M409	Front sports seats trimmed with black cloth upholstery		1973 to end of 1974 (1300) and end of production (1303)	1300 and 1303
M416	Safety steering wheel	Austria, Switzerland, Japan, Australia	1975 to end of production	1200
M444	Sports wheel – 5½J × 15		1973 to end of production	1303 and Cabriolet
M527	Exhaust emission control system	Switzerland, Japan	To end of 1971	
M528	External rear view mirror to right as well as left		1969 to end of production	All Sedan models
M549	Three-point safety belts for front seats	Not USA or Canada	1974 to end of production	All models
M550	Front valance with air slots US market – for air conditioning		1973 to end of production	Super Beetle
M551	Halogen headlights (normally tungsten)		1968 to end of production; includes 1302/3 and Cabriolet	Not 1200
M559	Front valance fitted with air vents		1971 to end of production	1302/3
M560	Steel sunroof with wind-back mechanism		1964 to end of production	
M562	Reclining front seats		1973 to end of 1974 (1300) and 1974 1200 L	
M565	Sports steering wheel		1972 to end of production	1300 and 1303
M568	Side (front and rear) and rear window fitted with heat insulating glass		1974	
M568	Green tinted glass to all windows		1976 to end of production	All models
M571	Rear fog light		1973 to end of 1974	1303 and 1303 Cabriolet
M599	50PS engine – disc brakes and compensating spring		1974 to end of production	1200

RIGHT: *M258 adjustable headrests.*
FAR RIGHT: *M976 sports wheel.*

factory-fitted optional equipment

M no.	Description	Country or excluded markets	Years	Model/s
M601	Deluxe equipment		1968	1300, 1500 Sedan and Cabriolet
M602	Deluxe equipment		1968	All models inc 1200
M602	Luxury equipment Padded dashboard, hazard warning lights and dual-circuit brake warning light system	USA and Canada	1968	
M603	Luxury equipment		1970 to end of 1974 (1300) 1971 to end of 1974 (RHD 1300) 1974 to end of production (1200) From start to end of production (1302 and 1303)	
M607	Windscreen wiper – two-speed 12V motor	Norway	1971–3	1200
M607	Windscreen wiper – two-speed 12V motor, plus locking back rest on rear seat	Norway	1974 to end of production	1200
M608	Automatic three-point seat belts for front seats	Australia	1975 to end of production	1200 and 1303
M610	12V system		1968 to end of production	1200
M611	12V system, sealed beam headlamps, hazard warning lights	Export markets	1968 to end of production	Torsion-bar models inc Cabrio
M613	12V system with suppression of interference	Police	1968 to end of production	
M616	Reversing lights fitted in rear light cluster		1968 to end of production	
M617	Washer reservoir with additional air take-off pipe and reduced air space		1968–70	
M618	50A 12V alternator	USA	1970s	
M622	Cigarette lighter		Production run	1303
M649	Lap belt attachments for three people in rear of car		1975 to end of production	1200
M652	Intermittent wipe for windscreen wipers		1972 to end of production	1302/3 including Cabriolet 1300
M659	Halogen fog lights		1972 to end of production all models except 1200 1972 to end of 1975 – 1200 with M610 package 1976 to end of production – 1200	
M671	Laminated windscreen – heat insulating		1974 to end of production	
M676	Dashboard clock		Production run	1303
M976	Sports wheels		1973 to end of production	1300 and 1200

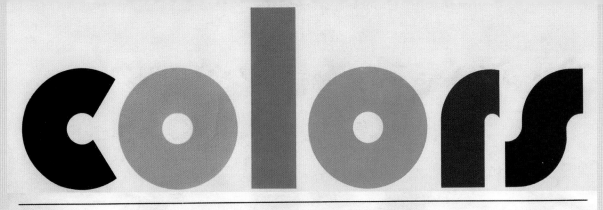

colors

BEETLE

Exterior Paint	Bright Orange	African Red	Marina Blue	Atlas White
Cloth Seats	Grey	Grey	Grey	Grey
Leatherette Trimming	Black	Black	Slate Grey	Slate Grey
Leatherette Seats	Black	Black	Slate Grey	Slate Grey

SUPER BEETLE

Exterior Paint	Sahara Beige	Bright Orange	African Red	Black
Cloth Seats	Mocha	Black	Bamboo	Red
Leatherette Trimming	Mocha	Black	Bamboo	Red
Leatherette Seats	Mocha	Black	Bamboo	Red

 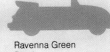  

Exterior Paint	Marina Blue	Rallye Yellow	Tropical Green
Cloth Seats	Slate Grey	Black	Bamboo
Leatherette Trimming	Slate Grey	Black	Bamboo
Leatherette Seats	Slate Grey	Black	Bamboo

SUPER BEETLE CONVERTIBLE

Exterior Paint	Phoenix Red	Ravenna Green	Amber	Bahia Red
Convertible Top	Black	Black	Black	Black
Leatherette Seats	Black	Black	Black	Bamboo

Exterior Paint	Saturn Yellow	Olympic Blue
Convertible Top	Black	Black
Leatherette Seats	Black	Black

7 — *paint and trim colours*

ABOVE: For the 1974 model year Volkswagen of America produced this handy colour chart to illustrate all the paint options available. Note the variances in description compared to those of the German market.

1) PAINT COLOURS AUGUST 1967– JANUARY 1978

The core range of colours for the home market is listed together with the identifying L codes. The restricted range of options for the base model 1200 is also listed and is again based on the home market. Additional colours pertinent to the Cabriolet are noted where possible, as are some colour details specific to the US market. Limited edition models with special paint colours are not included, as these are covered elsewhere to a large extent. It is well worth noting that export markets did not necessarily receive all the colours offered for the home market. For example, for

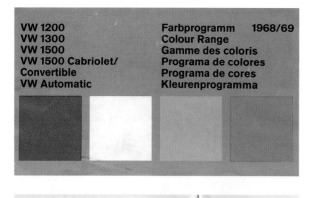

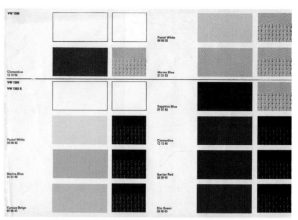

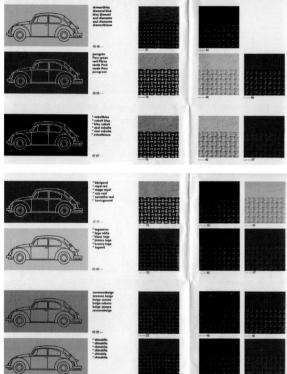

This multilingual brochure covered the paint and fabric options for all models in the Beetle range during 1968 and 1969.

The 1971 Volkswagen Colors

SEDAN			CONVERTIBLE		
Body	Cloth with leatherette trim	Leatherette	Body	Convertible top	Leatherette
Sapphire Blue	Grey	Alabaster	Sapphire Blue	Silver Grey	Alabaster
Elm Green	Cork	Alabaster	Clementine	Black	Black
Clementine	Grey	Black	Marina Blue	Black	Black
Marina Blue	Blue	Black	Iberian Red	Black	Black
Iberian Red	Grey	Black	Canary Yellow	Black	Black
Shantung Yellow	Grey	Black	Kansas Beige	Black	Cork
Kansas Beige	Cork	Cork			

The limited range of paint colours and choices in leatherette offered to British purchasers in 1971 compares badly with the three options in cloth upholstery and a further three in leatherette presented to American buyers.

the '71 model year, of the eleven paintwork options on offer in Germany, only seven were available to US buyers, the excluded colours being: Pastel White, L90D; Silver Metallic, L96D; Colorado Metallic, L97D; Gemini Metallic, L96E. Similarly, while a shade might be available on the home market in conjunction with the base model 1200 for another country, it could well be restricted to Deluxe offerings.

Promotional material produced in the early 1970s entitled *The Birth of a Volkswagen* included a section allocated to the painting process at the factory:

Paint application by electrophoresis
First the body is washed for twenty-five minutes. After eight minutes under hot air blowers the car is dry again. Now comes the actual painting. First the body is immersed in a giant tank full of primer paint. Here the first layer of paint is applied by the so-called electrophoresis process. This process resembles that used in applying metal coatings, e.g. chromium plate. The next step is the electrostatic application of the undercoat, the second layer of paint which gives the paintwork its thickness and durability. Finally the finishing coat is sprayed on by experts

using hand-held guns and is baked hard at high temperatures.

By 1974 Volkswagen of America Inc. could describe the process thus:

While you're deciding on the color of your new Volkswagen, you might like to know what's under it. For most of the finish is hidden from view. To get the colour blue, for instance, we have to start three layers down. Here the body gets dipped in a bath of zinc phosphate, to defend it against rust and corrosion. A primer coat goes on next. And the way we put it on

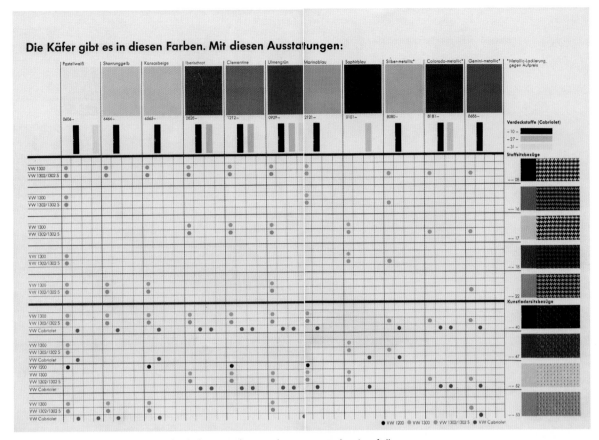

As might be anticipated, the 1971 options for the home market were the most comprehensive of all.

represents a major advance in the state of the art.

The car is given a positive charge of electricity and submerged into a vat containing a mixture of 92 per cent water, 8 per cent pigment. The pigment is negatively charged. You can imagine what happens. The car and the pigment develop an irresistible and lasting attraction for each other. When the car is lifted from the vat, it actually feels dry to the touch. Only the pigment has adhered. Not the water.

Every inch of metal, inside and out, is smoothly covered. With 3½ times the amount of primer paint as the former 'straight dip method' would have given it. And to give the front end the little extra protection it needs, we've developed a somewhat ingenious, but still very effective method. We dunk the car nose first. And then we go through the whole primer routine a second time. For a very sound reason. An economy car wouldn't be very economical if the finish didn't hold up as well as the rest

of the car (we spare nothing to make the Volkswagen economical).

Now the body gets washed, sanded and rewashed. At this point the car passes through a drying tunnel, and finally receives its outer coat of blue enamel. Sprayed on by hand. Then we bake on the durable shine. In an oven set at 265 degrees.

The whole process has taken 3½ hours. At the end of which, the Volkswagen emerges wearing 13 pounds of colorful armor. …

Marino Yellow, L20A, on a 1200L.

Chrome Yellow (US colour description), L20A, on a 1303 Cabrio.

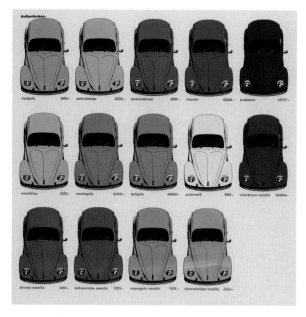

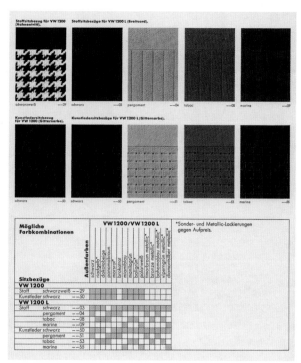

ABOVE AND RIGHT: Despite the Saloon range having been reduced to the basic 1200 and the more luxurious 1200L, home market options both in paint and upholstery were still plentiful in 1977.

The new Beetle. Custom-make it yourself.

To add insult to injury, for the 1975 model year British buyers were shown not only what they could have, but also the options unavailable in the UK.

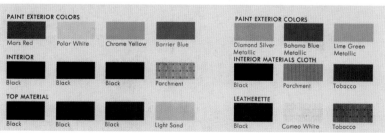

American-market Saloon and Cabriolet paint and upholstery options for the year 1977.

August 1967–July 1968 ('68 model year)

1500 and 1300

Royal Red, L30A; Chinchilla, L70F; Delta Green, L610; Savannah Beige, L620; VW Blue, L633; Zenith Blue, L639; Lotus White, L282.

1200

VW Blue; Royal Red; Chinchilla; Lotus White – only.

Notes

The Cabriolet was also available in Poppy Red (L54) and Yukon Yellow (L19K) for certain markets. The US market was offered Sedans in Black (L41), but not Chinchilla, although this colour was available in Canada.

August 1968–July 1969 ('69 model year)

1500 and 1300

Royal Red, L30A; Chinchilla, L70F; Savannah Beige, L620; Cobalt Blue, L630; Toga White, L90C; Peru Green, L60B; Diamond Blue, L50B.

1200

Cobalt Blue; Royal Red; Chinchilla; Toga White.

Cobalt Blue, L630, on a 1300.

Diamond Blue, L50B, on a 1300L.

Sahara Beige, L13H, on a 1303.

Clementine, L630, on a 1300.

Hellas Metallic, L98C, on a 1303.

Chinchilla, L70F, on a 1200.

Kasan Red, L30B, on a 1303.

Brilliant Orange, L20B, on a 1303.

Elm Green, L60D, on a 1300.

Marina Blue, L54D, on a 1303.

Pastel White, L90D, on a 1302S.

Savannah Beige, L620, on a 1300.

Sumatra Green, L61B, on a 1302S.

Turquoise Metallic, L95B, on a 1300.

Laguna Blue, L50C, on a 1303 Cabrio.

Texas Yellow, L10B, on a 1302S.

Ancona Metallic, L97B, on a 1303 Cabrio.

Barrier Blue, L52K, on a 1303 Cabrio.

Royal Red, L30A, on a 1300.

Lofoten Green, L61H, on a 1200 Super.

Gentian Blue, L51B, on a 1300.

Notes

As per 1968 model year, plus Cabriolets in the US were available in Poppy Red, L54, and Yukon Yellow, L19K.

August 1969–July 1970 ('70 model year)

1500 and 1300 (1600 in the USA)

Royal Red, L30A; Chinchilla, L70F; Savannah Beige, L620; Cobalt Blue, L630; Pastel White, L90D; Elm Green, L60D; Diamond Blue, L50B; Clementine, L630.

1200

Cobalt Blue; Royal Red; Chinchilla; Pastel White.

Notes

For the US market Royal Red, Elm Green and Pastel White were only available on the Sedan, while Clementine was only offered with the Cabriolet. Poppy Red continued to be available for the Cabriolet, but Yukon Yellow was now offered with both the Sedan and the Cabriolet. Most lists indicate that Black was no longer offered as an option.

August 1970–July 1971 ('71 model year)

1302 and 1302S, 1300

Sapphire Blue, L50D; Iberian Red, L31F; Shantung Yellow, L12D; Kansas Beige, L91D; Pastel White, L90D; Elm Green, L90D; Marina Blue, L54D; Clementine, L20D; Silver Metallic, L96D; Colorado Metallic, L97D; Gemini Metallic, L96E.

1200

Marina Blue; Clementine; Kansas Beige; Pastel White.

Notes

The Cabriolet was available for some markets in Canary Yellow, L11E. For the American market Clementine and Marina Blue were available for all models, although Shantung Yellow and Elm Green were not available with the Cabriolet. Iberian Red, Sapphire Blue and Kansas Beige were available on the Super Bug and the Cabriolet, but not the Custom model. Finally Iberian Red, Sapphire Blue and Kansas Beige could not be specified if the vehicle was fitted with a sunroof.

August 1971–July 1972 ('72 model year)

1302 and 1302S, 1300

Kasan Red, L30B; Brilliant Orange, L20B; Texas Yellow, L10B; Sumatra Green, L61B; Gentian Blue, L51B; Kansas Beige,

Diamond Silver, L97A, on a 1200L.

Toga White, L90C, on a 1300.

L91D; Pastel White, L90D; Marina Blue, L54D; Silver Metallic, L96D; Colorado Metallic, L97D; Gemini Metallic, L96E; Turquoise Metallic, L95B.

1200
Texas Yellow; Marina Blue; Brilliant Orange; Pastel White.

Notes
The Cabriolet was available in Saturn Yellow, L13M, for some markets.

August 1972–July 1973 ('73 model year)

1303 and 1303S, 1300
Kasan Red, L30B; Biscay Blue, L52B; Brilliant Orange, L20B; Sumatra Green, L61B; Maya Metallic, L98A; Alaska Metallic, L96B; Marathon Blue Metallic, L96M; Turquoise Metallic, L95B, Marina Blue, L54D.

1200
Texas Yellow; Marina Blue; Brilliant Orange; Pastel White.

Notes
For the American market Texas Yellow was available with all Sedans. British market lists also indicate that Texas Yellow was available in conjunction with the 1303 and 1300 models, but not as an option with the 1200, while Pastel White was available whatever the model. Kansas Beige was also still an option for models ranging from the 1300 Deluxe upwards. Black was available for some markets. Biscay Blue and Marathon Metallic were not options for the British market, the latter colour only appearing in the UK in conjunction with the special edition World Champion Beetle.

In the United States the Cabriolet was offered in: Saturn Yellow, L13M;

Amber, L20E; Bahia Red, L30E; Phoenix Red, L32K; Olympic Blue, L51P; Ravenna Green, L65K.

August 1973–July 1974 ('74 model year)

1303 and 1303S, 1300
Atlas White, L91Z; Brilliant Orange, L20B; Senegal Red, L31A; Sahara Beige, L13H; Marina Blue, L54D; Tropical Green, L60A; Rally Yellow, L10A; Cliff Green, L61A; Hellas Metallic, L98C; Moss Metallic, L95C; Alaska Metallic, L96B; Marathon Blue Metallic, L96M.

1200
Atlas White; Marina Blue; Brilliant Orange; Senegal Red; Sahara Beige.

Notes
Black was also available as an option for the 1303 range for some markets. In the United States Cabriolet colours for the Standard model were described thus: Bright Orange; African Red; Marina Blue; Atlas White. The Super Beetle was not available in Atlas White, but was offered in the other three colours listed for the Custom model as well as: Sahara Beige; Black; Rally Yellow; Tropical Green. The Cabriolet had its own set of colours which were: Phoenix Red; Ravenna Green; Amber; Bahia Red; Saturn Yellow; Olympic Blue.

August 1974–July 1975 ('75 model year)

1303 range
Atlas White, L91Z; Senegal Red, L31A; Miami Blue, L51C, Lofoten Green, L61H; Rally Yellow, L10B; Cliff Green, L61A; Blue Black, L52M; Ceylon Beige, L13H; Marino Yellow, L20A; Phoenix Red, L32K; Hellas Metallic, L99B; Marathon Blue Metallic, L96M; Ancona Metallic, L97B; Viper Green Metallic, L98B.

1200
Atlas White; Miami Blue; Lofoten Green; Marino Yellow; Senegal Red; Ceylon Beige.

Notes
More prominence was given to the 1200, with some of the shades listed above relating to the L version rather

than the base model. The American market was dominated by special edition Beetles with their own colours. Basic and Custom Beetles were available in most of the colours listed above, but some names were adjusted: African Red (Senegal Red); Chrome Yellow (Marino Yellow); Rally Green (Cliff Green); Alpine Green (Lofoten Green).

Cabriolet colours in the United States were: Sunflower Yellow, L13K; Fiesta Orange, L20C; Scarlet Red, L31M; Laguna Blue, L50C. Some add: Mayan Green, L11D; Malaga Red, L30C.

August 1975–July 1976 ('76 model year)

Deluxe options
Atlas White, L91Z; Senegal Red, L31A; Ocean Blue, L57H; Lofoten Green, L61H; Rally Yellow, L10A; Blue Black L52M; Marino Yellow, L20A; Phoenix Red, L32K; Viper Green Metallic, L96N; Topaz Metallic, L99D; Diamond Silver Metallic, L97A.

1200
Atlas White; Ocean Blue; Lofoten Green; Marino Yellow; Senegal Red; Blue Black.

Notes
The following shades are not depicted in home-market material covering the 1200 and 1200L published at the start of the 1976 model year: Blue Black L52M; Viper Green Metallic, L96N; Topaz Metallic, L99D; Diamond Silver Metallic, L97A.

The Cabriolet in the United States was available in: Sunflower Yellow, L13K; Fiesta Orange, L20C; Scarlet Red, L31M; Laguna Blue, L50C. Some add: Light Ivory, L80E. The Sedan in the United States was restricted to: Lime Green (Viper Green Metallic), L96N; Topaz Metallic, L99D; Diamond Silver Metallic, L97A.

August 1976–July 1977 ('77 model year)

Deluxe options
Blue Black, L52M; Riyad Yellow, L11A; Dakota Beige, L13A; Panama Brown, L12A; Mars Red, L31B; Brocade Red, L32A; Miami Blue, L51C; Manila Green, L63Y; Bali Green, L62A; Polar White,

L90A; Timor Brown Metallic, L97F, Bronze Metallic, L95D; Bahama Blue Metallic, L99F; Viper Green Metallic, L96N; Diamond Silver Metallic, L97A.

1200
Blue Black; Riyad Yellow; Dakota Beige; Panama Brown; Mars Red; Miami Blue; Manila Green; Bali Green; Polar White.

Notes
Some lists also include Achat Brown, L86Z, although this shade doesn't feature in publicity material that included representations of the paint colours available.

The Cabriolet in the United States was available in: Chrome Yellow, L20A; Mars Red, L31B; Barrier Blue, L52K; Polar White, L90A. The Sedan in the United States was restricted to: Lime Green (Viper Green Metallic), L96N; Bahama Blue Metallic, L99F; Diamond Silver Metallic, L97A.

August 1977–January 1978 ('78 model year)

Deluxe
Alpine White, L90E; Malaga Red, L30C; Riyad Yellow, L11A; Dakota Beige, L13A; Panama Brown, L12A; Mars Red, L31B; Miami Blue, L51C; Manila Green, L63Y; Bali Green, L62A.

1200
Blue Black; Riyad Yellow; Dakota Beige; Panama Brown; Mars Red; Miami Blue; Manila Green; Bali Green; Alpine White.

Until the '70 model year the outer rims of the Beetle's wheels were painted in varying shades of white/cream, dependent on the body colour of the car. The inner hubs were painted in Grey Black.

With effect from August 1969 the whole Beetle wheel was painted silver.

As the basic 1200 became more spartan, one economy measure taken was to delete hubcaps as part of the specification. The 1200 Beetle lacked these items at least in Germany with effect from August 1974. Plastic nut covers and a centre cap avoided the saving appearing too miserly.

The Big Beetle of 1974 vintage, the 1200 Super and the special edition UK market GT Beetle were amongst the first Beetles to benefit from so-called Sports wheels of varying dimensions. Towards the end of Beetle production these wheels became increasingly commonplace.

Limited to the Special Edition World Champion Beetle, the so-called Marathon wheels were manufactured in Germany by Lemmertz. The steel wheels were sprayed in silver with a black centre section. An attractive polished alloy centre cap stamped with the VW roundel and grey plastic 19mm nut covers completed the story. Today these are the most sought-after of all Beetle wheels.

The Cabriolet in the United States was offered in the same colours as in the previous year, with the exception of Polar White, which was replaced by Alpine White.

USA Cabriolet colours '79 model year and '80 model year

Mars Red, L31B; Alpine White, L90D; Diamond Silver Metallic, L97A; Lemon Yellow, LA1D; Florida Blue, LA5A; River Blue Metallic, LK6V.

2) TRIM COLOURS – EXTERIOR

At first glance the trim specification per year looks immensely complicated. However, compared to earlier cars of pre-1967 vintage the programme is both simpler and on many occasions repetitive from one year to another.

August 1967– July 1968 ('68 model year)

Wheels

The outer rims of the wheels of the Beetle Saloon were painted in Lotus White, L282, or Cumulus White, L680, dependent on the body colour of the car. All cars except those painted in VW Blue, Zenith Blue, or Chinchilla had outer wheel rims painted in Lotus White. The inner hubs were painted in dull gloss Grey Black LD43 through-out. As Cabriolets' wheels were embellished with trim rings – M218 – the whole wheel was painted in Grey Black in all instances.

Running boards

All Cabriolet and most Saloon running board covers were offered in black. The exceptions for the 1968 model year were cars finished in Lotus White and Savannah Beige, which had Savannah Beige covers, and Zenith Blue cars, which had matching Zenith Blue covers.

Bumper brackets and bumper tape

Bumper brackets and the 1300's and 1500's defining bumper tape were all black.

Cabriolet hood

Silver Grey or Black, dependent on the body colour of the car. Silver Grey

pertains to Black and VW Blue cars only.

August 1968–July 1969 ('69 model year)

Wheels

The outer rims of the wheels of all Beetle Saloons were painted in Cloud White, L581, while the inner hubs were painted in dull gloss Grey Black LD43. As previously, the Cabriolets' wheels were embellished with trim rings – M218 – and as a result the whole wheel was painted in Grey Black in all instances.

Running boards

All Cabriolet and Saloon running board covers were offered in black.

Bumper brackets and bumper tape

Bumper brackets were painted black, L41, while the bumper tape adorning the Europa bumpers of the 1300 and 1500 was also black.

Cabriolet hood

With the exception of cars finished in Cobalt Blue, where the vinyl hood was Silver Grey, all hoods were black.

August 1969–July 1970 ('70 model year)

Wheels

The wheels of all Beetles, Saloons and Cabriolets, were painted Chrome Silver, L91. To coincide with this change Cabriolet models were now beautified with trim rings.

Running boards

All running boards were covered in black rubber.

Bumper brackets and bumper tape

Bumper brackets were painted black, L41, while the bumper tape adorning the Europa bumpers of the 1300 and 1500 was also black.

Cabriolet hood

As with the '69 model year, with the exception of cars finished in Cobalt Blue, where the vinyl hood was Silver Grey, all hoods were black.

August 1970–July 1971 ('71 model year)

Wheels

The wheels of all Beetles, Saloons and Cabriolets were painted Chrome Silver, L91.

Running boards

All running boards were covered in 041 black rubber.

Bumper brackets and bumper tape

Bumper brackets were painted black. The bumpers of European cars with the L package and US Super and Cabriolets were embellished with black rubber impact strips. European models without the L pack, but excluding the 1200, which still had curved chromed bumpers of the general pre-'68 style, and US Custom models, had black bumper tape.

Cabriolet hood

All hoods were black, V1, with the exception of cars finished in Sapphire Blue, where the hood was finished in Silver Grey, V100.

August 1971–July 1972 ('72 model year)

Wheels

The wheels of all Beetles, Saloons and Cabriolets were painted Chrome Silver, L91.

Running boards

All running boards were covered in 041 black rubber.

Bumper brackets and bumper tape

Bumper brackets were painted black. The bumpers of European cars with the L package and US Super and Cabriolets were embellished with black rubber impact strips. European models without the L pack, but excluding the 1200, which still had curved chromed bumpers of the general pre-'68 style, and US Custom models, had black bumper tape.

Cabriolet hood

All hoods were black, V1, with the exception of cars finished in Gentian

Blue, where the hood was finished in Silver Grey, V100.

August 1972–July 1973 ('73 model year)

Wing beading
Although wing beading remained colour-coded to the paintwork of the Saloon, as it had done for many years previously, Cabriolets now featured contrasting black beading.

Wheels
The wheels of Saloon Beetles were painted Chrome Silver, L91, as previously. However, Cabriolet wheels were now painted Aluminium Grey, L97U.

Running boards
All running boards were covered in 041 black rubber.

Bumper brackets and bumper tape
Bumper brackets were painted black. The bumpers of European cars with the L package and US Super and Cabriolets were embellished with black rubber impact strips. European models without the L pack, but excluding the 1200, which still had curved chromed bumpers of the general pre-'68 style, and US Custom models, had black bumper tape.

Cabriolet hood
All hoods were black, V1, there being no exception to the general rule on this occasion.

August 1973–July 1974 ('74 model year)

Wing beading
Wing beading for Saloons was colour-coded to the body of the car. Cabriolets featured contrasting black beading.

Wheels
The wheels of Saloon and Cabriolet Beetles were now painted Aluminium Grey, L97U.

Running boards
All running boards were covered in 041 black rubber.

Bumper brackets and bumper tape
Bumper brackets, including the energy-absorbing type allocated to US models, were painted black. The bumpers of European cars with the L package and US Super and Cabriolets were embellished with black rubber impact strips. European models without the L pack had black bumper tape. The 1200 model, which now had black painted versions of the Europa-style bumper, featured a central bumper tape finished in silver.

Cabriolet hood
All hoods were black, V1, there being no exception to the general rule on this occasion.

August 1974–July 1975 ('75 model year)

Wing beading
Wing beading for most Saloons was colour-coded to the body of the car, but base models, including the US-specification cars finished in Rally Yellow, African Red and Miami Blue, now had contrasting black beading. Cabriolet models continued to enjoy black wing beading whatever the body colour of the car.

Wheels
The wheels of all Saloon and Cabriolet Beetles were now painted Chrome Silver, L91.

Running boards
All running boards were covered in 041 black rubber.

Bumper brackets and bumper tape
Bumper brackets, including the energy-absorbing type allocated to US models, were painted black. The bumpers of European cars with the L package and US Super and Cabriolets were embellished with black rubber impact strips. European models without the L pack had black bumper tape. The 1200 model, which now had black painted versions of the Europa-style bumper, featured a central bumper tape finished in silver.

Cabriolet hood
All hoods were black, V1, there being no exception to the general rule on this occasion.

August 1975–July 1976 ('76 model year)

Wing beading
All models, Saloons and Cabriolets, had black wing beading.

Wheels
The wheels of all Saloon and Cabriolet Beetles were painted Chrome Silver, L91.

Running boards
All running boards were covered in 041 black rubber.

Bumper brackets and bumper tape
Bumper brackets were universally black, bumper rubbers or tape were black, except in the instance of the 1200 with black painted bumpers where the tape was silver.

Cabriolet hood
All hoods were black, V1, although special edition models might vary from this norm.

August 1976–July 1977 ('77 model year)

Wing beading
All models, Saloons and Cabriolets had black wing beading.

Wheels
The wheels of all Saloon and Cabriolet Beetles were painted Chrome Silver, L91.

Running boards
All running boards were covered in 041 black rubber.

Bumper brackets and bumper tape
Bumper brackets were universally black, bumper rubbers or tape were black, except in the instance of the 1200 with black painted bumpers where the tape was silver.

Cabriolet hood

Although black was dominant as a hood colour, some standard issue Cabriolets were now produced with a Light Sand, V3, hood.

August 1977–Jan 1978 (Saloon) and July 1978 Cabriolet ('78 model year)

As per the '77 model year, Light Sand hoods were more prominent in the Cabriolet range. Cabriolet specification stayed as per '77 model year until the end of production in Jan 1980.

3) TRIM COLOURS – INTERIOR

Owners of UK-specification Beetles dating from 1968 and into the earlier years of the 1970s might well be surprised to discover that potential buyers of German and US cars could select between cloth upholstery and basket-weave leatherette when the latter appeared to be the only option available. A further surprise for such buyers was to discover that, for example, in Canada not only were the 'seating surface and front sides of the backrests available with cloth', but also if 'air permeable leatherette' was selected it was only available at 'extra cost'! On the other hand, the introduction of the 1300A – a basic-specification Beetle with the 1300 rather than 1200 engine – to the British market in the summer of 1972 and a description of it, the 1200 and the 1300 Deluxe as 'economy' models, might help to explain why even the last-mentioned car of these three could only be purchased in the UK with black leatherette upholstery, providing it can be assumed that cloth implied a higher specification as the 1970s advanced. To confirm the logic

behind this argument, by the onset of the '74 model year for UK buyers the 1200 was still inevitably restricted to black leatherette, as were all other models in the range unless extra-cost metallic paint was specified when three colour options in cloth became available.

Essentially, the whole topic of upholstery is incredibly complicated if all markets are taken into consideration, but on the other hand tedious in its repetitiveness if every option for each major Volkswagen importing country is listed. As a result, a selection is presented with an emphasis being placed on the home market, North America and the UK.

1968 North American market

A particularly enlightening back page from a 1968 model year brochure illustrating and naming every option of cloth and leatherette available and how they were attributed to the various paint options offered sets the scene for the ensuing examples covered here. The page is accordingly reproduced, but for clarity's sake the names are reproduced here in chart form (*see* below).

1969 European market

A listing covering several languages implies that buyers in each country were offered the same degree of choice, although this was blatantly not the case as far as UK would-be owners were concerned, the importer, Volkswagen Motors Ltd., choosing to restrict the offer to leatherette upholstery only.

VW 1200 models were offered in Royal Red, Toga White, Chinchilla and

Cobalt Blue. Standard fabric upholstery was offered in shade 23, Grey, while extra-cost leatherette was available in shade 50, Light Grey.

The VW 1300, VW 1500 and VW Automatic came with fabric upholstery as standard. Royal Red, Peru Green and Cobalt Blue cars were offered with shade 19, Grey upholstery; Toga White, Savannah Beige and Chinchilla cars came with shade 20, Red upholstery; while Diamond Blue vehicles had shade 21, Dark Blue, upholstery.

The VW 1300, VW 1500, VW Automatic could all be specified with leatherette upholstery at extra cost, but for owners of the Cabriolet this material was standard and thus incurred no extra charge (to confirm, the Cabriolet was not available with cloth upholstery). Toga White and Chinchilla cars were offered with the choice of shade 40, black and shade 47, red. Royal Red cars were available either with shade 40, black or shade 46, cream. Savannah Beige cars were available with black upholstery, shade 40, but were also offered with darkish brown upholstery, shade 48. Diamond Blue cars were the only vehicles to be offered with just one shade of leatherette upholstery, namely shade 40, black. Peru Green and Cobalt Blue cars were both offered with shade 46, cream upholstery, while the former was also available with shade 48, darkish brown and the latter with shade 47, red.

Two shades of hood fabric were available for Cabriolet models. Royal Red, Peru Green and Cobalt Blue cars came with a grey hood, shade 27, while Toga White, Savannah Beige, Chinchilla and Diamond Blue cars were offered with shade 10, black hoods.

The 1968 US market. Volkswagen colors			
Body colour – Sedan and Cabriolet as applicable	**Cloth – leatherette trim on sides and reverse of seat**	**Leatherette**	**Cabriolet hood**
Savannah Beige – Sedan and Cabriolet	India Red, Sedan only	Gazelle	Black
Zenith Blue – Sedan and Cabriolet	Water Blue, Sedan only	Black	Black
Black – Sedan and Cabriolet	Platinum, Sedan only	India Red	Black
VW Blue – Sedan and Cabriolet	Platinum, Sedan only	Platinum	Silver Grey
Royal Red – Sedan and Cabriolet	Platinum, Sedan only	Black	Black
Delta Green – Sedan only	Platinum	Platinum	N/A
Lotus White – Sedan and Cabriolet	India Red, Sedan only	Black	Black
Poppy Red – Cabriolet only	N/A	Black	Black
Yukon Yellow – Cabriolet only	N/A	Black	Black

1971 home market. Upholstery options

Cloth upholstery (with leatherette)

Paint shade	Grey (Black)	Blue (Blue)	Grey (Alabaster)	Red (Red)	Cork (Cork)
Pastel White	1300, 1302 and 1302S	1300, 1302 and 1302S		1300, 1302 and 1302S	1300, 1302 and 1302S
Shantung Yellow	1300, 1302 and 1302S				1300, 1302 and 1302S
Kansas Beige	1300, 1302 and 1302S				1300, 1302 and 1302S
Iberian Red	1300, 1302 and 1302S		1300, 1302 and 1302S		
Clementine	1300, 1302 and 1302S		1300, 1302 and 1302S		
Elm Green	1300, 1302 and 1302S		1300, 1302 and 1302S		1300, 1302 and 1302S
Marina Blue	1300, 1302 and 1302S	1300, 1302 and 1302S			
Sapphire Blue			1300, 1302 and 1302S	1300, 1302 and 1302S	
Silver Metallic	1302 and 1302S	1302 and 1302S		1302 and 1302S	
Colorado Metallic	1302 and 1302S		1302 and 1302S		
Gemini Metallic	1302 and 1302S		1302 and 1302S		1302 and 1302S

Leatherette upholstery

Paint shade	Black	Red	Alabaster	Cork
Pastel White	1300, 1302 and 1302S	1300, 1302 and 1302S	1200	1300, 1302 and 1302S
Shantung Yellow	1300, 1302 and 1302S			1300, 1302 and 1302S
Kansas Beige	1300, 1302 and 1302S		1200	1300, 1302 and 1302S
Iberian Red	1300, 1302 and 1302S		1300, 1302 and 1302S	
Clementine	1300, 1302 and 1302S		1200, 1300, 1302 and 1302S	
Elm Green	1300, 1302 and 1302S		1300, 1302 and 1302S	1300, 1302 and 1302S
Marina Blue	1300, 1302 and 1302S		1200, 1300, 1302 and 1302S	
Sapphire Blue		1300, 1302 and 1302S	1300, 1302 and 1302s	
Silver Metallic		1302 and 1302S		
Colorado Metallic			1302 and 1302S	
Gemini Metallic			1300, 1302 and 1302S	1302 and 1302S

1971 German, North American and British markets

Home market

The complexities of five options of cloth upholstery – subdivided into one instance where Grey material was coupled with leatherette trim in either Alabaster or Black – and four when considering leatherette, is most easily summarized in a chart (above) matching paint colours to interior trim.

The Cabriolet was available in the same range of paint colours as the 1302S on which it was based. All upholstery was finished in leatherette. Hood covers varied from paint shade to paint shade, while on some occasions more than one shade of material was available.

Pastel White cars were offered with either black or cream tops. Shantung Yellow, Kansas Beige, Marina Blue, Silver Metallic and Gemini Metallic were all only available with a black hood. Iberian Red, Clementine and Colorado Metallic cars were offered with either black or Silver Grey hoods. Sapphire Blue cars were only available with a Silver Grey hood, while the remaining paint colour, Elm Green, was obtainable with all three shades of top.

North American market

The chart below covering options for the American market is essentially a slimmed-down version of the ones reproduced above covering the home market. Omissions included both the Metallic options and the paint shade on the Cabriolet where, in Germany the choice of all shades for the hood was offered. Red upholstery was absent in either guise.

All Cabriolet hoods were made of black material, other than cars painted Sapphire Blue, where the single shade offered was Silver Grey.

British market

The VW 1200 was offered in three shades of paintwork: Pastel White, Clementine and Marina Blue. All such cars came with Alabaster basketweave leatherette upholstery. However, when

Paint shade	Upholstery	
	Cloth – with leatherette trim – Sedan only	Leatherette
Sapphire Blue	Grey	Alabaster
Elm Green – Sedan only	Cork	Alabaster
Clementine	Grey	Black
Marina Blue	Blue	Black
Iberian Red	Grey	Black
Shantung Yellow – Sedan only	Grey	
Kansas Beige	Cork	Cork
Canary Yellow – Cabriolet only		Black

such paint shades were offered on the VW 1300 and VW 1302S the leatherette upholstery colour switched to black. This was also the colour offered with all remaining paint shades, namely Iberian Red, Elm Green and Kansas Beige, the sole exception being Sapphire Blue when Alabaster was the single option.

1973 British market

The upholstery offer couldn't have been simpler, with all paint shades regardless of the specification being offered with black leatherette upholstery, while the Cabriolet's hood material was similarly straightforward, with black being the only option available. The restricted choice presented to British buyers by Volkswagen GB Ltd is highlighted by the design of the brochure to promote the Beetle. A whole page is devoted to just two tiny blocks of colour with a vast acreage of white paper, indicating that Volkswagen's corporate design was intended to accommodate far more in the way of options for many a market.

1974 North American and British market

North American market

The Custom model was offered with either Grey cloth seats, or black leatherette seats when the car was painted in Bright Orange or Africa Red and Slate Grey when it was finished in Marina Blue or Atlas White.

The Super Beetle was also offered with a choice of cloth or leatherette seats. However, in this instance and unlike the Custom model, the colour was identical whatever the finish of the car. Bright Orange and Rally Yellow cars had black upholstery; African Red and Tropical Green cars – Bamboo upholstery; Sahara Beige – Mocha upholstery; Black – red upholstery; Marina Blue – Slate Grey upholstery.

Cabriolets were only offered with leatherette upholstery. Phoenix Red, Ravenna Green, Amber, Saturn Yellow and Olympic Blue cars had black upholstery, while standing on its own was the Cabriolet finished in Bahia Red, as this had Bamboo-coloured leatherette upholstery. The hood

material of all Cabriolets was finished in black.

British market

No doubt reacting to the offer made by other importers and manufacturers in Britain by August 1973, and the '74 model year, cloth was on offer as a luxury market item. The irony of cloth being basic to the Beetle range in many European countries and for the American market, with leatherette offered as an extra-cost option, cannot be overlooked. However, as the 1970s developed, latter-day observers could note that the age of leatherette's fashionable appeal was over. Fabric came to rule supreme, the only challenge coming many years later when genuine leather became an extra-cost option on a wide variety of family cars.

The VW 1200 not unsurprisingly was only available with black leatherette trim. Other options in the range, namely the 1300, 1303 and 1303S were offered with black leatherette if painted in one of the same three body colours as the 1200 options of Atlas White, Marina Blue and Brilliant Orange. Additionally, when offered with the restrained tones of Senegal Red or Sahara Beige the same group of models were similarly only available with black leatherette.

However, when the Deluxe models were offered with paintwork options at extra cost – two bright colours, Rally Yellow and Cliff Green, and three metallic hues of cloth, Marathon Metallic, Alaska Metallic and Hellas Metallic, not only became available in three shades of material, but also leatherette was deleted from the choices available. Rally Yellow and Marathon Metallic cars sported black, 37, upholstery, Cliff Green and Alaska Metallic Beetles were trimmed with Bamboo, 01, coloured fabric, while Hellas Metallic vehicles were the only ones to luxuriate in Mocha, 04, cloth.

1975 Home, British and American market

Home and British market

Would-be British Beetle owners were presented with a particularly confusing chart of paint and upholstery colours

for the 1975 model year as a number of both leatherette and cloth options were included that in reality were only available for the home market. (Conversely some paint options that didn't extend to the UK weren't depicted – these being L10B; Cliff Green, L61A; Blue Black, L52M; Ceylon Beige, L13H; and Hellas Metallic, L99B. However, Phoenix Red, L32K, which also wasn't available, was shown.) The perplexity was partially rectified within a few months with a revised chart that still included all colours and materials, but included as a suffix where applicable the damning words 'not available in the UK'.

The range of cloth upholsteries encompassed: Yellowstone, Nutbrown, Pine Green, Lava Black and for the 1200, black and white houndstooth. Of these Yellowstone, Pine Green and black and white were not available in Britain. Leatherette was offered in four shades, black, Yellowstone, Pine Green and Nutbrown, but only the first mentioned was offered in the UK and then only in conjunction with the basic 1200 Beetle.

For the British market the 1200 was available in just three paint colours: Senegal Red, Miami Blue and Atlas White. Marino Yellow and Lofoten Green were added for 1300 models, while elements of the 1303 range were additionally obtainable in three metallic shades: Marathon, Ancona and Viper Green. All but Lofoten Green and Viper Green Metallic were offered with Lava Black cloth upholstery; the remaining shades being presented with Nutbrown upholstery.

The chart in its more confusing mixed-market state of all upholstery colours but selective paint shades is shown overleaf.

North American market

Regular flat-screen model and Basic 110 (Super Beetle now restricted to Special Edition, Le Grande Bug).

American buyers were offered seven paint colours to select from: Rally Yellow*, African Red*, Miami Blue*, Ceylon Beige, Rallye Green, Alpine Green and Chrome Yellow. Model 110 was only offered in the colours marked with an asterisk and came with black/white houndstooth cloth upholstery, which in America was referred

Paint shade	Yellowstone – cloth (C) Yellowstone – leatherette (L)	Nutbrown – cloth (C) Nutbrown – leatherette (L)	Upholstery Black/White – cloth	Pine Green – cloth (C) Pine Green – leatherette (L)	Lava Black – cloth (C) Black – leatherette (L)
Rally Yellow				1300/03 C and L	1300/03 C and L
Marino Yellow	1200 L		1200	1300/03 C and L	1300/03 C and L 1200 L
Phoenix Red	1300/03 C and L				1300/03 C and L
Senegal Red	1300/03 C and L 1200 L		1200		1300/03 C and L 1200L
Miami Blue	1300/03 C and L 1200 L		1200		1300/03 C and L 1200 L
Lofoten Green – also known as Lynx Green	1300/03 C and L 1200L	1300/03 C and L	1200		1200L
Atlas White	1200 L		1200	1300/03 C and L	1300/03 C and L 1200 L
Marathon (Metallic)		1300/03 C and L			1300/03 C and L
Ancona (Metallic)	1300/03 C and L				1300/03 C and L
Viper Green (Metallic)		1300/03 C and L			1300/03 C and L

to as Grey. This sole cloth option was also offered on the Deluxe cars, but owners could also select leatherette. Rally Yellow, Ceylon Beige, Rally Green and Chrome Yellow cars came with black leatherette trim; African Red and Miami Blue Beetles sported white leatherette and Alpine Green vehicles could be specified with Tan leatherette upholstery.

1976 Home and American market

Home market
The options can be quickly summarized in a chart (below); however, it is worth noting that for the 1976 home market not only was the number of upholstery choices slimmed down in line with the reduction in Beetle models offered, but also that name changes occurred for what to all intents and purposes appeared to be the same products.

North American market
The Sedan was offered in a choice of three metallic paint shades: Diamond Silver, Topaz and Lime Green. The first two options mentioned were paired to Grey houndstooth cloth, or Anthracite leatherette. Lime Green cars were available with either Saddle Tan houndstooth cloth, or Saddle Tan leatherette.

Cabriolets were offered in four paint shades – *see* paint section above – and all were mated to Anthracite leatherette upholstery and black hood material.

1977 Home and North American market

Home market
Home market buyers were offered both the basic 1200 and the more luxurious 1200L. Although the lower priced model was available in a reasonable number of paint shades, the options in upholstery were limited to one colour in leatherette – black and, in a break with traditions of earlier years, one style of cloth upholstery. This took the form of a dogtooth check, the pattern reproduced in a combination of black and white.

Purchasers of the 1200L were offered leatherette in a variety of colours as well as cloth, which, as might

Paint shade	Upholstery Black/White	Cloth Lava Black	Cloth Cognac	Leatherette Anthracite	Leatherette Cognac
Rally Yellow		1200L		1200L	
Marino Yellow	1200	1200L		1200 and 1200L	
Phoenix Red		1200L		1200L	
Senegal Red	1200	1200L		1200 and 1200L	
Ocean Blue	1200		1200L	1200	1200L
Lofoten Green	1200		1200L	1200	1200L
Atlas White	1200		1200L	1200	1200L

be anticipated, appeared more upmarket than the dogtooth fabric of the straightforward 1200. However, it is worth noting that the Deluxe model's velour upholstery hasn't stood the test of time as well as might have been expected.

The matching of upholstery to paint colour was identical whether leatherette or cloth was selected, hence the abbreviated nature of the chart.

North American market

Although there were similarities between the range of paint shades offered in 1976 and in 1977, it is worth noting how different the upholstery choices were – even down to the decision to change the name on occasion despite use of the same colour!

US Sedans were available in three paint colours, all of which were metallic in finish. These were Diamond Silver, Bahama Blue and Lime Green. Unlike their German counterparts, the shade

of leatherette and cloth material was not necessarily the same.

Diamond Silver was always paired with black; Lime Green was similarly always trimmed with Tobacco, but Bahama Blue featured Parchment cloth and what was referred to as Cameo White leatherette.

US Cabriolets were offered in Mars Red, Polar White, Chrome Yellow and Barrier Blue paintwork. All but the last mentioned colour were matched to both black leatherette upholstery and a black hood. Barrier Blue cars featured Parchment leatherette and a Light Sand hood.

4) SUNDRY FITTINGS COLOURS

1968 and 1969 specification cars

The steering column, gear lever, handbrake and frames of the seats were all painted Grey Black, LD43. (The

exception was the right-hand heater knob which was produced in red.) All knobs and buttons – for example, gear lever knob and door lock button – were finished in 043 Grey Black plastic.

The carpet in the body of the car was issued in Lava Grey, 045, while the PVC carpet material in the rear luggage compartment was finished in Medium Grey, 901/148. The rubber mats were Lava Grey coloured, 046. The kickboards under the rear seat were also finished in Lava Grey, 192.

The headlining, sun visors and door pillar covers were all finished in Cloud White plastic, 581.

1970

The carpet in the body of the car changed to Anthracite, 469. The right-hand heater knob was now produced in 043 Grey Black plastic (formerly red). The Grey Black paint used on, for example, the gear lever was now referred to as Dull Grey Black, but retained the code LD43.

1971

The 1302/1302S Super Beetles gained Lava Grey carpet now coded 192, while other models retained Anthracite carpet.

1972

All carpets were now finished in Anthracite. The style of carpet used in the body of the car now extended to the rear luggage compartment on all models except the 1200, which was formerly PVC carpet material.

There were no further significant changes to the specification.

Paint shade	Black	Parchment	Tobacco (Brown)	Marine (Blue)
Black	✓	✓		
Riyad Yellow	✓		✓	
Dakota Beige	✓		✓	
Panama Brown		✓	✓	
Mars Red	✓	✓		
Brocade Red	✓	✓		
Miami Blue	✓			✓
Manila Green	✓		✓	
Bali Green	✓		✓	
Polar White	✓			✓
Timor Brown Metallic	✓	✓		
Bronze Metallic	✓		✓	
Bahama Blue Metallic	✓	✓		
Viper Green Metallic	✓		✓	
Diamond Silver Metallic	✓			✓

8

accessories

ABOVE: *Although no longer as desirable as they were three or four decades ago, some owners still endeavour to load their Beetles with as many accessories as possible.*

RIGHT: *Thirty-six delightful options for US market owners to produce an individualistic car circa 1969.*

As might be anticipated with the world's most produced car of a single type, and particularly so with a vehicle that was renowned for its simplicity, a wealth of accessories – both those marketed under the Volkswagen umbrella and ones entirely emanating from the aftermarket – were available. Such a diversity existed that here it is necessary to restrict specification details to those produced by or for Volkswagen for distribution through their dealerships.

TWO CLARIFICATION CLAUSES

In its promotional literature, Volkswagen often referred to equipment that could either only be built into the specification of the car on the assembly line, or would most likely be included at that point under the M system of factory-fitted optional equipment, as accessories. Typical is the following

Volkswagen Accessories

1 Golden Miler Snow Tire	13 Fender Shields	25 Outside Mirror
2 Wheel Trim Rings	14 Fog Light	26 "Sapphire" Radio
3 Air Intake Grill	15 Engine Sump Heater	27 Magnetic Hood Lock (Rear)
4 Collapsible Roof Rack	16 Trailer Hitch	28 Polish
5 Steering Wheel Cover	17 Mud Flaps	29 Liquid Wax
6 Tool Kit	18 Taper Tips	30 Chrome Cleaner
7 Headrest Cushion	19 Front Fender Shields	31 Paint Spray Can
8 Tow Rope	20 Bumper Guards	32 Touch-up Sticks
9 Ski Rope, Roof Type	21 Rubber Bumper Strips	33 Trunk Light
10 License Plate Frame	22 Door Sill Panel Guards	34 Walnut Gearshift Knob
11 Sports Gearshift Lever	23 Underdash Shelf	35 Cigarette Lighter
12 Rubber Floor Mats	24 Coco Mats	36 Door Handle Shield

extract from promotional literature to promote the Beetle range of 1974 vintage, the text being set against a photographic backdrop depicting an open sunroof, heated rear window, anti-dazzle rear-view mirror, rubber bumper inserts and light clusters including lenses, bulbs and the other paraphernalia associated with reversing lights.

Choose the Beetle. With a little extra.

If we were to make all the extras a standard feature of the Beetle, a lot of people would be unhappy. Not everyone wants the same things. And not everyone can afford the same things. But if you want more comfort, more luxury, more safety, order some of the VW accessories when you're ordering your car; you'll get them expertly built in at a bargain price. For all-weather drivers there are special bad weather accessories – Halogen fog and spot lamps. A special rear fog light. Mudflaps. And stoneguards for the front and rear. A car radio will provide entertainment and information on the way. Three models are available – some simple, some with all the trimmings.

An American sales brochure of similar vintage, which although non-specific in detail, leans more heavily to genuine accessories rather than factory add-ons:

If you're the type who likes to consider his options (or accessories), consider these. Snazzy sports wheels. Air conditioning. Radial tires. A special soft steering wheel. AM/FM Radio. Ski and luggage racks. Even racing stripes. And automatic stick shift transmission. Of course, the nice thing about all the little VW extras is that they're only a little extra.

ACCESSORIES FOR THE BEETLE

All listings produced here are restricted to those items which would be most likely to be purchased from a VW dealer and either fitted by their service department, or by the Beetle's owner at home.

Accessories produced and sold under the Volkswagen umbrella might well vary dependent on the market, this being nowhere more noticeable than when a comparison is drawn between 'European' and US catalogues of such items. All listings include reference to the source from which it originates.

1970 home market

A third A4-sized leaflet was issued in Germany specific to sporting accessories for the Beetle. The list was relatively short and by today's standards far from sportily exotic:

- Halogen driving lights
- Halogen fog lamps front and rear
- Windscreen-mounted searchlight
- Rev counter
- Ammeter
- Centre console with push-outs to fit above two items
- Sports gearstick and knob
- Gear knob – wooden with Wolfsburg crest
- Gear knob – wooden with VW roundel
- Standard gear knob with Wolfsburg crest

Black fingerplates.

'Silver' fingerplates – seen much more often than the black version.

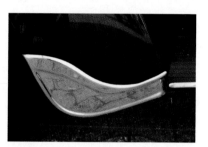

Front stoneguard – of little practical use, but a collection point for mud and other road debris..

Black mudflap with 'white' VW roundel (also available in white with black VW roundel and in black with white background for the Wolfsburg crest).

Jacking point cover (the car is a Cabriolet, hence the strengthening of the sills).

The US marketing men perfected an eye-catching way of promoting the individuality that might be achieved through the purchase of accessories.

Original-Volkswagen-Zubehör.
Für alle, die gut und sportlich fahren.

trims

		£·s·d	£·d	Part Number
a.	Finger plates—2 in a set	0·12·2	0·61	000-071-061A
b.	Jacking point caps—2 in a set	0·17·3	0·86	000-093-001
c.	Lockable petrol cap	2· 2·6	2·13	211-201-551C
d.	Hinge pillar kick plates—2 in a set type 1	1· 6·0	1·30	000-063-111A
e.	Sill guards—2 in a set type 1	2· 5·9	2·29	000-063-101A
f.	Door edge kick plates—2 in a set type 1	1· 5·7	1·28	000-063-121A
g.	Front stoneguards—2 in a set type 1	1· 2·11	1·15	000-071-021
h.	Rear stoneguards—2 in a set type 1	1· 0·9	1·04	000-071-035

LEFT, ABOVE AND RIGHT:
From fingerplates to kickplates, but presented in a rather lacklustre way.

VW Accessories
Volkswagen Motors Limited

- Detachable headrest
- Check bonnet bib
- Bumper-mounted horns
- Vinyl sports seats – black with red trim stripe
- MW/LW push button radio – Emden.

1970 British market

In 1970 Volkswagen Motors Ltd produced less of a brochure and more of a fold-out leaflet to describe and illustrate the range of accessories available for the Beetle and other members of the Volkswagen family. The list that follows includes all products specific to the Beetle and those applicable to all models, with the exception of breakdown kits and car-care products, but excludes items relating only to the Transporter, VW 1600 and the VW 411, and is conveniently divided into the subdivisions Volkswagen Motors created.

Lights
A	Rear fog lamp	000-053—322A
B	Halogen fog lamp	000-053-046
C	Halogen spot lamp	000-053-501
D	Reverse warning lamp	000-053-102A

Interior
A	Vanity mirror	000-761-971
B	Adjustable headrest	000-061-775A-041
C	Steering wheel glove	000-063-131-041
D	Wooden gear-shift knob VW roundel	000-064-225
E	Wooden gear-shift knob Wolfsburg Crest	000-064-223
F	Cigarette lighter	411-919-305
G	Sports gear-shift lever	000-064-231A
H	Anti-mist cloth	000-096-165
I	Tunnel tray	000-061-115

Steinschlagschutz
aus Kunstleder,
für vordere Haube.
Auch einfarbig silbergrau
lieferbar

ABOVE: The bonnet bib proved popular, but potentially lethal due to condensation and trapped rainwater.

Grilles

A	Front air-intake grille	000-071-291
B	Rear air-intake grille	000-071-309
C	Wind deflector for sliding roof	000-072-305
E	Grilles for engine hood 1500cc – type 1, two in a set	000-071-310

Parcel shelves

A	Rear parcel shelf	000-061-131-581
B	Front parcel shelf	000-061-092

Trims

A	Fingerplates – two in a set	000-071-061A
B	Jacking point caps – two in a set	000-093-001
C	Lockable petrol cap	211-201-551C
D	Hinge pillar kick-plate – two in a set	000-063-111A
E	Sill guards – two in a set	000-063-101
F	Door-edge kick-plates – two in a set	000-063-121A
G	Front stoneguards	000-071-021
H	Rear stoneguards	000-071-035

1970 North American market

In 1970, just a couple of years into the period cover by this volume, Volkswagen of America produced a twenty-page brochure under the simple heading of *Accessories*, outlining all the ancillary products available for the range of Volkswagen cars on sale through the company's dealers. After siphoning out the 'Station Wagon and Truck', the 'Squareback and Fastback' and the 'Karmann Ghia', the list is still mightily impressive. Note also the use of the 'Formula Vee' branding, fuelling

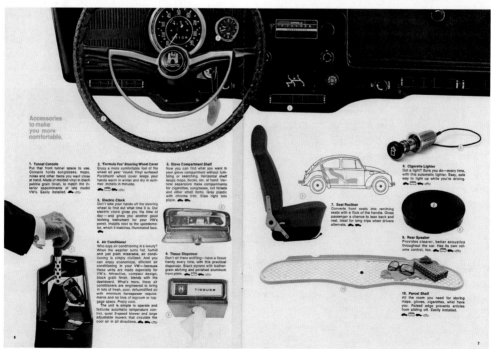

Accessories to make your VW look nicer.

3. Mag Wheels
What will mag wheels do for your VW? Look to the right and see. They're made of a special aluminum-magnesium-beryllium-titanium alloy. Gleaming. Lightweight. Very strong. And very striking. For use with tubeless tires.

1. 'Formula Vee' Stripe Kit
These racing stripes add a look of dash to your VW. Kit contains 4 pre-aligned self-adhesive strips, each 2½" x 40". Choice of gold, white or black. Easy to apply.

2. Wheel Trim Rings
Highly polished aluminum, chromed steel or stainless steel slotted type. Add a dash of flash to your wheels.

4. 'Formula Vee' Taper Tip Exhaust Pipes
Add a sporty look and a sporty sound to your VW, while improving performance at the same time. Heavy chrome plated tapered pipes reduce exhaust back pressure, improve gas consumption. Easily installed.

5. Right Side Mirror
This mirror matches your left side mirror, gives extra rear visibility when passing and parking. Heavy chrome finish, fully adjustable. (Standard equipment on Squareback.)

Accessories to protect your Volkswagen.

1. 'Formula Vee' Bumper Overriders
Here's extra protection for your VW when you're on the road, and when you're parked. Overriders have live rubber strips to cushion against shocks. And they're made to match your VW: heavy chrome finish for the Sedan, Fastback and Squareback; baked enamel for the Station Wagon.

2. Vent Shades
Highly polished stainless steel. Not only dresses up your VW, but gives draft-free ventilation, reduces window fogging, keeps rain out, keeps car cooler in summer.

3. Gas Door Guard
Prevent paint chipping and scratching caused by gas station hose nozzles. Stainless steel trim protects the side and the bottom of the gas door opening.

4. Door Handle Shields
The area around the door handle gets a lot of wear. Keep it gleaming with a high-polish aluminum shield.

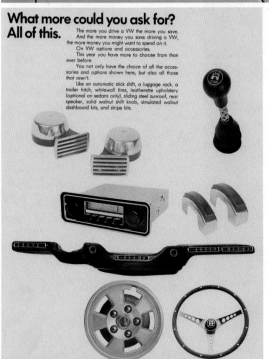

What more could you ask for?
All of this.

The more you drive a VW the more you save. And the more money you save driving a VW, the more money you might want to spend on it.

On VW options and accessories.

This year you have more to choose from than ever before.

You not only have the choice of all the accessories and options shown here, but also all those that aren't.

Like an automatic stick shift, a luggage rack, a trailer hitch, whitewall tires, leatherette upholstery (optional on sedans only), sliding steel sunroof, rear speaker, solid walnut shift knob, simulated walnut dashboard kits, and stripe kits.

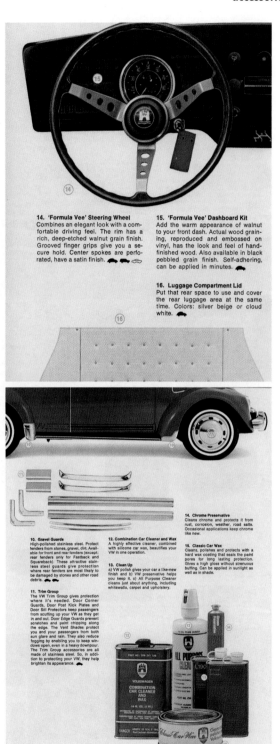

14. 'Formula Vee' Steering Wheel
Combines an elegant look with a comfortable driving feel. The rim has a rich, deep-etched walnut grain finish. Grooved finger grips give you a secure hold. Center spokes are perforated, have a satin finish.

15. 'Formula Vee' Dashboard Kit
Add the warm appearance of walnut to your front dash. Actual wood graining, reproduced and embossed on vinyl, has the look and feel of hand-finished wood. Also available in black pebbled grain finish. Self-adhering, can be applied in minutes.

16. Luggage Compartment Lid
Put that rear space to use and cover the rear luggage area at the same time. Colors: silver beige or cloud white.

10. Gravel Guards
High-polished stainless steel. Protect fenders from stones, gravel, dirt. Available for front and rear fenders (except: rear fenders only for Fastback and Squareback). These attractive stainless steel guards give protection where rear fenders are most likely to be damaged by stones and other road debris.

11. Trim Group
The VW Trim Group gives protection where it's needed. Door Corner Guards, Door Post Kick Plates and Door Sill Protectors keep passengers from scuffing up your VW as they get in and out. Door Edge Guards prevent scratches and paint chipping along the edge. The Vent Shades protect you and your passengers from both sun glare and rain. They also reduce fogging by enabling you to keep windows open, even in a heavy downpour. The Trim Group accessories are all made of stainless steel. So, in addition to protecting your VW, they help brighten its appearance.

12. Combination Car Cleaner and Wax
A highly effective cleaner, combined with silicone car wax, beautifies your VW in one operation.

13. Clean Up
a) VW polish gives your car a like-new finish and b) VW preservative helps you keep it. c) All Purpose Cleaner cleans just about anything, including whitewalls, carpet and upholstery.

14. Chrome Preservative
Cleans chrome and protects it from rust, corrosion, weather, road salts. Occasional applications keep chrome like new.

15. Classic Car Wax
Cleans, polishes and protects with a hard wax coating that seals the paint pores for long lasting protection. Gives a high gloss without strenuous buffing. Can be applied in sunlight as well as in shade.

Many of the accessories depicted in the spreads opposite and on this page might not be quite as desirable as they were in 1970. The same could once be said of 1950s accessories, but no longer is that the case. The wise will hoard what they can now!

**Beetle.
Accepted
in every
situation.**

The Beetle has built up a reputation of being a sturdy and reliable worker. But few people seem to realise how elegant our car can become with Volkswagen accessories.
You'll be surprised at the transformation yourself.

1. Door storage tray, extra room for books, maps, etc. Also available for other Volkswagen models.
000 061 025A
2. Rear mudflaps, in black and white rubber, with VW roundel.
113 821 805 black
113 821 805A white
3. Front stoneguards.
000 071 201
4. Rear stoneguards.
000 071 035
5. Overriders, sturdy construction with a solid rubber buffer.
113 707 153 left
113 707 154 right
113 707 195 beading
6. Tunnel tray, in black leather grained vinyl.
111 999 172
7. Parcel shelf, for extra storage under the dashboard.
000 061 092 (excluding 1303)
8. Door area trims, attractive and functional.
000 063 111A la. hinge pillar kick plates, pair)
000 063 131A lb. sill guards, pair)
000 063 121A lc. door edge kick plates, pair)
9. Locking petrol cap, with two keys.
113 201 551H (different designs available for all VW models).
10. Cigarette lighter, with automatic 'hot wire' system.
000 054 122B (also available for all VW models)
11. Rear trims for air intake and engine hood vents.
000 071 310A (engine hood vents)
000 071 309 (rear air intake)
000 071 309A (rear air intake for 1303)
12. Dipping rear view mirror to prevent headlight dazzle.
114 857 511J (Beetle)
136 857 511 (1303 Beetle only)
(different designs available for other VW models).
13. Finger plates, available in pairs.
000 071 061C
14. Front air intake trim.
000 071 291

Volkswagen approved accessories carry the 'Votex' trade mark.

Votex

options open to you.

the inside it's insulated and fully upholstered. (Even the metal braces are covered.) It flips up and down with the flick of a wrist. (There are no complicated motorized devices to get stuck when you're stuck in a rainstorm.)

In addition, the rear window is a real window. Made of glass, not plastic.

Under the top is the same dependable and economical Volkswagen you get when you buy a regular Beetle. Which means that this year, you can definitely afford not to have a roof over your head.

You can also afford to choose from many accessories. Like mag-type wheel covers (1). Floor mats (2). Fog lamps and a front spoiler (3).

Bumper overriders (4). Vent shades (5). Even a tunnel console and a sports gearshift lever (8).

A luggage rack (6), lockable ski rack (10) or trailer hitch (7) can help you bear a heavy load.

An AM/FM radio (9) is a sound investment. As is optional air conditioning (9).

After all, when you own an economy car like the Beetle, you can afford the luxury of adding on to it.

speculation that the Special Edition Formula Vee Beetle was little more than a dealer-fitted package of off-the-shelf accessories (*see* Chapter 9 for further details).

1. Rear-mounted ski rack
2. Ski rack – mounted on the rain channels
3. Luggage rack – galvanized and highly polished; mounted on rain channels
4. Sapphire AM radio – push-button tuning
5. Sapphire FM/AM radio – push-button tuning
6. Radio/tape-player combination
7. 'Formula Vee' tachometer – 'lets you watch your engine's rpms in each gear range ... made to match your instrument panel.'
8. Trailer hitch
9. Tunnel console – 'made of moulded vinyl in black pebble grain finish to match the interior appointments of late model VWs'

ABOVE: British market 1976.

LEFT: US market 1976.

THE COOL LINE

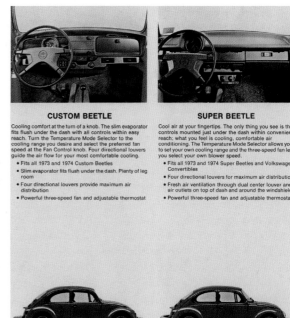

CUSTOM BEETLE

Cooling comfort at the turn of a knob. The slim evaporator fits flush under the dash with all controls within easy reach. Turn the Temperature Mode Selector to the cooling range you desire and select the preferred fan speed at the Fan Control knob. Four directional louvers guide the air flow for your most comfortable cooling.

- Fits all 1973 and 1974 Custom Beetles
- Slim evaporator fits flush under the dash. Plenty of leg room
- Four directional louvers provide maximum air distribution
- Powerful three-speed fan and adjustable thermostat

SUPER BEETLE

Cool air at your fingertips. The only thing you see is the controls mounted just under the dash within convenient reach; what you feel is cooling, comfortable air conditioning. The Temperature Mode Selector allows you to set your own cooling range and the three-speed fan lets you select your own blower speed.

- Fits all 1973 and 1974 Super Beetles and Volkswagen Convertibles
- Four directional louvers for maximum air distribution
- Fresh air ventilation through dual center louver and air outlets on top of dash and around the windshield
- Powerful three-speed fan and adjustable thermostat

10. 'Formula Vee' steering wheel cover – 'vinyl surfaced Porotherm wheel cover keeps your hands warm in winter and dry in summer'
11. Electric clock
12. 'Air conditioner'
13. Glove compartment shelf – 'horizontal shelf keeps maps, books, etc. at hand. Vertical separators make compartments for cigarettes, sunglasses, toll tickets and other small items. Grey plastic with chrome trim …'
14. Tissue dispenser – 'black styrene with leather grain etching and polished aluminium front plate'
15. Seat recliner – 'converts front seats into reclining seats with a flick of the handle'
16. Cigarette lighter
17. Rear speaker
18. Parcel shelf
19. Hinged side windows – 'Give your passengers in the back a break. These side windows are adjustable for draft-free ventilation. Safety lever holds the windows open or tightly shut. Comes in sets of two'
20. Door storage compartment
21. Child's safety seat
22. Utility light – 'illuminates engine and/or luggage compartment. Light goes on and off when hood is opened and closed'
23. Sunroof wind deflector
24. 'Formula Vee' stripe kit – 'These racing stripes add a look of dash to your VW. Kit contains four pre-aligned self-adhesive strips, each 2½in × 40in. Choice of gold, white and black. Easy to apply'
25. Wheel trim rings – 'Highly polished aluminium, chromed steel or stainless steel slotted type. Add a dash of flash to your wheels.'
26. Mag wheels – 'made of special aluminium-magnesium-beryllium-titanium alloy …'
27. 'Formula Vee' taper-tip exhaust pipes
28. Right-side mirror
29. Sill panel reflector – 'glass reflectors pick up the headlights of vehicles approaching from either side. Aluminium moulding enhances your car's appearance. Packaged in sets of two ...'
30. 'Formula Vee' fanfare horn set
31. Rubber bumper inserts
32. 'Formula Vee' air intake grille
33. 'Formula Vee' walnut gearshift knob – 'Custom designed of warm walnut. Top shows VW shift pattern … Also available with Wolfsburg City Crest insert.'
34. 'Formula Vee' steering wheel
35. 'Formula Vee' dashboard kit – 'Add the warm appearance of walnut to your front dash. Actual wood graining, reproduced and embossed on vinyl, has the look and feel of hand-finished wood. Also available in black grain finish. Self-adhering …'
36. Luggage compartment lid (behind rear seat)
37. Luggage compartment mat (boot)
38. 'Formula Vee' bumper overriders
39. Vent shades – 'Highly polished stainless steel. Not only dresses up your VW, but gives draft-free ventilation, reduces window fogging, keeps rain out, keeps car cooler in summer.'
40. Gas door guard – 'Prevent paint chipping and scratching caused by gas station hose nozzles. Stainless steel trim protects the side and the bottom of the gas door opening.'
41. Door handle shields
42. Terry cloth seat covers
43. Nylon-foam seat covers
44. Rubber floor mats
45. Mudflaps
46. Coco fibre mats
47. Gravel guards (front and rear stoneguards)
48. Trim group – 'The VW trim group gives protection where it is

The coolest of stickers!

needed. Door corner, doorpost kickplates and door sill protectors keep passengers from scuffing up your VW as they get in and out. Door edge guards prevent scratches and paint chipping along the edge …'

49. Hub cap removal tool
50. Glove compartment lock
51. Gas tank lock

1976 North American market

Literature produced to promote both the Sedan and the Cabriolet included one section designed to emphasize the somewhat more limited range of options open to Beetle owners in the car's declining years. Stressing the value of the Beetle in both hard- and soft-top guises the copywriter continued with the reassuring statement that owners could:

> also afford to choose from many accessories. Like mag-type wheel covers. Floor mats. Fog lamps and a front spoiler. Bumper overriders. Vent shades. Even a tunnel console and a sports gearshift lever. A luggage rack, lockable ski rack or trailer hitch can help you bear a heavy load. An AM/FM radio is a sound investment. As is optional air conditioning. After all, when you own an economy car like the Beetle, you can afford the luxury of adding on to it.

(See page 94 for an image taken from this brochure.)

1976 British market

In late 1975 and theoretically for the '76 model year, Volkswagen GB Ltd produced a brochure entitled *VW Accessories to Suit All Tastes*. Like the American offering of five years previously, this was designed to cover all models in the range and therefore included models such as the Golf, Passat, Polo and Scirocco. However, despite the Beetle's increasingly peripheral role in Volkswagen's overall sales strategy, the list of accessories available was extensive

and perhaps even more surprisingly included products for now redundant models such as the 1303. Accessories were promoted under the umbrella of the Votex brand, the brochure being liberally smattered with two messages: 'Volkswagen approved accessories carry the "Votex" trade mark' and '"Votex" is the name you'll find on Volkswagen factory made or approved accessories.' The catalogue of Beetle-specific items was complemented by a range of general items including seat covers, steering wheel gloves and radios.

1. Door storage tray, extra room for books, maps, etc.
   000 061 035A
2. Rear mudflaps, in black and white rubber, with VW roundel
   113 281 805 black
   113 821 805A white
3. Front stoneguards
   000 071 201
4. Rear stoneguards
   000 071 035
5. Overriders, sturdy construction with a solid rubber buffer
   113 707 153 left
   113 707 154 right
   113 707 195 beading
6. Tunnel tray, in black leather grained vinyl
   111 999 172
7. Parcel shelf, for extra storage under the dashboard
   000 061 092 (excluding 1303)
8. Door area trims, attractive and functional
   000 063 111A (hinge pillar kickplates, pair)
   000 063 101A (sill guards, pair)
   000 063 121A (door edge kick plates, pair)
9. Locking petrol cap, with two keys
   113 201 551H
10. Cigarette lighter, with automatic 'hot wire' system
    000 054 122B
11. Rear trims for air intake and engine hood vents
    000 071 310A (engine hood vents)
    000 071 309 (rear air intake)
    000 071 309A (rear air intake for 1303)

12. Dipping rear-view mirror to prevent headlight dazzle
    114 857 511J (Beetle)
    136 857 511 (1303 Beetle only)
13. Fingerplates, available in pairs
    000 071 061C
14. Front air-intake trim
    000 071 291

(See page 94 for an image taken from this brochure.)

SPECIFIC LINES

In addition to brochures either promoting the car and its attendant accessories, or specific to the extra-cost items designed either to improve the functionality of the car, or to enhance its appearance, literature in the form of glorified flyers might well have been available to endorse one particular item, a typical example being the US-produced *The Cool Line*, a fold-out leaflet about air conditioning.

The Cool Line covered all the models in the range including both the Custom Beetle and the Super Beetle, as well as: The Thing, Type 181; Karmann Ghia; Type Four; Type Two Station Wagon; and Campmobile.

The text for the Custom Beetle ran as follows, while the words used to describe the system as fitted to the Super Beetle were similar in content and identical in purpose.

> Cooling comfort at the turn of a knob. The slim evaporator fits flush under the dash with all controls within easy reach. Turn the Temperature Mode Selector to the cooling range you desire and select the preferred fan speed at the Fan Control knob. Four directional louvers guide the air flow for your most comfortable cooling.
>
> ■ Fits all 1973 and 1974 Custom Beetles
> ■ Slim evaporator fits flush under the dash. Plenty of leg room
> ■ Four directional louvers provide maximum air distribution
> ■ Powerful three-speed fan and adjustable thermostat'

special edition Beetles

ABOVE: *Surely the most special of all: a press shot of the British version of the 'World Champion' Beetle – launched to coincide with the occasion of Volkswagen's Beetle overtaking the legendary Ford Model 'T' as the most produced car of all time.*

Special edition Beetles grew out of Volkswagen's fear in the post-Nordhoff era that the car was outdated and had to be replaced as a matter of urgency. A logical way to boost sales against ever-stiffer competition was the introduction of limited edition cars with additional equipment and, on occasion, 'exclusive' paint colours at a price which represented exceptional value when compared to the standard models in the Beetle range.

Additionally, Volkswagen decided to take advantage of its continuing good fortune in terms of breaking production barriers by issuing celebratory models which were again limited in number – increasing their perceived value – and which were laden with additional trim and special paint colours.

Unfortunately, due to their limited edition status and most definitely where the onus was placed on the dealers to add the attributes to make the special model, specification records are comparatively brief and on occasion unclear. In theory, but certainly not in practice, every factory-instigated special had a three-digit code prefaced by an 'S' – standing for *Sonderausführung*, or special model.

As a starting point to a specification guide to selected special edition models, the known S codes are listed together with any M codes that formed all or part of the make-up of the vehicle. Where possible, the model

year in which the special was produced, the model on which it was based and the market it was intended for are also included. Unfortunately, more than one special model was allocated the same S code, while a further hindrance to clarity comes with the allocation of special model numbers to cars with features specific to a given market; these are also listed.

A CHRONOLOGICALLY ARRANGED SELECTION OF SPECIAL MODELS

The June Beetle – 1970

This was the first special to be offered to UK buyers. Based on the 1500, then

S Code	Description	Model/s	M information	Year/s
S708	Special wraparound rear bumpers USA	All	M108, M113	1976/7
S710	Rear light cluster Amber/Red instead of Amber/ Red/Clear *Bundespost*	1200 Beetle		1974/5
S714	Special trim and paint	1200 Beetle		1973
S714	Yellow and Black Racer West German market	1303 1200		1974
S714	Jeans 74 West German market	1200		1974
S715	Love Bug USA	Super Beetle		1974
S715	Leisure Beetle West German market	1200		1975
S716	Jeans 74 Export	1200		1974
S717	1200L Herringbone West German market	1200	M603	1974
S719	1200L Herringbone Export UK market – known as 1200 Super	1200	M603	1974
S723	Special for North America	Super Beetle		1974
S723	Special for North America The Champagne Edition	Cabriolet		1977
S729	Luxury Beetle Export, excluding USA and Canada	1303		1974
S736	Sun Beetle USA, Canada	Custom	M108, M110	1974
S736	Spring Messenger West German market	1200, 1303		1973
S736	Luxury Beetle – sometimes referred to as La Grande Bug USA, Canada	Super Beetle		1975
S739	Special for the USA	Cabriolet		1976
S744	Jeans 111 West German market	1200		1975
S759	Black is Beautiful Export (excluding USA and Canada)	1200, 1303		1973
S761	Jeans Beetle	1200		1974
S763	Big Beetle	1303		1974
S764	City Beetle	1303		1974
S765	Champagne Edition 11 USA	Cabriolet		1978
S785	Spring Messenger Export (excluding USA and Canada)	1300, 1303		1973

the top-of-the-range model, it was available from dealers with effect from June 1970 – hence its name. Apart from a heated rear window and overriders, neither of which were standard to the regular range of Beetles on offer, plus anodized aluminium wheel trims which were a popular accessory of the time, the June Beetle's most striking attribute was its paintwork. Signal Orange, L20E, had previously been

the preserve of Volkswagens built by Karmann and this proved a convenient way of creating a special without a great deal of effort!

The Super Vee – 1971

Reference to the accessories chapter and the availability list for the American market in 1970 indicates a wealth of options under the 'Formula Vee'

brand, one notably being a 'Stripe Kit', an essential part of the Super Vee's make-up. There is more than a suggestion that US Super Vees were standard cars to which dealers added a predetermined marketing-led list of accessories. In the UK rumours persisted of the Dovercourt St John's Wood operation having a grand clear-out of Super Vee accessories a few years after the edition was launched, thus enabling

Der Weltmeister

In 1927, when production of the Model T Ford finally ended over 15,000,000 of that same vehicle had been manufactured. This established a world record in motor car production.

In 1972, with production still in progress the Volkswagen Beetle established a new world record in motor car production. 15,007,033 was the recorded figure for the 17th February 1972. The Beetle is now World Champion.

This medallion has been minted to celebrate the Volkswagen Beetles World Record. And this certificate records the fact that one of a limited fifteen hundred distinctive commemorative models released to the U.K. is in the possession of

A section of the certificate presented to UK World Champion owners. Printed on thick card, a recess was cut into the material to house the specially minted medallion.

ABOVE: Cover of the booklet issued to all purchasers of Weltmeister cars in Germany. Oddly, the English language version still featured a 1302S, although the UK World Champion edition was based on the 1300.

BELOW: Highly polished alloy centre cap stamped with the VW roundel, plus grey plastic 19mm nut covers.

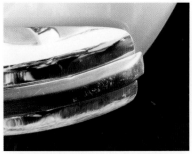

Rubber bumper strip.

RIGHT: The much sought-after Lemmertz steel wheel – exclusive in special edition terms to the Weltmeister.

enthusiasts to create their own 'Super Vee'. Theoretically based on the top-of-the-range 1302S model of the day and finished in either Gemini Metallic, L96E, or Turquoise Metallic, L95B, more than one 1300 torsion-bar model has been recorded in the UK, raising the odds that the Super Vee was not originated at the factory but in the showrooms of the dealers.

Special features of the American version included: 4½J Lemmertz pressed steel wheels; three-spoke, padded rim steering wheel in matt black; brightwork gutter trims; door window vent shades; front and rear stoneguards; grille for rear air intake, grilles for engine lid air intakes; sill; pillar and door-edge kickplates; bumper overriders front and rear; taper-tip tailpipes; twin fanfare horns; walnut grain trimmed dash and walnut gear-lever knob; radio cassette player; and under-dash tissue dispenser.

Understandably, the UK version was somewhat more restrained, with items like the brightwork gutter trims, the walnut grain dash trim and taper tips being dropped from the recipe handed to the dealers. All Super Vees should have been identifiable by a specially minted Super Vee engine lid badge that replaced the standard model identifying decal and which would normally have read 1302S.

Der Weltmeister (The World Champion) – 1972

Without doubt, when the Beetle's production numbers finally overtook those of Ford's legendary Model T, the era of the special edition car had arrived and would remain an important ingredient to the boosting of sales until the end of German production and beyond.

The package offered to would-be buyers varied from country to country, with, for example, the US celebratory model being entwined with off-road racing success at Baja, while the British special cars were based on the 1300 torsion-bar car rather than the 1302S that was standard to the rest of the world.

The unifying attributes of a World Champion Beetle were two-fold. First and foremost, all cars were painted in the attractive shade of Marathon Blue Metallic, L96M. Although this colour, purloined from Audi and the latest 80 model, became standard to the upper echelons of the Beetle range at the start of the '73 model year, at the time it was unique to the special edition model, leading to the misnomer of such cars being referred to as Marathon Beetles. Secondly, the World Champion Beetle sported distinctive ten-spoke pressed steel wheels. Manufactured

ABOVE: Probably the best-known surviving World Champion Beetle in the UK today, even though for photography purposes the car's number plates have been removed.

RIGHT: This World Champion has its certificate on display behind the windscreen.

in Germany by Lemmertz, the wheels were sprayed in silver with a black centre section. An attractive polished alloy centre cap stamped with the VW roundel and grey plastic 19mm nut covers were the other components to what has since become a sought-after item amongst enthusiasts of post-'68 model year Beetles.

The other seemingly universal attribute of the World Champion Beetle was hardly earth-shattering, as it came in the form of rubber bumper inserts. However, associated regalia helped to increase the edition's appeal. In Germany, new owners were given a small key ring medallion bearing the words 'Der Weltmeister, Wolfsburg, Germany, 1972', as well as a thirty-two page booklet charting the car's progress from concept to world champion. In Britain, purchasers received an English language version of what was otherwise the same booklet, plus a

board-mounted certificate measuring 305mm × 415mm, which included a 50mm diameter medallion for mounting on the dashboard if the new owner so wished. Australian World Champion Beetle owners were perhaps the most fortunate, as their medallions bearing the simple legend, 'fifteen-millionth commemorative VW 1972' were individually numbered.

American Baja SE owners received a confusing plaque making no reference to the Beetle's achievement, but instead carrying an image of seven cacti and the words 'Baja Champion SE 1967 – 1971'. Leatherette upholstery was justifiably added to the extras list for a market where cloth was the norm. Some, but certainly not all, Baja Champion SE models were adorned with Baja side stripes, while an extra-cost option was the inclusion of Bosch halogen fog lamps. To confuse matters further, a dealer-instigated second edition Baja

Beetle followed closely on the original and included taper-tip tailpipes, over-riders, Bosch fog lamps, walnut-effect dash trim, Baja side stripes and the biggest giveaway of all, clip-on wheel trims in imitation of the mag wheels fitted to the Super Vee.

Of greatest significance and typical of most special edition models whichever market the car was destined for, the 'genuine' Baja Champion SE sold at $2,284.50, making it only $70 more expensive than a normal Superbug. Similarly, the 6,000 Weltmeisters offered on the home market were priced at DM6,930, which, when the extras were accounted for, equated to a DM300 saving on the amount charged for a regular 1302S.

The British edition of the World Champion extended to 1,500 cars, with main dealers acquiring six vehicles each and other agents being limited to just three. A national newspaper advertising campaign under the banner heading, 'If you buy one of these, you deserve a medal' helped to ensure that the edition sold out very quickly.

The GT Beetle – December 1972

Introduced to celebrate the arrival of the 300,000th Beetle in Britain on 15 December 1972, the GT Beetle was a vehicle known to the home market as a 1300S, a torsion-bar, flat-screen Volkswagen with front disc brakes and the 50PS 1600 engine. Never officially imported to the UK in this guise, the 1300S became the GT Beetle thanks

For £19 more than the price of a 1300 Beetle, GT owners had the advantage of a very special edition.

All GT colours might be best described as vibrant. This is Lemon Yellow.

'Hot property' – the cover of a four-page bro-chure produced to sell the GT Beetle.

The centre spread of the GT brochure and the striking use of colour to promote three 'special fruity colours'.

ABOVE: The fifth 4½J × 15 Sports wheel in the GT's boot.

LEFT: Tomato Red GT Beetle.

RIGHT: This image of the door card is a good guide to the colour of the GT's upholstery. Very few cars with original upholstery survive.

to a higher standard of fittings than British owners were used to, a series of dealer-fitted accessories and three paint shades which had not as yet fil-tered through to the general market.

Somewhat unusually for the special Beetles, a four-page sales brochure was produced to sell the limited edition of just 2,500 cars. Useful though the bro-chure is in confirming the specification of the GT, Volkswagen probably could

have saved itself the expense, as the extremely good value special sold very quickly, most if not all having gone by March 1973.

For just £19 more than a normal 1300 Beetle and at a price conven-iently just under the £1,000 barrier, in addition to the 1600cc engine and front disc brakes owners benefited from the following:

- 4½J × 15 (M976) Sports wheels shod with radial ply tyres.
- A choice of three 'fruity special colours', described as and illustrated in the form of Tomato Red, Lemon Yellow and Apple Green (*Tomatenrot*, L30M; *Zitrongelb*, L15M; *Apfelgrün*, L64M). It has been assumed that these colours were Anglicized versions of three future popular shades, namely Phoenix Red, L32K, Lemon Yellow, L15M, and Cliff Green, L61A, but in two out of three instances this appears to be erroneous.
- The new style of rear light cluster, so far only seen on the recently introduced 1303 range and known in enthusiast circles as the 'elephant's foot' due to its size and shape ('80 square inches of winker, stop light and reflector').

The desirable and in the past frequently stolen GT badge.

- Bamboo (01) coloured cloth upholstery – the norm of the day still being black basketweave-design vinyl: 'It's warm in winter, cool in summer. It won't shine your suit. Or take the creases out of your jeans.' (In later life, this upholstery was extremely prone to rot due to the effects of the sun.)
- 'There's also a non-reflective, matt black padded dashboard' – M228, previously the preserve of the L models, which hadn't filtered through to the British market.
- A tunnel tray (Part No. 111 999 172) and a sports gear shift (Part No. 321 064 231), the onus being on the dealer to fit these two items.

The most envied item of all, though, was a specially minted 'GT Beetle' engine lid badge. Amazingly, some dealers forgot to fit the badge (Part No. 1H 999 17), and it wasn't uncommon to see cars on the road bearing the original 1300S legend.

The Black and Yellow Racer, S714 – January 1973

Launched in January 1973, the 3,500 run of Black and Yellow Racers was specially designed for the home market only. The car's most recognizable attribute was its striking paint scheme, with the main panels being finished in Saturn Yellow, L13M, but complemented by a black bonnet and engine lid. The bumpers were similarly finished in black, while clever touches came in the form of a yellow centre stripe for these, the replacement of the normal bright trim on the bonnet with a yellow painted strip and similar treatment for the 1303S legend on the engine compartment lid. Side trim

strips were finished in black, although headlamp surrounds and indicator covers remained in standard chrome finish, while bright inserts in the window rubbers were deleted to give the car a sportier look. (During the restoration of the car photographed, later front wings have been fitted, in the process transferring the indicators from the wing tops to the later-style bumper.)

Inside the car featured special rally seats, M409, and a smaller than standard 38cm diameter sports steering wheel, while the décor throughout was black.

5½J sports wheels, M444, were shod with tyres specially developed for the car by Pirelli, Veith-Pirelli 175/70 SR 15, and these became generally available for all Beetles fitted with 5½J rims. Considering that the

Black and Yellow Racer appeared to be little more than a trim package, as it sported the standard 1584cc, 50PS engine attributed to all 1303S models, the fitting of M550, the perforated front valance designed to supply air-conditioned Beetles with cooling air, but equally suited to assisting an oil cooler sited behind the apron, seems odd. Clearly there was no intention to offer air conditioning as an option, so it has to be assumed that Volkswagen expected that owners would choose to tune their engines and fit an oil cooler.

Unlike most specials, the Black and Yellow Racer, at DM7,760, carried a relatively hefty premium over the price of an equivalent 1303S, which stood at DM7,000. Nevertheless, the cars were eagerly snapped up and remain a sought-after special to this day.

This carefully restored Black and Yellow Racer betrays only one inaccuracy – for Concours presentation the front indicators should be wing-mounted. Note the air-conditioning grille in the front valance, which was apparently installed for those intending to improve the car's performance.

The Sports Bug, S714 – 1973

Essentially an American version of the Black and Yellow Racer, this special edition proved exceptionally popular and despite Volkswagen's advertising department's assertion that 'If you don't get it now you may not be able to get it at all', 20,000 Sports Bugs were sold.

The Sports Bug extended to what Volkswagen of America called 'snazzy mag-type' wheels, but in reality were the same 5½J Sports wheel attributed to its European counterpart, 'Indy-type' steering wheel, which again was as offered in Germany, and 'true sports bucket seats, with contoured vinyl sides and no-slip fabric', identical to those on the Black and Yellow Racer. Similarly, both cars featured black-dominated interiors.

Where the two vehicles differed was in paintwork, for the Sports Bug lacked the black engine and boot lids, although it retained other black accoutrements, while it was available not only in Saturn Yellow but also in Marathon Metallic. Unlike the Black and Yellow Racer, Volkswagen of America openly promoted a series of add-ons to the basic package. These included what were described as 'racing stripes' – black, red-edged vinyl, ZVW146120, that ran from along the driver's door, the rear quarter panel, across the air intake vents above the engine lid, along the passenger side of the car, to terminate where the door met the A-pillar; flare-tip tailpipes; and a stereo

Volkswagen announces a limited-edition Volkswagen.

The Sports Bug

Bet you thought we'd never do it.
Well, catch this:
Oversize radial tires. Mounted on snazzy mag-type wheels.
Indy-type steering wheel. Covered in simulated leather over thick padding.
True sports bucket seats. With contoured vinyl sides and no-slip fabric. To hold you comfortably while cornering.
Short-throw synchro stick shift. The faster you shift, the faster it shifts.
Spirited air-cooled engine. Cast with lightweight aluminum-magnesium alloy Just like in Super Vee racing engines.
Four-wheel independent suspension. McPherson-design coil/shock combo up front. Double-jointed rear axle with independent trailing arms in back.
Special high-gloss paint job. In Saturn Yellow. Or Marathon Silver Metallic. Jet black trimming.
Options? All kinds. Like racing stripes.
©VOLKSWAGEN OF AMERICA, INC.

Flare-tip pipes. Stereo radio. And more.
If this sounds like what you've been waiting for from us, wait no more.
We built only a limited number of our special-edition Sports Bug.
After all, we can't make too much of a good thing.

ABOVE: Volkswagen of America promoted the Sports Bug through magazine advertising and the wit of the DDB agency.

RIGHT AND BELOW: The promotional brochure to promote the Jeans Beetle in the UK took as its base the size and format of a newspaper page. These three extracts form the nub of the publication. Note the lack of a big picture of the car.

Everyone knows you're one of the few amongst the many. But if you're worried that being different always works out to be an expensive pastime we'd like to casually let this slip. The Jeans Beetle is something special in more ways than one. It's dressed with a lot more than you'll actually be paying for.

Side stripes.

Handy pockets in seat backs.

Sports gear shift.

3 wave radio.

J Rally wheels.

Tunis yellow body.
Cool black exterior trim.

Twin reversing lights.

1200 power unit. The economical one that lets you cruise at a speed the law doesn't.

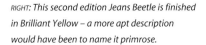

Decal details from the original Jeans Edition and the only one to make it to the UK.

RIGHT: *This second edition Jeans Beetle is finished in Brilliant Yellow – a more apt description would have been to name it primrose.*

radio. (Note, however, that the beltline stripe was also available as an accessory for the regular Custom model Beetle, Part No. ZVW146121, thus negating the exclusivity of this special.)

The Jeans Beetle, S761 – 1974 model year; S714 & S716 – 1974 model year; plus S744 – 1975

The Jeans Beetle was probably the most successful of all the special edition Beetles, with the initial run alone consisting of some 25,000 cars. Add to this three more batches of Jeans Beetles – making a total of three during the 1974 model year and one in 1975 – and it is likely that in excess of 50,000 Jeans Beetles were produced.

The secret of this success was probably two-fold. First the package was at one with the spirit of the age – the elderly and increasingly staid Beetle was reborn as a trendy fun car beloved of students and those with either anti-establishment sentiments, or a wish to regain a long-lost youth.

Second, in times of rampant inflation, recession and world oil crises, the Jeans Beetle was reassuringly cheap; a basic 1200 Beetle but without the austerity of the lowest cost Beetle in the range. To illustrate this point, in Britain in May 1974 compared to the basic

1200 Beetle at £1,029, the Jeans Beetle cost just £31 more at £1,060.

The specification of the Jeans Beetle not only varied slightly from edition to edition, but also from market to market. Amazingly, as late as 1974 buyers of a basic Beetle on the home market suffered the ignominy of 6V electrics and the humiliation of reliance on a fuel tap due to the lack of a fuel gauge. That the Jeans Beetle carried both such basics as part of its specification was of obvious merit in Germany but of little value in the UK, where all 1200 cars were equipped with such essentials.

The first Jeans Beetle was the only one exported to Britain and was instantly recognizable externally by its Tunis Yellow, L16M, paintwork, a shade best described as a muddy yellow with a hint of brown, and its complete lack of chrome or brightwork. As a special based on the 1200, which by this time had adopted the 1303's and 1300's Europa-style bumper, but finished in black rather than chrome, the presence of this colour wasn't out of the ordinary. However, that the headlamp rims, door handles and even the trim strips down each side of the car were also finished in matt black was ground-breaking for Volkswagen, albeit very much in keeping with the spirit of this special. A bold matt black lower

side strip with the word 'Jeans' etched out of the vinyl on the rear quarter panel and a similarly obvious brand-name on the engine compartment left no one in any doubt that this was a special Beetle. Use of the increasingly ubiquitous 4½J sports wheel, M976, further set the car apart from the ordinary 1200, although the fact that the wheels were shod with cross-ply tyres must have come as a disappointment to some would-be owners.

Inside, there was no mistaking that this was a Jeans Beetle, as the seats were covered with a blue denim material (No. 30), which featured both large red stitches and reinforcing rivets. The back of the front seats were decorated with large pockets.

Volkswagen in Britain produced a most unusual newsprint-style, fold-out, full colour brochure to promote both the Jeans Beetle and the Big Beetle. Clearly emanating from the stable of the legendary DDB advertising agency, the text summarized the car's attributes to full fun Beetle effect:

A bright today idea that comes with a bright Tunis Yellow body and blue denim seats with coloured stitching and attractive decorative riveting. It's the Beetle that goes everywhere in Jeans. …

There are rally wheels that certainly look the part, a three-wave radio, sports gearshift and twin reversing lights. Lights to make certain you'll know your way around any place backwards. And to keep it looking rather cool we've kept all the outside trimmings in black. (When you're out to be different you might as well be seen as such.)

Back on the inside you'll find the seats have back pockets. Useful back pockets. Whoever heard of Jeans without them. And of course your Jeans Beetle will come suitably emblazoned with side stripes. Just to make sure everyone knows you're different. …

The Jeans Beetle is something special in more ways than one. It's dressed with a lot more than you'll actually be paying for.

As the ad-man's text implies, the Jeans Beetle was laden with additional items, ones that ranged from the rudimentary such as a passenger sun visor, singular by its absence on an ordinary 1200, and a passenger grab handle, to the genuinely supplementary to a standard specification. These included a heated rear window, a dipping interior mirror, sports gearstick and, quite a luxury in 1974, a three-band Wolfsburg radio.

The second Jeans Beetle followed rapidly in January 1974 – the initial run having been produced in December 1973 – and was available to selected export markets and on the domestic front, but only in the last two colour options mentioned. Although essentially the same as the first issue in that all the trimmings were finished in black, while the value of the extras included totalled considerably more than the purchase price of the car, Tunis Yellow was consigned to the archives in favour of three different paint options. Marino Yellow, L20A, cars came with the same Jeans Blue upholstery that owners of the original edition were familiar with. However, Phoenix Red, L32K, Jeans Beetles were trimmed with a Jeans Black, B1, upholstery, while Brilliant Yellow, L11C, vehicles were paired with Jeans Dust Green interiors. (Brilliant Yellow as a description for a paint colour was

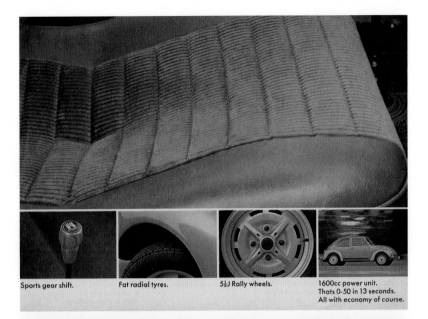

Sports gear shift.   Fat radial tyres.   5½J Rally wheels.   1600cc power unit.
Thats 0-50 in 13 seconds.
All with economy of course.

Side stripes.   Go for the Big Beetle   Wood-look fascia.   Sports steering wheel.
in a big way.

The Big Beetle promotional material sat on the reverse of a newspaper format-style brochure devoted in part to the Jeans Beetle. Inevitably taking the same format as that of the Jeans, the main image of the car was of its seats, part of which has been included here. However, the content of the thumbnail pictures is of more significance in terms of specification.

somewhat misleading, as the shade in question equated to a pastel primrose shade, as illustrated in a couple of the accompanying pictures.) One or two markets benefited from Jeans Beetles that included front seats with integral headrests and a black padded dashboard.

The third and final edition of the Jeans Beetle manufactured in West Germany – Mexican Jeans Beetles would follow later – emerged in 1975. Undoubtedly the best equipped of the editions, as these Jeans Beetles all had a fuel gauge, heated rear window, front seats with integral headrests, halogen headlamps, a rear fog light,

padded dash and, no doubt to the delight of many an enthusiast, radial ply tyres, sadly some of the individuality and originality of the earlier cars was lost. Depressingly, the exterior of the cars were painted in L28N Orange, while upholstery and door cards were matched to this colour accordingly, thus losing the denim appeal of earlier editions.

The City Beetle, S764 – 1974

Based on the straightforward 1303 Beetle with a 1300, the City Beetle was offered in three shades of paintwork, which was duly colour-coordinated

A publicity shot of the Luxury Bug released by Volkswagen of America's press office at the time of its launch . (VWoA)

with matching upholstery. Ibiza Red, L31M, Ontario Blue Metallic, L95M, and Ischia Green Metallic, L99M, City Beetles were adorned with Jeans Beetle-type side stripes, which read '1303/City', and 4½J Sports wheels. Apart from their special seat fabrics, the interior specification of the City Beetles included deep pile carpet, a padded steering wheel, inertia seat belts, dipping rear-view mirror, heated rear window and the three-wavelength VW Emden radio. External luxuries extended to an engine lid lock, rubber bumper strips and reversing lights, while publicity shots at least indicated that the City Beetle was shod with radial tyres.

The Big Beetle, S763, S719 – 1974

The fold-out newspaper-style brochure already referred to with reference to the Jeans Beetle included a massive double-page spread allocated to the Big Beetle's inviting front seats and a series of thumbnail pictures captioned thus: 'Side stripes; Go for the Big Beetle in a big way; Wood-look fascia; Sports steering wheel; Sports gear shift; Fat radial tyres; 5½J Rally wheels; 1600cc power unit. That's 0–50 in 13 seconds. All with economy of course.'

The text from the same brochure follows in full:

A Beetle with big ideas about itself. That's why we've called it, quite simply, the Big Beetle. There's a 1600 power unit which will take you from 0 to 50 in just 13 seconds and after that you can cruise all day at 81mph. This Big Beetle is really something rather special, in fact its special effects certainly make quite a list. There's wall to wall carpeting, wide ribbed corduroy seats and a range of Big Beetle metallic paint finishes.

To continue. There's a sports gear shift, a wood-look fascia, and a sports steering wheel that's a real pleasure to get to grips with.

There's still more however, very sensible rubber faced bumpers and a pair of powerful reversing lights.

All in all this Big Beetle will take some missing, its big extras are more than noticeable. But just to make certain it's recognized for what it is there are some special side stripes to make the point. That point being of course, 'The Big Beetle'.

Try one for size, feel its quality. We know you'll love its big difference. It's also something we haven't mentioned. A Big Bargain.

The ad-man's text for the UK-market version of the Big Beetle more or less includes all the vehicle's attributes, but inevitably doesn't include the minutiae of the car's specification and couldn't possibly have been expected to outline the variations in the package between markets.

The paintwork options were initially Ontario Blue Metallic, L95M (with either Blue, 28, or Dark Blue, 73, interior), Moss Green Metallic, L95C (with Bamboo Beige, 72, interior), Hellas Gold Metallic (with Nutbrown, 71, interior) and Diamond Silver Metallic, L97A, with Dark Blue, 33, interior. Not all markets received all the colour options; for example, in Britain Silver was not initially included, but was added in a second tranche, together with more blue cars.

Similarly, the specification varied a little between countries. As examples, some markets received front seats with integral headrests, while the package for others didn't include a heated rear window. UK-market cars were offered with plain black stripes on the lower body sides, while those seen on the German highways featured the words 1303/BIG built in.

Big Beetles came with meaty wheels in the form of 5½J × 15 sports design steel shod with 175/70 HR15 radials. Other luxuries included an engine lid lock, rubber bumper strips, dipping rear-view mirror and reversing lights. Inside there was a padded steering wheel and a dash trimmed with a wood-effect plastic strip. The gearstick had a genuine wooden knob, while the seat belts were of the reel variety.

A highlight was undoubtedly the attractive and seemingly hardwearing corduroy panels in the seats, while a low point had to be the exclusion of a radio from what was theoretically the highest-specification special on the top of the range 1303S Saloon.

The Herringbone, or VW 1200 Super Beetle – 1974/5

Although in Britain only some £31 more expensive than the Jeans Beetle described above, the VW 1200 Super Beetle, S719, a forerunner of the widely available 1200L and known in Germany as the VW1200L Herringbone, S717, was more or less eclipsed by its popular stablemate. The Herringbone Beetle was a 1200 fitted with an L pack, M603, the luxury extending to chrome bumpers, a full headlining, two-speed wipers, and so on, but which nevertheless retained the base model two-spoke steering wheel and plain rubber window surrounds. For the home market the colours available were Phoenix Red and Lofoten Green, but for UK buyers Marino Yellow was added. 4½J sports wheels were part of the package in most cases, while the seats were finished in a combination of velour cord material and colour-coordinated vinyl.

1303 Campaign and the Sun Beetle – 1975

The price list issued by Volkswagen (GB) Ltd in June 1975 illustrates the exceptional value of many of the special models. The chart below demonstrates exactly what the cost implications of purchasing two specials were.

The 1303-based Campaign Beetle was a British-market special that was released in the spring of 1975 and finished in Agate Brown Metallic, L86Z, a colour normally reserved for Audis. Inside it sported yellow stone, 22, cloth upholstery, a wood-look dash trim and a heated rear window. 4½J sports wheels completed the package. Working on basic prices, to add metallic paint to the £1,323.93 1303 would have cost £29.19, while a heated rear window would have added a further £13.09, giving a grand total before car tax and VAT of £1,366.21. Considering the Campaign model cost £1,366.67, just pence more than the standard model with these attributes, but also featured sports wheels and cloth upholstery, here was exceptional value.

The UK-market Sun Beetle was essentially a well-packaged 1300 with a sunroof. Launched in the late spring of 1975, the special was available in either Sun Yellow or Sun Orange, presenting another case where the cars' paintwork might have attracted special paint shades, but were more likely to be Anglicized versions of existing colours, probably from the Karmann stable – Sunshine Yellow, L13K, and Nepal Orange, L20C. The Sun Beetle's main attributes apart from the sunroof were 4½J sports wheels, heated rear window and a padded dash. Again comparing a standard 1300 with some of the Sun Beetle's extras added to the

A gathering of Last Edition Beetles – an active register chivvies owners to display their cars at events across the UK.

price shows that the special was particularly keenly priced, the sunroof alone accounting for the higher price tag.

The Luxury Bug

In the final years of Beetle export to the USA, the emphasis was placed on luxury against a backdrop of declining sales and ever-rising prices. 1974 saw the emergence of two specials, the

Sun Bug, which was launched in the spring, and the Love Bug, a product of the last months of the model year. The latter, based on the torsion-bar flat-screen Beetle, was a Disney 'Herbie' promotion, although it bore little relation to the car in the film. Clad in a coat of either Phoenix Red, L32K, or Ravena Green, L65K, paint its upholstery was houndstooth black and white cloth. Sports wheels and Love Bug decals

Model	Basic £	Car Tax £	VAT £	Total £
1200	1,110.26	95.52	96.22	1,299.00
1300	1,238.46	103.21	107.33	1,449.00
1303	1,323.93	110.33	114.74	1,549.00
1303 Campaign	1,366.67	113.89	118.44	1,599.00
Sun Beetle	1,273.51	106.12	110.37	1,490.00
Metallic Finish	29.19	2.43	2.53	34.15
Steel sunroof	80.07	6.67	6.94	93.68
Heated rear window	13.09	1.09	1.13	15.31

Advertising material supplied to dealers followed a black and yellow theme, while the content served to confuse the situation somewhat.

ABOVE: One of only a handful of Last Edition Beetles in unrestored, pristine original condition. Another example belongs to Volkswagen UK.
BELOW: A straightforward 1200L interior.

completed the package. In 1975 production of the Super Beetle in Sedan form was apparently limited to La Grande Bug, although it is possible that a second edition of the Sun Bug in Super Beetle format only emerged. As for La Grande Bug, here was a Beetle that was sufficiently popular to warrant both a second and third run, the last-mentioned hovering into the '76 model year, but classified as a 1975 car to avoid falling foul of US and Canadian certification rules.

A US press release with the simple heading of 'Luxury Bug' summarized all the US late specials:

The 1976 Beetle, now on display at area VW dealerships, comes with so many luxury 'extras' included as standard equipment that it may still be the best automotive bargain on the market today. Among the features VW includes as standard are fuel injection, wall-to-wall carpeting, metallic paint, an electric window defogger, front vent windows and sports wheel rims …

The Sun Bug concept extended not only to the Super Beetle and the torsion-bar, flat-screen Sedan, but also to the Cabriolet and in this last instance paintwork was crucial to its specification, as the other main feature of the edition was a factory-fitted steel sunroof. Sales literature indicates that all the variants on the Sun Bug theme were painted in 'gold metallic sun colour'. Translated from marketing speak into a recognized paint code the edition was finished in Hellas Metallic, L90C. Other features were 4½J sports wheels, a padded rim steering wheel, a specially commissioned embellished gear-lever knob, and the by-now almost commonplace wood-effect grained dash inlay, which on this occasion was in the style of Rosewood.

La Grande Bug was similar in nature to the European Big Beetle, but with a sunroof. It was available with either Ancona Blue Metallic, L97B, or Viper Green Metallic, L98C, paintwork, although the latter colour was known as Lime Green in the USA. The seats were finished in the same leatherette

velvet cord combination as those of the Big Beetle; Ancona cars were paired to Dark Blue upholstery and Lime Green to Bamboo. Similarly, La Grande Bug boasted a padded steering wheel, a dashboard trimmed with a mock Rosewood veneer strip, and 4½J sports wheels.

The Last Edition Beetle – 1977/8

With the knowledge that Beetle manufacture on German soil was due to end in January 1978, the end of the road as far as right-hand-drive cars were concerned was in sight. (Plans were afoot to import Beetles from Mexico to satisfy the demands of would-be owners in Germany and a selection of other European countries.) As a result, Volkswagen in Britain arranged to import 300 perfectly ordinary 1200L models, save that they were finished in Diamond Silver, L97A, one of fifteen established paint options for the home market, but not previously a part of the much more restricted range available in the UK.

The plaque endorsing the car's status as a Last Edition model. Sadly, not all owners seem to have been supplied with a plaque, possibly due to their arrival sometimes weeks after the purchase had been made.

The '78 model year paint options for the UK consisted of: Miami Blue, L51C; Alpine White, L90E; Riyad Yellow, L11A; and Mars Red, L31B. These cars were matched to Marine Blue upholstery in the first two instances and to Tabac and Parchment respectively in the latter cases. The significance of the detailed inclusion of the other cars can only be appreciated when Volkswagen's marketing of the Last Edition model is assessed.

A series of newspaper adverts announced that the Beetle was soon to be no more. 'Going, going …' read the headline, while the text urged would-be owners to 'move fast', as the 'time has come. The Beetle is about to bid adieu.' Time was of the essence, 'because the very last of the Beetles have already been brought into the country'. Not that many were trampled in the subsequent rush. The 300 Diamond Silver Beetles had been built in the earlier days of September 1977 and a percentage were still available to register in August 1978, as cars bearing a registration with a T suffix testify. (Most Last Edition Beetles bear an S plate, August 1977–July 1978; T covered the period August 1978–July 1979.) Perhaps part of this apparent lack of enthusiasm was due to a wider availability of Last Edition Beetles!

Volkswagen's dealers were supplied with marketing material that included banners, flags and, significantly, a large freestanding poster with yellow print on a black background. The text on the poster ran as follows:

Last Edition. This is one of the last gallant 600 in Britain. First created more than forty years ago, the Beetle has become a legend in the history of the motor car. Loveable and ever reliable, the Beetle is a breed apart. Your very last chance to buy a piece of motoring history. The Last Edition.

Somewhere along the line the decision had been taken to order a further 300 cars finished in the standard colours of the day. That they were built later than the silver cars is attested by reference to their chassis numbers; most date from the latter part of September 1977, although a percentage lurch into the early days of October. As a result of this additional order, cars in a variety of colours jostled position with the silver Beetles.

If the author's recollections of the purchase of a Last Edition Beetle are typical the value of a silver car could not have been appreciated at the time of purchase. Some six weeks after buying a Diamond Silver Last Edition Beetle, having chosen this colour in preference to Alpine White, the owner received a call from the dealer to collect something for the car. This proved to be a plaque to mount on the dashboard which read: 'This is one of the last 300 Beetles to be produced for the United Kingdom. Number XX.' This plaque, which bore no relation to the sequence of manufacture of the silver cars, wasn't offered to the owners of other colour Last Edition Beetles and sadly wasn't necessarily even offered to all owners of such cars.

Nevertheless, the Last Edition Beetle's specification can be summarized as being a Diamond Silver 1200L with Marine Blue cloth upholstery, bearing a numbered plaque mounted on the dashboard. Two erroneous theories relating to the Last Edition Beetle can be summarily dismissed. The first was that the cars were built to celebrate twenty-five years of the Beetle in Britain, 1953–78. The second relates to the Silver Jubilee celebrations of Her Majesty Queen Elizabeth II's elevation to the throne in 1977.

SPECIAL EDITION CABRIOLETS

A number of limited edition Cabriolets were designed for the American market as the end of Beetle production in Germany drew inevitably closer. Of these, both the Epilog, an all-black Cabriolet, and the Champagne Edition II have been claimed as the last. The funereal appearance of the former, the finality of its name, and the fact that each dealer received just one car to increase its rarity value, might suggest that the Epilog really was the final edition. However, literature produced by Volkswagen of American to promote the Champagne Edition II included the message that it was the 'rarest of the rare. This is the last special Bug sold in North America. Your VW dealer will have a few of them, but not many, for those who want to drive the rarest of a rare breed.' Perhaps as two cars were offered to each dealer the implication is that the Epilog, a rarer breed still, was the last Cabriolet and that events superseded what had once been a truthful text.

The irony of the first Champagne Edition, S723, offered in 1977, was that it was created to celebrate production of the millionth Golf, realistically the vehicle that spelled the end of the road for the Beetle. One point to note is that the Champagne Edition extended to special colours for the Rabbit, Dasher or Passat, Scirocco and even the Transporter. Inevitably, the Cabriolet offering was the most attractive, consisting of Alpine White, L90B, paintwork, with an Opal leatherette interior (referred to as Cameo White in the sales brochure) and a Pale Sand hood, leading in some circumstances to it being referred to as the Triple White Cabriolet.

Curiously, the second edition Champagne model bore no striking resemblance to its predecessor, as the paint colours offered were Ancona Blue Metallic and Indiana Red Metallic. Although identical to the Opal leatherette of the first series Champagne model, the seat upholstery on this occasion was now described as White Hermlin. Both Champagne editions featured the old regulars of: a padded rim steering wheel; plastic mock Rosewood dashboard strip; and sports wheels. These cars also came equipped with a radio and intermittent wiper controls, as well as the normal Cabriolet luxuries.

The VW Convertible.

One of life's lasting little pleasures.

the Karmann Cabriolet

ABOVE: Cover of 1974 US brochure dedicated to the Cabriolet.

If the changes to the Cabriolet's specification between the '68 model year and the end of production – the numbers manufactured on a year-by-year basis, the paint colours available and more – are all comprehensively covered in other sections, why is this chapter required? With the exception of a few summary facts, the answer has to be one of indulgence: the opportunity to produce a gallery of Cabriolet imagery and the option to reproduce a selection of period lifestyle shots taken from contemporary literature. After all, the Cabriolet was the top-of-the-range model, the chance to own a brand-new example being restricted not by availability but by price.

This atmospheric Cabriolet image was produced by Volkswagen in the era of the 1302's supremacy.

The 1974 UK market Beetle family brochure included this image of the Cabriolet.

ABOVE: Towards the end of Cabriolet production VW of America decided to cut the size of its brochure dedicated to it to just 50 per cent. LEFT: With effect from August 1966 and the '67 model year, the 1500 Beetle became the flagship Saloon of the range. This top-of-billing status was transferred to the Cabriolet too. The image is taken from a 1968 model year brochure.

US-market Cabriolets

A cluster of late US-specification Cabriolets, all with a humped rear valance and single tailpipe.

Home-market Cabriolets

All the Cabriolets pictured in this cluster bear the specification appropriate to the European market.

In Germany in August 1969, and the start of the '70 model year, the basic 1200 Beetle cost DM4,525. The top-of-the-range Saloon with a 1500cc engine was priced at DM4,896. At a total of DM6,268, the Cabriolet was 38.5 per cent more expensive than the 1200 and 28 per cent dearer than the 1500 Saloon.

Towards the end of the Beetle's production run and at a time when the range had been trimmed in Britain to just the 1200L Saloon and the Cabriolet, the former cost £2,228 inclusive of taxes, while the latter was priced at £3,620, or a massive 62.5 per cent more than Saloon. Theoretically, a would-be Cabriolet owner could buy any model in Volkswagen's range, whatever the specification, at a cheaper price.

UK-market Cabriolet circa 1978

LEFT AND BELOW: *The Ancona Blue, L97B, Cabriolet featured here dates from the '78 model year. Many of the items photographed in detail have been described elsewhere in this book. This selection endeavours to bring them all together in one specification package.*

BELOW: *Hoods in black or 'white'.*

Twin tailpipes, chromed – bumper with rubber trim strip.

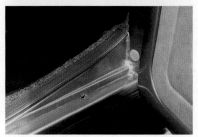

Cabriolet identification marks: from Karmann badge on the front quarter panel, to sill strengtheners, extra metalwork around the lower doorposts.

Humped rear valance.

UK-market Cabriolet circa 1978

Late model's simple 1303 badge – despite 1600 engine.

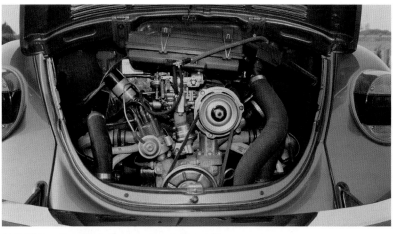

1600, 50PS engine with plastic case, paper element air filter.

Cabriolet interior rear-view mirror.

The interior from the rear of the car with the hood down. (Headrests have been removed for photography.)

LEFT: Engine lid catch – lockable. RIGHT: Final style of rear light cluster – introduced 1972 with 1303 series of cars initially.

RIGHT: The sign of a Deluxe – the dashboard clock. Note the handbrake warning light (red circular) and rocker switch for the lights.

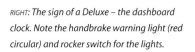

Rear mudflaps – an almost standard accessory!

The steel sports wheel with black plastic wheel nut covers and centre cap.

The substantial nature of the Cabriolet's quarter light window.

The interior looking in from the driver's door.

Inevitably, Volkswagen played the price differential down, or in the case of VW of America was particularly clever in spinning a different story:

This year, Volkswagen offers, among other options, the sun, the moon, and the stars. Which come your way courtesy of the 1977 Beetle Convertible. Ours is the most inexpensive four-seater convertible you can find today. But that doesn't mean we cut corners … underneath it all, the same dependable and economical Volkswagen you get when you buy a regular Beetle. Which means that this year, you can definitely afford not to have a roof over your head.

At the start of the period covered by this book the message was simple and made no reference to price:

'The VW Convertible. The convertible that's just as much of a pleasure to drive in winter' was a story of craftsmanship that took the Cabriolet into a league of its own and a feature that must be reiterated in this soft-top overview:

Thanks to the sturdy top. With its double layer of padding. Inside it has a white plastic headlining which hides the bows … And on the outside there's a weatherproof and virtually indestructible PVC covering. It's an absolutely tight fit because it overlaps the windows … The rear window is made of safety glass and not – as is so often the case – of celluloid. Just like the side windows. Which are fully lowerable …

The essence of the Volkswagen Cabriolet throughout its production run was that it wasn't built at Wolfsburg and its German satellites, but instead was subcontracted to the Osnabrück-based specialist coachbuilding firm of Karmann. (As an aside, this also explains the reference in many a Volkswagen Beetle sales brochure requesting potential Cabriolet customers to refer to the brochure produced to promote the VW Karmann Ghia for details of the paint options available for the soft-top version.)

As such, every Cabriolet's body was lovingly assembled and more or less finished by hand. To ensure body rigidity without the reassurance of a metal roof, the sills were reinforced via a rail on each side, which was welded to the bottom plate of the sill. Inner strengthening panels to the rear of the front door pillars and the base of the B-post, plus transverse reinforcement under the rear seat and substantially different, rear quarter panels, and a heftier short panel above the engine lid, all not only distinguished the soft top from the Saloon, but also in the quality of workmanship distinguished the vehicle from many of the convertibles produced in-house by other manufacturers.

Extending this theme one stage further, the Beetle Cabriolet's hood was superior to those fitted to virtually every convertible on the market no matter what the vehicle's price-point. Key to the hood's quality was its watertight and windproof nature, as well as its glass rather than perspex window. The hood's durability and other qualities could be explained by its layers of combination rubber padding and heavy horsehair and even when in 1976 a more modern foam material replaced this combination standards hadn't deteriorated.

Throughout, the Cabriolet was based on the top Saloon in the range. Hence for the 1968 model year, the first period covered here, the Cabriolet had its foundation embedded in the 1500 Beetle Saloon. The addition of an L package as an option for both the 1300 and 1500 Saloon at the start of the '70 model year and comprising such extras as a padded dash, rubber bumper strips and more, were automatically passed on to the Cabriolet, even for a few years extending to incorporating a distinctive L in the badge on the engine lid.

From the start of the 1971 model year the soft top was modelled on the 1302, and two years later on the curved-screen 1303. While this last-named model might not necessarily be the most favoured among enthusiasts, without doubt the curved screen afforded the neatest of all joins from metalwork to hood. Following the deletion of the 1303 from the Saloon range in the summer of 1975, for once the Cabriolet branched away from the norm of the previous twenty-five years. There was no Cabriolet version of the 1200L; instead, sufficient 1303 panels had been squirrelled away to allow production to continue for a few more years.

One footnote is worthy of mention. Although the Cabriolet was always based on the Deluxe, or top model of the Saloon range, the vehicle's engine could not necessarily be guaranteed to be the most powerful of the selection offered on the Saloon. For example, for taxation purposes some Italian Cabriolets were fitted with the 34PS 1200 engine. A final confusion arises in the Cabriolet's last days, as the decision was taken to delete the L description from the car's engine lid badge. However, the absence of the L on a late model does not imply that the nature of the vehicle's trimmings had been simplified – far from it.

11 *Beetle exports, assembly and manufacture outside Germany*

ABOVE: Beetle legions ready to embark to their destinations across the world. (Volkswagen AG)

Although most would assume the Beetle not only to be a product of Germany but of the factory at Wolfsburg, by the time of the period covered by this book the story was far more complex.

BEETLE EXPORTS FROM WEST GERMANY

West German registrations compared to total manufacture serve to demonstrate that more than 70 per cent of production was either built in Germany for export, or assembled overseas.

The USA's love affair with the Beetle ensured that exports to North America alone outperformed Volkswagen's domestic market (the five-millionth

Year	Total worldwide Beetle production	Beetle registrations in West Germany	West German registrations as a percentage of total production
1967	925,787	258,185	27.9%
1968	1,186,134	261,450	22.0%
1969	1,219,314	314,336	25.8%
1970	1,196,099	328,715	27.5%
1971	1,291,612	291,312	22.6%
1972	1,220,686	257,742	20.0%
1973	1,206,018	236,308	19.6%
1974	791,053	121,511	15.4%
1975	441,116	43,145	9.8%
1976	383,277	19,121	5.0%
1977	258,634	10,524	4.1%

Beetle was shipped to the USA on 27 August 1971). Even considerably less populous countries, whose native car manufacturers tended to specialize in production of smaller cars, could muster more than respectable Beetle sales figures. As reference to the Special Edition British market GT Beetle described in Chapter 9 reveals, 300,000 Beetles had arrived in Britain by 15 December 1972. Nevertheless, it is worth noting that whenever the opportunity arose, further countries were added to the export drive. Typical then of this expansion was the addition of Hawaii and Japan as export markets in 1967. 1966 had seen the five-millionth export vehicle and on 28 April 1970 this figure had doubled when a Pastel White Beetle destined for France rolled off the assembly line.

While in 1968 Wolfsburg could still be regarded as the main Beetle assembly plant worldwide, the car's engine was brought in from what is generally known as the home of the Transporter at Hanover (Hannover), while the Cassel (Kassel) plant supplied the transmission units and the oldest and smallest factory of all situated at Brunswick (Braunschweig) submitted the front axles.

Such was the demand for the Beetle globally that with effect from 8 December 1964 Wolfsburg's activities had been supplemented by a new, purpose-built factory at Emden, specifically designed with export to North America in mind. With Wolfsburg supplying Beetle bodies and the other factories delivering the components they already offered Wolfsburg, only the seats and wiring harness were produced locally. With an initial production capacity of 500 vehicles per day, which had already increased to 1,100 Volkswagens by March 1966, vehicles were despatched from the company's own port to both the USA and Canada.

Following the partial acquisition in 1964 and complete purchase by 1966 of Auto-Union from Daimler Benz AG, Volkswagen ensured that the Ingolstadt factory was at full capacity by adding the Beetle to its portfolio of models. This arrangement continued until 1969.

To appreciate the scale of the exports to 140 countries all over the world it is worth a momentary

Two of the sixty trains per day to leave Wolfsburg station loaded with Volkswagens circa 1971.

Sometimes the press departments could be a little premature in their announcements, as the photo and extract from a release of 25 July 1974 indicate, but that Volkswagen led the way in accommodating the needs of a given state or country indicates why they topped the export listings for so long: 'VW Beetle adds a bustle for 1975 – the 1975 Volkswagen Beetle sports a slotted and bustled "skirt" below its rear bumper. Bustle and louvres are there to cover and ventilate a platinum-coated catalytic converter whose performance is now being tested on a fleet of 1975 Beetles based in Van Nuys, California ...'. (VWoA)

diversion to look at Volkswagen's transport arrangements in the first years of the 1970s. Wolfsburg's goods station had to deal with around sixty trains per day. Ten diesels, the largest of which had a capacity of 1,000PS, were given over to shunting duties, and in a twenty-four-hour period the Wolfsburg signal box would record

the arrival or departure of around 1,500 trucks. Each train, which had a total length of approximately 650m, housed a maximum of 300 Beetles on double-tier transporter trucks. Additionally, in the region of seventy special ships, each resembling a multi-storey car park and capable of carrying up to 3,000 vehicles, were chartered

Volkswagens in the bush and outback.

by Volkswagen. Beetles destined for North America were despatched from the port at Emden, but were also sent across the Atlantic from Bremen. For the UK exports both Emden and Bremen were used, while for Scandinavia the port was Lübeck. Exports to the Middle and Far East, Africa, Australia and South America were sent via regular shipping companies.

ASSEMBLY AND MANUFACTURE IN COUNTRIES OTHER THAN GERMANY

Volkswagen's Corporate Press Department described the road to manufacture and assembly in countries outside Germany thus:

To keep up with the rising demand, Volkswagen established assembly plants in many countries with the domestic importers. This made it possible to ship above all voluminous body parts completely knocked down [CKD] which cut costs. It also became possible to make use of domestic raw

materials and semi finished parts. The number of new assembly plants established around the world over the last three decades is accordingly quite large.

In the summer of 1967 Beetle manufacture or assembly was accounted for in eleven different countries apart from Germany. The ensuing chronological list indicates not only the date when the first Beetles were assembled in a given country, but also when manufacture or production of the car finally ceased:

■ Southern Ireland 1950–77
■ South Africa 1951–79
■ Brazil 1953–86 and 1993–6
■ Australia 1954–76
■ Belgium 1954–75
■ New Zealand 1954–72
■ The Philippines 1959–82
■ Uruguay 1961–82
■ Venezuela 1963–81
■ Portugal 1964–76
■ Peru 1966–87.

In 1968 assembly was started in Malaysia under the auspices of an independent importer and continued apace until 1977. An operation in Singapore was opened in the same year, but Beetle production there ceased in 1974.

In 1970 an independently owned plant in Costa Rica started to assemble Beetles and continued to do so for the next five years.

In 1972 independent importers in Thailand and Indonesia commenced operations, with Beetle assembly ceasing in 1974 and 1977 respectively. The following year, 1973, assembly of Beetles commenced in Sarajevo, Yugoslavia, following the establishment of a company in which Volkswagen AG had a 50 per cent holding. Production of the 1200 Beetle assembled from CKD kits, but with an increasing percentage of materials being sourced locally, came to a halt three years later in 1976. Yugoslavian-built Beetles can be identified by a VW 1200J badge in the engine lid.

The last country to begin assembly of Beetles was Nigeria and this occurred as late as 1975, at a time when Wolfsburg no longer produced Beetles, thereby giving rise to the clue that other operations within the Volkswagen family supplied CKD kits.

As can be determined from the details given above, with the change in the car's fortunes as the 1970s began to gather pace it wasn't long before the numbers of plants and countries involved started to reduce.

Typical of these was the New Zealand operation, which in the years between 1954 and March 1972 (when the decision was taken not to order any more CKD packs), assembled 24,640 Beetles. Initially obtaining the kits from Wolfsburg, between 1962 and 1967 CKD packs were the responsibility of Volkswagen Australasia Pty, before a return in the final years to German supply. Hence a car of New Zealand assembly was virtually identical to a German model for many years and only deviated during the Australian supply period, purely because the latter operation didn't retool after the massive investment there in 1960–61. Motor Holdings, the company responsible for the VW operation in New Zealand with one

RIGHT: Note the four unequal ranks of engine lid ventilation louvres, which are reminiscent of some Karmann Cabriolets but not of a Wolfsburg produced Saloon.

ABOVE: 1600L – not a designation to be found on a German-built Beetle.

ABOVE: A temperate climate might explain why the 1600L featured opening rear side windows as standard.

ABOVE: Apparently softer and more obviously trimmed in vinyl, South African seats don't necessarily appear to have the most attractive of finishes.

South African Beetles were not that dissimilar to German models, although by the final years of production some anomalies had arisen. The car depicted is a late model 1600L.

FAR LEFT: The South African steel sports wheel – note the number of wheel bolts. South African cars retained five to the end of production, instead of Germany's four of later years.

Wood-grain trim panels on the dashboard. US-bound Cabriolets based on the 1303 carried similar features, but the effect depicted on a torsion-bar dashboard was unique.

Volkswagen of South Africa's press office released a photograph and write-up to enable editors to write about the Beetle's latest dashboard (circa 1978 in relation to the 1300 model). (Volkswagen of South Africa)

This Volkswagen of South Africa press office image depicts not only the oldest Beetle to have survived in South Africa, a model which dates from 1949, but also a 1978 Super Bug, which outwardly looks like a MacPherson strut 1303, but in reality embraces old-fashioned torsion-bar technology. Note the five-stud wheels! (Volkswagen of South Africa)

name or another from the start, faced a two-fold problem in the early 1970s. First, but of no more significance than the other issue, the Japanese were making significant inroads into the international market. Second, following the revaluation of the Deutsche Mark, the Beetle's price had risen to an uneconomic level. The appeal of the gizmos associated with the opposition and the unhealthy price increase in the product spelled the end for the Beetle, not just in New Zealand but in many other countries too.

Here too a paragraph has to be devoted to Beetle assembly in Belgium, particularly as owners of a 1970s car might, on checking, discover that their vehicle, identical in specification to the products coming from Wolfsburg or Emden, possibly even right-hand drive, was a product of the Brussels plant. D'Ieteren Frères, with origins dating back to 1805, had been one of the first to see a need for the Beetle in postwar Europe, signing up for 300 cars on 17 March 1948. In the same year, the company had commissioned work on a new assembly plant for Studebakers. Heartened by the Belgian Government's wish to encourage the assembly of foreign cars in the country, D'Ieteren added the Beetle to its portfolio, the first such car rolling off the assembly line on 11 February 1954. The 500,000th Beetle, a car virtually indistinguishable from the West German product, came off the assembly line on 12 January 1967. In 1970, ownership of the Brussels factory passed from the D'Ieteren family to Volkswagen without in truth affecting assembly, while in 1976 the operation, Volkswagen Bruxelles SA, became 100 per cent owned by Volkswagen AG. In total, in excess of 1,000,000 Beetles were produced in Brussels, the last ones rolling off the assembly line in 1975, when the car's manufacture retrenched to Emden.

However, one notable exception to the trend, the South American operations based in Puebla, Mexico, and São Paulo, Brazil, were destined to carry the Beetle's mantle forward for many years; the former even supplying Germany and other European countries with the car for a number of years, while the latter helped to extend the Beetle's influence by supplying CKD

kits to operations in Africa, Asia and beyond.

The history of Volkswagen's activities in selected countries follows, while specific reference is made to the specification of the cars produced where it differed from the home market. The order is deliberately neither alphabetical nor chronological, as will be appreciated when the Beetle's future beyond the period covered by this volume is touched upon.

Volkswagen of South Africa (Pty) Ltd

The Beetle's links with South Africa dated back to August 1951, when the first locally assembled Volkswagen came off the assembly line at the works of South African Motor Assemblers and Distributors Ltd (SAMAD) in Uitenhage. In 1956 the controlling interest of SAMAD was acquired by Wolfsburg, a move which led to the emergence of the 100,000th VW assembled on South African soil in 1963. Three years later the company name was changed to Volkswagen of South Africa and heavy investment in the factory led to expansion of the manufacturing block. In 1974 Volkswagen AG assumed 100 per cent control of the Uitenhage operation, while in the same year the 250,000th locally produced Beetle came off the assembly line. The last South African Beetle was manufactured on 18 January 1979.

Although the South African Beetle wasn't as quirky as its Brazilian cousin, often it didn't really keep pace with developments at Wolfsburg, or adopted a second-rate variation on the theme emanating from Germany. As examples of South African progress, a 1970s Beetle benefited from 12V electrics, the larger rear window of German '72 model year vintage, a collapsible steering column and twin port cylinder heads. Indeed, in one instance such cars were ahead of Germany, as, like cars exported to the USA, they were possessed of a 1600 engine a full twelve months before Germany and the rest of the VW empire. However, in other respects South African cars lagged behind quite dramatically. Throughout the seventies, the South African

Beetle retained: a single brake circuit; drum brakes on all four wheels; five-stud wheels; domed hub caps (unless five-stud sports wheels were fitted); king pins; and a generator rather than an alternator.

Briefly, for the twelve-month period of the '74 model year, South African Beetles adopted the large US-specification front indicator lights, but for 1975 these were dropped in favour of the European-style indicators in the front bumper. Similarly, 1974 saw the arrival of the much larger rear light clusters, first seen at Wolfsburg with the introduction of the 1303 for the '73 model year. However, Uitenhage decided not to update the rear wings of the Beetle at the same time, with the result that a spacer had to be designed to sit between the wing and the light cluster, leading to both a clumsy and rather droopy appearance.

Engine options varied from the pattern established by Wolfsburg, in that the range was generally more restricted. For 1968 and 1969, only the 1500 engine was available. In 1970, curiously while the 1500 was still offered, the 1300 made a comeback, having last been an option in 1967, while, as previously mentioned, South Africa joined the USA as the only countries where a 1600 engine was available. This arrangement of three engine options continued until 1973, when the 1500 was dropped. The 1600 engine was deleted from the range in August 1978, leaving the 1300 to power all Beetles produced between that date and the end of production in January 1979. 1600 engines fitted to a model known as the SP1600 and produced between 1976–8 profited from twin Solex 32/34 PDSI carburettors.

The most unusual South African produced Beetle had to be the 1600 Super, a car which was built between June 1975 and July 1978. Although Uitenhage never embraced MacPherson strut technology, this model had the external appearance of a German-built 1303, complete with curved windscreen, plastic moulded dashboard and the characteristic pregnant stance enjoyed by such models. Despite the adoption of such trendsetting features, old-style rear wings were still employed, so that spacers had to be used between the elephant's foot rear lights and the body of the car, while underneath this skin of modernism lay not only drum brakes, five-stud wheels, king pins and rear swing axles, but also under the boot lid an upright spare wheel in the tradition of all torsion-bar Beetles.

A grand total of 209,916 Beetles was assembled or manufactured in South Africa between August 1951 and January 1979.

Volkswagen Australasia Ltd

Assembly of Beetles started at a factory in Clayton, Australia, in June 1954, the first cars to have been imported officially occurring the year before. The urgency with which Wolfsburg demanded the transition from import to assembly was due to the strict import tariffs imposed by the Australian Federal Government. In 1955, 6,351 vehicles, a combination of Beetles and Transporters, were produced, equating to no more than a mere 3.4 per cent of the car market, and less than one per cent of commercial vehicle sales in the country. Nevertheless, a visit from Heinz Nordhoff at the end of 1956 resulted in a commitment to 95 per cent local manufacture until 1969 in return for a guarantee of duty-free imports from the Australian Federal Government for a decade. Arrangements for presses and dies were duly made in preparation for full manufacture, which started in 1959. 1960 saw 24,652 Beetles manufactured rather than assembled and a sales boom ensued, while Volkswagen Australasia worked towards a second goal of exporting Australian-made CKD kits and fully assembled cars to both South East Asian and Pacific countries. Production wavered between the tens of thousands and the low twenties, until in 1964 there came a final push to achieve 22,150 cars, but all was not well on the horizon. Not only did sales decline dramatically from this point, but also when compared to production forecasts set in 1959 for the next decade, even in the best years only some 50 per cent of the target was being achieved.

At the start of the period in the Beetle's history covered by this book, Australian manufacture was coming

While the Brazilian Beetle resident in the Stiftung Museum, Wolfsburg, might date from 1986, it bears the hallmarks of the breed as the years went by which visually included pre-'65 model year window specification and unique 15in wheels with twenty-four vent holes.

to an end, with a return to German-built CKD assembly. Production of the Australian-built Deluxe Beetle ceased in March 1968, and of the Custom (the successor to the basic standard model) in September. The return to CKD assembly had the overnight effect of bringing the time-warp Australian-market Beetle – carefully lodged in 1962 in all respects other than its engine – up to date, with 12V electrics, larger windows all round, Europa bumpers, dual-circuit brakes and an external fuel filler amongst many other items making their first appearance. Production to meet a rekindled demand rose to 13,684 for 1968, but was soon to ebb away once more. CKD production ceased in June 1976, at the point when a decision had been taken to withdraw the Beetle as a model appropriate to the Australian market; such was the stockpile of cars that the last vehicle wasn't sold until March 1977.

Inevitably, specification variations in a period of German CKD assembly were strictly limited, being more or less restricted to local content items such as paint, glass, tyres and electrical components. Surprisingly, upholstery was despatched from Germany. (A list of the paint colours offered in 1972 indicates the extent of such differences, particularly when it is stressed that this is not a simple renaming exercise: Antarctica White; Regatta Blue, similar to the German Sea Blue of the sixties; Avocado Green, a pale lime green; Radar Red, not that dissimilar to

Mars Red; Honey Brown, a mid brown; Mustard, a muddy orange; Wattle, a brilliant yellow; Gemini Blue, similar to the 1980s Mexican Beetle shade of Atlantic Blue; and Marine (Flipper) Blue, slightly brighter than the German Marina Blue.)

From 1968–70, the range was restricted to the 1300 and 1500 Beetle, while for 1971 the MacPherson strut 1302 with a 1600 engine replaced the 1500, and bore a Volkswagen S badge on its engine lid. From 1972 all Australian Beetles, both 1300 and Volkswagen S models, sported both a padded dashboard and US-style front seats with integral headrests. 1973 saw the curved-screen 1303 arrive, complete with a Volkswagen L badge on its derrière and this model, together with the 1300, would remain in the range until the end of 1975. Despite the badge names allocated to the 1302 and the 1303, both cars were marketed as the Superbug. The final year of CKD assembly saw the reversion to flat-screen, torsion-bar territory, but with the advantage of a 1600 engine, CV joint rear axles and disc brakes. Marketed simply as the Beetle, this car also carried a fully padded dashboard and US-style front seats and integral headrests.

Volkswagen do Brasil Ltda

With the exception of Volkswagen's West German plants, no factory across the world played a more important role in boosting total Beetle production

Beetle exports, assembly and manufacture outside Germany

Model year	Main variations of Brazilian Beetles compared to German production
1950s onwards	Dished pistons to accommodate low 72 octane fuel, as per optional equipment M240 in Germany (1966 onwards).
1960	From 1960–73 Brazilian wheels were of a Porsche 356 style – ventilated, five-stud, open centre, rims.
1965	Retention of smaller windscreen, rear and side windows. This would be the case until the end of production in 1986.
1966	Retention of king-pin front suspension. Ball joints only fitted when disc brakes became an option on the 1500 Beetle introduced in 1973. (Disc brakes fitted to European-specification 1500 Beetles when model introduced on 1 August 1966.)
1966/7	Retention of five-stud wheels until 1973. (Four × 14mm diameter by 1.5mm thread bolts replaced five 12mm diameter by 1.5mm bolts securing the wheels on German 1300 and 1200 models. The newly introduced 1500 Beetle of '67 model year vintage – not US examples – had been fitted with four-stud wheels, but previously not any other members of the Beetle family.)
1969	Replacement of 6V electrical system with 12V German 1500 and 1300 Beetles had changed to 12V at the start of the '68 model year. American-bound Beetles were fitted with a 12V system from August 1966.
1972	German Beetles other than the 1200 acquired four sets of cooling slots (outer banks numbering seven each and inner ones six each, totalling twenty-six overall). Brazilian cars were also fitted with cooling slots, but with a different layout – two banks of eight (outer positions) and two banks of six (inner positions), totalling twenty-eight overall, plus a central area of plain metal between.
1970	Introduction of Europa bumpers – German built Beetles, other than the 1200, had adopted this style of bumper from the start of the '68 model year.
1973	Disc brakes optional on 1500 Beetle (*see* 1966 above) – as a result four-stud wheels with twenty-four square vents were fitted to all Brazilian Beetles.
1974	Introduction of crescent-shaped ventilation vents behind rear side windows – introduced to German models (1302S and 1300) for the start of the '71 model year.
1975	Retention of wing-mounted indicators, a feature of all Brazilian Beetles to the end of production.
1976	Optional twin-port 1600 engine introduced – first available on the German market for the '71 model year. The Brazilian version was fitted with twin Solex carburettors.
1976	1600 models were fitted with 14in wheels as used on the Brazilia, a car designed for the Brazilian market that might be mistaken at first glance for a German-market Type 4 – VW 411, VW 412.
1976	Disc brakes standard (disc brakes fitted to European-specification 1500 Beetles when model introduced on 1 August 1966).
1978	Introduction of dual-circuit brakes – German models except 1200, 1 August 1967.
1978	While rear swing axles remained as part of the Beetle's make-up until the end of production, the camber compensating z-bar was only introduced in 1978 (added to the German Beetle on 1 August 1966).
1978	New style of steering wheel unique to the Brazilian market – two-spoke with large padded centre horn pad.
1979	Introduction of the large rear light clusters, 'elephant's foot', first seen on the German-produced Beetle with the introduction of the 1303 at the start of the '73 model year.
1981	Thicker rubber bumper insert than the German type.
1981	1300 Beetle with alcohol-fuelled engine – 10.1:0 compression.
1982	Replacement of traditional German dashboard with homespun variation – padded with square dials and a dished steering wheel and a large, square horn button.
1983	Use of Fusca badge on the engine lid.

numbers than the Brazilian operation. Just weeks before the period covered by this book, on 4 July 1967 the Brazilian factory had celebrated the arrival of the 500,000th Beetle to be built at São Bernardo do Campo, some 14 miles from São Paulo, which was then the Brazilian capital. Due to the manufacture of 223,453 Beetles in 1972, plus the export of a further 6,000 cars, March 1972 had seen the magic million achieved, while just four years later in June 1976 the two-millionth Beetle to be built in Brazil rolled off the assembly line. As late as 1980, 146,000 Beetles were sold in the country, equating to 18.5 per cent of the domestic car market for this single model. When in 1986 the decision was finally taken to cease production and the last car

eased its way off the assembly line on 7 December, in excess of 3,300,000 Beetles had been built. (As a footnote, as the years involved are outside the remit of this book, against all odds the Fusca, Portuguese for Beetle and the name by which the car was and is known in Brazil, made a comeback in 1993 due to direct pressure from a Brazilian Government eager to see more cheap new cars. For the next three years, until the Government's tax incentives came to an end, the Beetle was once more produced at a rate of one hundred cars per day!)

The first CKD German-made, Brazilian-assembled Beetle rolled off a somewhat *ad hoc* assembly line in rented premises in Ipirango in March 1953. However, in 1956 work started

on a 10,000m² purpose-built plant, where it was anticipated that Beetles and Transporters would be assembled in state-of-the-art surroundings. The plant opened at the end of the year, but thanks to new Government import restrictions taking effect on 1 July 1957, requiring 40 per cent of any finished product to be manufactured locally, the planned function of assembly was rapidly expanded to encompass full manufacture. Transporter manufacture ensued, but it wasn't until 3 January 1959 that the first Beetle rolled off the assembly line. Soon, Volkswagen was making Beetles that were of 95 per cent Brazilian content and as a result the German and Brazilian specification began to vary. The chart above indicates the progress of variation.

Außen sonnig. Innen wonnig.
Der Sunny Bug
zum Sonnenscheintarif.

The Mexican-built Beetles always followed the pattern of the German product very closely, making the Puebla factory the ideal candidate to take on the mantle of supplier to Europe once production at Emden ceased. The car featured here, which dates from the early 1980s, appears virtually identical to the last German 1200L models.

Der letzte Käfer.

The last batch of Beetles to be delivered from Mexico to Germany included in their specification Zinngrau Metallic paintwork, green-tinted heat-resistant window glass, sports wheels, heated rear screen, reversing lights, electric screenwash and a Golf-style steering wheel – a natural progression from German production of the '78 model year to Mexican manufacture in 1985.

Volkswagen of Nigeria

As the last country to embrace Beetle manufacture, Nigeria holds an important place in this book. Although the first Beetle had arrived in the country in 1953 and the importers Mandilas Ltd had subsequently developed a network of branches to cope with the demand, it wasn't until 1974 that Volkswagen of Nigeria, a company with manufacturing pretensions, was established. This new company was founded as a result of an agreement between the Federal Government of Nigeria and Wolfsburg, the major shareholders being the Government with 35 per cent and Volkswagenwerk AG with 40 per cent. The BHF Bank of Frankfurt accounted for a further 11 per cent, the Lagos state Government 4 per cent and the distributors 10 per cent. Work immediately started on a new factory and on 21 March 1975 the first Beetle emerged from the production line, one of the sixty cars to be

built each day. Constructed from CKD kits supplied by the Brazilian operation, both 1300 and 1500 cars were offered. Save the single deviation from the Brazilian specification through the fitting of the South African brand of large rear light clusters with a spacer to accommodate the earlier style wings, a practice that didn't last long anyway, Nigerian cars religiously followed the model pattern of their South American suppliers. Hence, at the end of the period covered by this book, Nigerian cars still exhibited the shallow windscreen and small side windows characteristic of a pre-'65 model year German-built Beetle, while when it came to locally produced items such as floor coverings the Nigerian Beetle appeared reminiscent of cars produced in the 1960s, with heavy ribbed matting throughout.

Volkswagen of Nigeria Ltd produced the 'twenty million plus one' Beetle worldwide in 1981 and continued to regard the car as its mainstay

until CKD kits were no longer available some three years after the Brazilian supplier had ceased production.

While annual Beetle production wasn't massive, by the time of the twenty million plus one celebrations, Volkswagen of Nigeria Ltd had produced more than 96,000 cars.

Volkswagen de México SA de CV

Certainly of less significance than the Brazilian operation if total output is considered to be the main criterion, as far as European countries are concerned the Mexican factory at Puebla played a significant role after the demise of German production, while Beetle enthusiasts far and wide cannot fail to know that Mexico was the last bastion of Beetle production, the final examples, the Última Edición, being produced as recently as 2003.

1955 had seen the first Beetles to be assembled in Mexico, a mere 250 examples out of a total sales level of 1,765 cars. It wasn't until 17 January 1964 that the Mexican operation became 100 per cent owned by Volkswagen. Throughout the intervening years, the Mexican factory had assembled German CKD kits and as such specification variations were strictly limited. Now, due to new import regulations making the import of both cars and kits increasingly difficult, Volkswagen decided to move from assembly to manufacture. A brand new factory was constructed in Puebla and became operational in November 1967; its manufacturing operations making extensive use of the products of Mexican suppliers in full accordance with Government-imposed quotas. 22,000 Volkswagens were sold in 1968, while on 12 June of that year total assembly/manufacture had grown to 100,000. By 1971 this figure had doubled, when on 21 October the 200,000th Mexican Beetle rolled off the assembly line. Volkswagen de México even dabbled with exports, when in March 1972 100 Beetles were despatched to Panama, El Salvador and Guatemala, while a lucrative contract to build taxis resulted in the first 500 Beetles of this nature being delivered in December of the same year.

With the end of German Beetle production imminent, 1,694 Mexican-built Beetles were despatched from the port of Veracruz on 1 December 1977 to arrive at Emden at the beginning of January 1978, their appearance being timed to ensure a constant supply of Beetles to those who wished to buy them in Germany and a selection of other European countries.

Although new Beetle registrations in Germany never reached the lofty heights of days gone by, Volkswagen considered it profitable to continue to import Mexican Beetles until 1985. In 1979, of the 112,511 Beetles built at Puebla, 19,242 were for export. German registrations accounted for 14,650 of these vehicles, but when this figure slipped to a paltry 5,087 cars six years later, the exercise seemed hardly worthwhile. Inevitably, the news that the Beetle would no longer be a part of the West German line-up of models brought a surge in sales. The final edition of 2,400 cars for this market, and a further 750 for other European countries, which arrived on German shores on 20 August 1985, marketed variously as the *50 Jahre Käfer*, to coincide with what Volkswagen claimed to be the Beetle's fiftieth birthday, and *Der letzte Käfer* boosted 1986 registrations to a more than respectable total of 13,043 cars.

The differences in specification between the last German-produced 1200L models and those manufactured in Mexico were at face value negligible, making the car much more suitable than the Brazilian Beetle to be the successor to the vehicle produced at Emden.

The specification variations between a 1978 model year German Beetle and one produced at Puebla can be summarized as follows:

- AC alternator replaced by DC generator
- rear window of the type fitted to German Beetles between 1965 and 1971
- rear valance flat as it had been on German cars until August 1974 and the '75 model year
- tailpipes chromed – final years of German production had been black
- trim strips on running boards – not a part of the '76 and onwards model specification German 1200L Beetle
- Mexican Beetle had cooling slots in the engine lid – not applicable to any German-built vehicle with a 34PS engine (Mexican Beetles lost this feature in July 1981)
- two-speed electric ventilation fan operated by a switch on the dashboard not applicable to Mexican cars.

Mexico was responsible for production of the landmark twenty-millionth Beetle on 15 May 1981.

bibliography

Bobbitt, Malcolm, *Volkswagen Beetle Cabriolet* (Veloce, 2002)

Copping, Richard, *VW Beetle – The Car of the 20th Century* (Veloce, 2001)

Copping, Richard, *Volkswagen – The Air-cooled Era in Colour* (Veloce, 2005)

Coyle, Phillip, *50 Years of Volkswagens in New Zealand* (Transpress, 2004)

Davies, Rod and Lloyd, *The Beetle in Australia* (AF Publications, 2004)

Etzold, H.R., *The Beetle – Volume 1 Production & Evolution* (Haynes, 1988)

Etzold, H.R., *The Beetle – Volume 2 Design & Evolution* (Haynes, 1990)

Etzold, H.R., *The Beetle – Volume 3 Beetlemania* (Haynes, 1991)

Fry, Robin, *The VW Beetle* (David & Charles, 1980)

Garwood, J.T, *Volkswagen Beetle – The Car of the Century – Vol 2 1961–1980* (J.T. Garwood, 1986)

Glen, Simon, *Volkswagens of the World* (Veloce, 1999)

Harvey, Jonathan, *Volkswagen Beetle* (Haynes, 2008)

Kuch, Joachim, *Volkswagen Model History* (Haynes, 1999)

Meredith, Laurence, *Original VW Beetle* (Bay View Books, 1994)

Nelson, Walter Henry, *Small Wonder – The Amazing Story of the Volkswagen* (Hutchinson & Co., 1970)

Price, Ryan Lee, *The VW Beetle* (HP Books, 2003)

Railton, Arthur, *The Beetle – A Most Unlikely Story* (Eurotax, 1985)

Richardson, James, *VW Beetle Specification Guide 1949–1967* (Crowood, 2008)

Schreiber, Gerhard (ed.) *A Never Ending Story* (Volkswagen de Mexico, 1998)

Seume, Keith, *The Beetle* (CLB International, 1997)

Seume, Keith & Shaill, Bob, *Volkswagen Beetle Coachbuilts and Cabriolets 1940–1960* (Bay View Books, 1993)

Sloniger, Jerry, *The VW Story* (Patrick Stephens Ltd, 1980)

Volkswagen AG (ed.), *Volkswagen Chronicle Vol 7 Historical Notes* (Wolfsburg, 2003)

LEFT: Volkswagen's photographers were on hand to record the sad day and time when the last Beetle left the Wolfsburg assembly line in July 1974. Few could have imagined that Beetle production would continue elsewhere in Volkswagen's empire for another 29 years.

index

WHAT YEAR IS IT?

WHAT YEAR IS IT?

VW 1978 EDITION

76

Chassis numbers:
116 2 000 001 — 116 2 176 287
1976 Beetle Convertible
Chassis numbers:
156 2 000 001 — 156 2 175 675

1. Beetle has plush appearance with many luxury "extras" as standard equipment: Two-coat metallic paint (Silver Metallic, Lime Green, Topaz Metallic);

full carpeting; sports-style wheel rims; rear window defogger.
2. New speedometer with outer scale in miles per hour and inner scale in kilometers per hour (on most '76 models).
3. Redesigned front seats with improved back adjustment, for added comfort and body support.
4. Two-speed fresh air blower.
5. All trim components chrome-plated.
6. Automatic stick shift (option) discontinued.

75

Chassis numbers:
115 2 000 001—115 2 267 815
Type 113 Chassis numbers:
135 2 000 001—135 2 267 815

1. Electronic fuel injection, with "fuel injection" insignia on rear deck lid.
2. Single tailpipe.
3. Increased horsepower; 48 hp, up from 46 (SAE net).
4. Clutch pedal pressure eased.

5. Larger exhaust valve stems for better heat transfer.
6. New heat exchangers for greater heater output.
7. Installation of battery ground cable with diagnosis contact for more accurate computer analysis readings.
8. Odometer triggers red warning light "EGR" in speedometer to notify driver of service requirements.
9. California models with catalytic converter require lead-free gasoline; fuel filler neck is smaller opening for nozzle.
10. Maintenance intervals extended to 15,000 miles.

74

Chassis numbers:
114 2 000 001—114 2 818 456
Type 113 Chassis numbers:
134 2 000 001—134 2 798 165

1. Self-restoring, energy-absorbing front and rear bumpers.

2. Ignition interlock prevents engine from being started before safety belts are fastened.
3. New cylinder head alloy for better heat dissipation.
4. Additional Computer Analysis sensor reads ignition timing and top dead center.
5. Front seat headrests redesigned and made slightly smaller.
6. Steering wheel made more elastic to "give" more in the event of an accident.
7. "Park" position for Automatic Stick Shift.
8. Warning light for hand brake.

73

Chassis numbers:
113 2 000 001—113 3 021 954
Type 113 Chassis numbers:
133 2 000 001—
133 3 021 860

1. Large, circular taillight complex combining stop light, turn signal, tail and backup lights.

2. Stronger bumpers add an inch to overall length.
3. Front seats adjustable to any of 77 different positions.
4. More durable, easier-to-operate clutch; softer transmission mounting.
5. Improved intake air pre-heating for faster cold-weather starts.
6. Windshield wiper arms have black finish.
7. Inertia-reel safety belts.
8. 6.00 x 15L tires with 4½ inch wide wheels.

72

Chassis numbers:
112 2 000001—112 2 961362

1. Larger rear window.
2. Air intake slots on engine compartment increased from two to four.
3. Smoother engine warm-up after cold-weather start.
4. New safety steering wheel with collapsible hub.

5. Lever mounted on steering column for fingertip control of both windshield wiper and washer.
6. Hinged parcel shelf to cover rear-end luggage well.
7. Restyled and easier-to-read speedometer.
8. Automatic electronic check of dual brake system warning light each time the engine starts.
9. VW Computer Analysis socket.

71

Chassis numbers:
111 2 000001— 111 3 143118

1. Increased horsepower, from 57 to 60.
2. Flow-through ventilation with exhaust ports behind rear side windows.
3. Headlights automatically go off and parking lights stay on when ignition is turned off.
4. Larger taillights.

70

Chassis numbers:
11 0 2000001 — 11 0 3096945

1. Air intake slots on engine lid.
2. Increased horsepower (from 53 to 57) and displacement (from 1500 cc to 1600 cc).

3. Enlarged front turn signals (combined with side marker lights).
4. Reflectors mounted on rear bumper.
5. Side reflectors built into taillight housing.
6. Tenths of mile indicator on odometer (also appears on late '69 models).
7. Head restraints reduced in size.
8. Buzzer sounds when door is opened and key is left in ignition.
9. Remote control knobs for warm air outlets discontinued.
10. Lock in glove compartment door.

69

Chassis numbers:
119 000 001—119 1 093 704

1. Rear window defogger and defroster; electric heating wires on inner surface of glass.
2. Double-jointed rear axle for improved ride and handling.

3. Warning lights in speedometer identified by letters or symbols.
4. Ignition lock is combined with a locking device for the steering wheel.
5. Gas tank filler neck flap has lock which has a release under the right side of the dash panel.
6. Front hood release is located in the glove compartment.
7. Day/night rear view mirror.
8. Warm air outlets at base of the doors moved rearward; remote control knobs on door columns.

68

Chassis numbers:
118 000 000—118 1 016 098

1. One-piece bumpers; bows and overriders eliminated (bumper height raised).
2. Head restraints combined with front seat backrests.
3. Automatic Stick Shift (optional) introduced.

4. External gas tank filler; spring-loaded flap.
5. Front hood air intake louver; push-button front hood catch.
6. Fresh air ventilating system.
7. Collapsible steering column.
8. Exhaust emission control system.
9. Flattened door handles with built in trigger release.
10. Back-up/brake lights and rear turn signals in single housing.
11. Certification sticker on door post that vehicle meets federal safety standards.

67

Chassis numbers:
117 000 001—117 844 892

1. Increased horsepower (from 50 to 53) and displacement (from 1300 cc to 1500 cc).
2. Single-unit headlights with chrome rim; fender indented.
3. Dual brake system; front/rear operate independently.
4. Back-up lights.
5. Parking lights incorporated into front turn signals.
6. Locking buttons on doors.
7. 12-volt electrical system (36-amp battery).
8. VOLKSWAGEN nameplate on engine lid.

66

Chassis numbers:
116 000 001—116 1 021 298

1. Increased horsepower (from 40 to 50) and displacement (from 1200 to 1300 cc); number 1300 on engine lid.
2. Ventilating wheel slots; flat hub caps.
3. Emergency blinker switch.
4. Headlight dimmer switch mounted on turn signal.
5. Center-dash defroster outlet.
6. Semi-circular horn ring.

65

Chassis numbers:
115 000 001—115 979 200

1. Windows enlarged; slimmer door and windshield posts.
2. Heat control levers mounted on tunnel; heater efficiency improved.
3. Rear seatback converts to platform.
4. Push-button catch on engine lid.
5. Thinner, deeply contoured front seats; increased rear seat knee room.
6. Swivel mounted sun visors.

Volkswagen of America went to great lengths to provide a 'What year is it?' guide every 12-months – in essence a specification guide covering the major changes made to the Beetle from its earliest days. The edition reproduced here dates from 1978 and a time when the saloon was no longer available.

Related titles from Crowood:

VW Beetle Specification Guide 1949–1967

James Richardson
ISBN 978 1 86126 940 9
128pp, over 300 illustrations

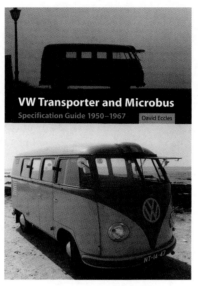

VW Transporter and Microbus Specification Guide 1950–1967

David Eccles
ISBN 978 1 86126 652 1
96pp, over 400 illustrations

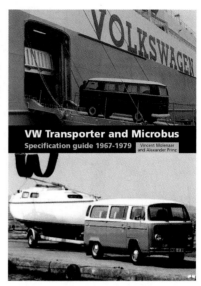

VW Transporter and Microbus Specification Guide 1967–1979

Vincent Molenaar & Alexander Prinz
ISBN 978 1 86126 765 8
128pp, over 400 illustrations

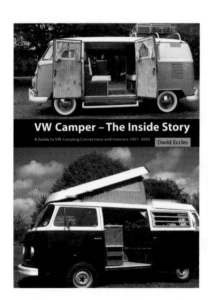

VW Camper – The Inside Story

David Eccles
ISBN 978 1 86126 763 4
160pp, over 400 illustrations

VW Camper Inspirational Interiors

David Eccles
ISBN 978 1 84797 070 1
224pp, over 700 illustrations

EXETER UNVEILED

EXETER UNVEILED

270 UNKNOWN IMAGES OF THE CITY'S PAST

Todd Gray

TODD GRAY

THE MINT PRESS

For Delphine and Andy

First published in Great Britain by The Mint Press, 2003

© Todd Gray 2003

Hardback edition ISBN 1-903356-25-3
Softback edition ISBN 1-903356-26-1

Cataloguing in Publication Data
CIP record for this title is available from the British Library

The Mint Press
18 The Mint
Exeter, Devon
England EX4 3BL

Typeset in Frutiger by Kestrel Data, Exeter
Cover design by Delphine Jones

Printed and bound in Great Britain
by Short Run Press Ltd, Exeter

Contents

Acknowledgements

I have incurred many debts to a number of colleagues while undertaking research for this book and I would like to record their help. It is impossible not to be aware of the debt owed to generations of collectors, librarians and archivists responsible for the rich legacy of images that exist in public hands and which makes this book possible. The majority of them passed away long before I came to Exeter but I hope the publication of these images would have provided some satisfaction to them. Nearly all of the images have lain unnoticed and some have not even been catalogued. It is particularly gratifying to know that these treasures will not only be given a wider audience but their reproduction will insure their survival in the off chance that something untoward happens to the originals. Only ten have previously been published: the three drawings by Willem Schellinks were printed in the 1950s and two images from the Ellis collection appeared in 1978 but neither the drawings of Schellinks or Ellis have been investigated to the degree to which they deserve. One painting of the Broadgate, which is included in order to provide a comparison with three other views, was used to illustrate the cover of Robert Newton's Eighteenth Century Exeter in 1984. Four additional images have been included to place others in their contexts; this comprises two drawings by James Crocker and two postcards that were published in the late nineteenth century. The remaining images are all 'discoveries' but with these I have been reliant on the work of many others in helping to place them within their context. I hope that I have fully recorded each debt. Historical images of Exeter are located in a number of locations and I owe a particular debt to the staff in the Westcountry Studies Library and the Devon Record Office for their patience over the years. In particular I would like to thank Ian Maxted and Tony Rouse of the Devon Library Service and John Draisey of the Devon Record Office. I am also very grateful to Josie Halloran and Mandy Caine for giving their time and assistance. At the Devon & Exeter Institution I have received considerable help from Roger Brien and I would like to thank Heinz Gruber of the Austrian National Library for his kind assistance. A number of specialists have been generous with their time and expertise: I have benefited from wide-ranging discussions on sites throughout Exeter with John Allan, Angela Doughty has given very useful guidance on the cathedral archives and Margery Rowe has allowed me to continually quiz her on matters relating to the city records. I am grateful to Charlie Page for his help with Tucker's reference to William Hogarth, to Richard Parker for conversations on various quirky parts of the city's history and I also owe a special debt to Mrs Audrey Erskine who pointed out the existence of a second Mol's Coffee House. I have also spent considerable time discussing the images with Chris and Kate Caldwell and I am grateful to them for their patience. Any and all mistakes are of course my own. The high quality of reproduction has been made possible by the work of Andrew Teed and Barry Phillips. Finally, I am compelled to note the work of Delphine Jones who has, once more, provided an exceptional cover. Permission to publish has been given by the Devon & Exeter Institution, Devon Library Service, Devon Record Office, Exeter City Council, the Picture Library of the Austrian National Library in Vienna and one private collection.

Sources of illustrations

Introduction: 1 Westcountry Studies Library (WSL), p&d07320; 2 WSL, p&d08346; 3 Devon Record Office (DRO), 76/20/4; 4 WSL, oversize box; 5 WSL, p&d04617; 6-9 WSL, sfdev/1949/mur; 10 DRO, Z19/2/4; main text 1-3 National Library of Vienna, Blaeu Atlas; 4-24 DRO, 76/20/1-8; 25-34 DRO, Z19/2/4; 35-41 WSL, p&d06547, p&d06690, p&d06691, p&d06624, p&d06546, p&d06623, p&d06550; 42-54 DRO, 75/20; 55 WSL, p&d06880; 56-7 DRO, exhibitions drawer; 58 WSL, p&d06503; 59 Devon & Exeter Institution (DEI), no reference; 60 WSL, p&d05680; 61 WSL, p&d06912; 62 DRO, 68/28; 63 DEI, no reference; 64 DEI, D78; 65 WSL, p&d06970; 66, WSL, SC1022; 67-8 DRO, D2/276 & 287; 69 James Crocker, Sketches of Exeter (1885), plate 5; 70 WSL, p&d43608; 71 WSL oversize no reference; 72 DRO, no reference; 73 WSL, p&d43613; 74 WSL, p&d40104; 75 James Crocker, Sketches of Exeter (1885), plate 27; 76 private collection; 77 DEI, D4; 78 WSL, p&d41637; 79 WSL, p&d41636; 80 WSL, p&d06983; 81 WSL, p&d06933; 82 WSL, p&d p&d43606; 83-4 Royal Albert Memorial Museum; 85 WSL, S757/Dev/Tuc; 86 WSL, sfdev/1949/mur; 87 private collection; 88 WSL, p&d40068; 89 p&d08410; 90 p&d08405; 91 p&d08406; 92 p&d08408; 93 p&d08409; 94 WSL, p&d07580; 95 WSL, p&d05613; 96 WSL, oversize box; 97 WSL, p&d05651; 98 WSL, p&d06869; 99 WSL, p&d43579; 100 WSL, p&d03737; 101 WSL, p&d05660; 102-103 DEI, no reference; 104-182 WSL, S757/Dev/Tuc; 183-264 WSL, sfdev/1949/mur.

Foreword

The people of Exeter are rightly proud of its long history. There was a settlement here even before the Romans came nearly two thousand years ago. One of the ways in which we can access those centuries of history is through the paintings, drawings and sketches left behind by generations of artists. The city is fortunate in that it attracted so many who worked to a high standard and that we have these treasures to understand more fully the city we live in. It is all the more exciting when hundreds of unknown historical images come our way. Their freshness challenges our perceptions of familiar places and intrigues us with those we have not seen. This collection will delight all those who love the city of Exeter and make us appreciate all the more the rich historical legacy that surrounds us.

I warmly recommend this book.

The Right Worshipful the Lord Mayor of Exeter
Councillor Margaret Dansk

1. This drawing is an example of an unknown fragment of Exeter's history. It shows a mill but the title was loosely given as 'Old Buildings in Exeter'. It has been attributed to Samuel Prout. The drawing was most likely made in the early nineteenth century. Unfortunately the mill has not been identified and could be one of many that were once situated along the river Exe.

2. An anonymous drawing entitled 'Exeter from Cowick Hill' from the middle of the nineteenth century. This is one of many general views that were popular, some of which were engraved. The Exe estuary is shown prominently on the right.

Introduction

This is a successor or companion book to *Lost Exeter*[1] in the sense that its research follows similar lines of thought. Both books look at the history of the city through images but this is attempted in two very different ways. *Lost Exeter*'s objective was to examine five centuries of topographical change mostly within the old city walls and it made use of a great number of historical illustrations that were previously unknown. *Exeter Unveiled* also introduces unknown images but it is entirely focused on them: these are used to explain aspects of the city's history as opposed to merely embellishing written text. Unknown images have been deliberately sought in order to introduce different perspectives and to stimulate perceptions of what may already be known or assumed.

Unknown historical images of a familiar place inevitably challenge the viewer's preconceptions. Altogether this collection of two hundred and seventy-six historical sketches, drawings, paintings and maps of Exeter includes images of buildings, parts of the city and of views along the river. Some are of familiar places, possibly seen by individual readers on a daily or regular basis, while others show buildings that disappeared long before the memory of anyone now alive. Each image depicts the city in a former guise, familiar to some degree but not as it is known today. There are several which illustrate places in different ways over the centuries, showing both change and the continuity. Each

3. *A drawing from the collection of Henry Ellis, 1828. This is a view of his new shop window at 200 High Street, near the Guildhall.*

4. Undated drawing entitled 'Near Countess Weir, Devon', attributed to F.J. Ellis, nineteenth century, of a view that is remarkably preserved today. It shows Lime Kiln Lane leading up from the river Exe near Countess Wear. The collection of cob cottages were probably built in the seventeenth or eighteenth centuries.[2] The cottage to the right is now known as Haldon View and that on the left is named Hillside.

5. An unnoticed drawing entitled 'The choir of the Cathedral Church of St Peter Exeter' by John Tozer (noted in pencil). The artist may have been the individual by that name who was elected Deputy Treasurer of the city's Workhouse in 1825.[3] The view is looking from the altar into the choir towards the West Window. The seventeenth-century organ can be seen in the foreground and the Bishop's Throne to the left. The box pews were installed in the 1760s and removed in the 1870s.

6-9. *Four drawings from the collection by Harold Murray, 1949. Clockwise from top left, a view of the Guildhall entitled 'There were many visitors in the ancient guildhall in 1949', a year in which 'the battle cry' for Exeter was 'Come to Exeter for your holidays'[4] (see illustrations 38 and 255); a view entitled 'In July 1949 the Cathedral Quire was closed while repairs proceeded, and the organ was shrouded to protect it from dust'; a drawing of the Exe bridge and finally, 'Tiger in the Museum shot by George V' (see illustrations 259 & 260). The tiger is still on display.*

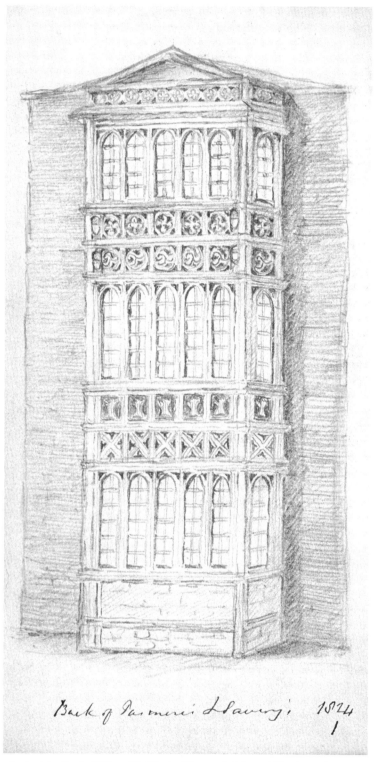

Back of Pasmore & Savery; 1824

10. *Drawing by John Harris, 1824, entitled 'back of Pasmore's & Savery'. The sixteenth-century oriel window looked out onto Cathedral Yard near the church of St Petrock. The building also has a front on High Street. The clothing firm of Passmore & Savery subsequently moved further along the High Street to the corner of South Street and were there until the late nineteenth century. In the early nineteenth century the window was removed and repositioned in the Bishop's Palace where it can be seen today.*

will add to an appreciation of the city in unveiling aspects of the past that have not been considered before. They also show that what we personally know also changes on a daily basis and remind us that, just like previous generations, we too are here on a temporary basis.

Nearly all these images are unpublished with only ten exceptions, notably two drawings by Willem Schellinks that appeared more than forty years ago in a national journal. Few of the images are known outside of a small number of individuals: some illustrations have hitherto been familiar to a handful of librarians, archivists or researchers while others are images unseen even by those who are responsible for their care.

The images are arranged in nine sections. One of the most unusual is the collection of caricatures by Mr Tucker, an Exeter artist whose name is known but whose identity is uncertain. His drawings provide glimpses into Victorian society. The caricatures are of a wide range of individuals, few of whom history has otherwise recorded and most no doubt have been long forgotten even by their descendants. Not all depictions are complimentary and some are particularly unpleasant. One of the most interesting caricatures is of two women who can be identified from other sources. Tucker wrote in his caption that they were the 'Alphington Ponies'. These women were two maiden sisters who were noted eccentrics. They acquired their nickname from being born in Alphington and from the two ponies they took with them when they moved to Torquay in the 1840s. The sisters were nearly identical in appearance and walked apart from other people and in step, arm in arm. Presumably they were as identical as their ponies.

They were particularly known for clothing thought to be 'peculiar' by nineteenth-century standards: visitors to Torquay were contemptuous because the sisters did not dress according to fashion. Sabine Baring-Gould described their clothing and it is interesting to compare it with Tucker's painting. Baring-Gould wrote:

'The style varied only in tone and colour. Their shoes were generally green, but sometimes red. They were by no means bad-looking girls when young, but they were so berouged as to present the appearance of painted dolls. Their brown hair worn in curls was fastened with blue ribbon, and they wore felt or straw hats, usually tall in the crown and curled up at the sides. About their throats they had very broad frilled or lace collars that fell down their backs and breasts a long way. But in summer their necks were bare, and adorned with chains of coral or bead. Their gowns were short, so short indeed as to display about the ankles a good deal more than was necessary of certain heavily frilled cotton investitures of their lower limbs. In winter over their gowns were worn check jackets of a 'loud' pattern reaching to their knees, and of a different colour from their gowns, and with lace cuffs. They were never seen, winter or summer, without their sunshades. The only variation to the jacket was a gay-coloured shawl crossed over the bosom and tied behind at the waist.'[5]

In contrast, Tucker's painting shows them in different dress. He noted them as the 'New' Alphington Ponies and this may have been because of a change in their clothing. The two women later returned to Exeter where they lived in the parish of St Sidwell.

There is also a small collection of drawings by George Townsend of local people celebrating the Fifth of November; these give an impression of the city's life in the nineteenth century that has long been forgotten. Another interesting collection is from the sketchbook of John Harris, a local surgeon; this provides images of places in the city and of Exonians from the 1820s, some were made of people of whom nothing is known and yet these are extremely intriguing. A few are of very unexpected subjects such as two individuals who appear to be aborigines, 'Bachapin', a chief, and 'Massisan', his daughter. In 1823 the 'Wild Venus' was exhibited in Exeter and it may have been in a similar situation that Harris saw these two strangers. There was public interest in seeing such 'curiosities'. One of Exeter's newspapers wrote of the Wild Venus that she was:

'Divested, in some degree, of her natural ferocity, and not sufficiently civilized to possess even a slight portion of the graces of her sex – at intervals displaying trifling symptoms of that cultivation which it has been attempted to instil into her mind since taken from her native wilds and bursting into paroxysms of primeval rudeness; her manners peculiarly interest the beholder.'[6]

It may have been this level of interest that prompted Harris to make his drawings. He also made ink sketches of familiar buildings such as the Guildhall and the Cathedral that are still very much a part of modern Exeter life and of others which have not survived. Harris provided no comment on them, only an identification of them and sometimes a date, and it is uncertain why he sketched these people and places.

More is known about the images made by Henry Ellis, a wealthy jeweller. He recorded his homes and businesses in both words and pictures over a period of some seventy years and wrote that his intention was to provide a record for the future. Ellis' drawings are interesting in that they provide a unique record of domestic life that was probably representative of his class in Exeter. George Townsend redrew many, if not all, of the sketches.[7] Two of the buildings he drew can still be seen today.

There are also sets of views by various artists of the river Exe, of buildings that have survived and of others that have been destroyed. The river scenes were all made in the nineteenth century at different locations on the Exe; some are of familiar places and others are of ones that have greatly changed. The eight subjects of lost buildings are ones that were destroyed at least sixty years ago. Most were taken down in the nineteenth century but some people in Exeter today, with longer memories, will have known the Abbot's Lodge or Dix's Field. Even the images of surviving buildings will challenge most viewers given the changes but there is also continuity in some of the subjects, for example Southernhay looks very similar to how it looked in the nineteenth century. The discovery of an early drawing of Mol's Coffee House prompted the research necessary to explain changes in the building's structure and the result is a history very much different from that previously told.

Another collection introduced here, which may well prove to be the most popular in the book, is that of Harold Murray, a religious writer, who came to Exeter in 1949 to see the plans for the rebuilding of the city. While here Murray decided he liked the city and stayed. His drawings were done in a style reminiscent of Lowry and depict the city with great charm in the years between the blitz and before the redevelopment. The eighty-nine images show a city coping with change but expectant of the future.

Perhaps the artist who made the greatest contribution to topographical studies of Exeter is John Gendall whose work appears throughout this collection. Nine drawings and paintings either by or attributed to him are reproduced here. When Gendall died in 1865 one newspaper enthused over his contribution to Exeter and commented 'the man is dead. Let all of us who can keep alive in our hearts the spirit of his genius by hanging something of his over the fireplace'.[8] George Townsend also features quite prominently. More than a dozen pictures are reproduced: in addition to his drawing of South Street and a number of sketches of figures on the fifth of November there are also his drawings made from Henry Ellis' sketches.

Another individual who has made a significant contribution to Exeter images is Thomas Shapter. Not only did he live at Cobham in Pennsylvania, which is illustrated here by a series of Victorian paintings for the first time, but he collected original paintings and drawings of Exeter. He redrew some, including one of St David's Hill which he saw on the walls of the Pack Horse.[9] Many were later left to the city of Exeter. At least five of these are reproduced in this book and it is uncertain what would have happened to them had he not had an interest in art and Exeter.

Two of the artists were in Exeter after particularly devastating periods in the city's history. Schellinks and Murray made sketches in which the effects of war are only too visible. Whereas the destruction of the civil war lay largely outside the city walls, in the 1940s the city suffered dramatically in the its very centre and much of Murray's work concerns how Exeter was then coping with the changes. Buildings that are familiar today can be seen as they were with bomb damage and great gaps around them.

This book is also about personal achievement and the impact an individual can make on history. Tucker, Harris, Ellis and Murray depicted the city in very personal ways and each image is a reflection not merely of them as artists but also of the times in which they lived. Willem Schellinks' two perspective drawings are the best earliest views of the city and the skill of this Dutchman is remarkable. Did others sketch the city at the time and their work not survive, or was he unusual? Like Murray he was new to Exeter whereas Ellis, Gendall, Townsend, and probably Harris and Tucker, were native sons. Unfortunately, we know nothing of the individual who sketched a map of the city from 1838 to 1839. He himself tells us that he lived in Exmouth, drew the map while on crutches and referred to himself as an invalid. It took nine months to complete the map and the detail with which he made it shows the high level of personal achievement. Was he connected with the city or did he merely see the making of a map of Exeter as a personal challenge? Until now it has remained in manuscript and there is no evidence that he intended it for publication. It would appear he did this for his own purposes. His work, as with all the others in this collection, reinforces the debt we owe to individuals who depicted the city in various forms.

1. Exeter in 1662: The drawings of Willem Schellinks

Willem Schellinks, a Dutchman, visited Exeter for little more than a fortnight in the summer of 1662 and yet the legacy of his short stay is remarkable: he was responsible for producing the earliest and most detailed drawings of Exeter. No resident, or other traveller, matched the quality of his work until the late eighteenth century when John Carter came to draw Exeter Cathedral. By the early nineteenth century a considerable number of artists were working in Exeter and produced a substantial number of topographical drawings, paintings and prints but Schellinks' three drawings remain of particular interest and significance.

The drawing of Exe Bridge has recently been reprinted[11] so only the two general views are reproduced here in full.

1-3. All three drawings are pen and ink over outlines of black lead or chalk with washes on several sheets.

English scholars have been aware of the works of Schellinks since the mid 1950s but the Exeter drawings still remain relatively unknown in the city itself: it is surprising that two were never been published locally but have only appeared in a volume of the Walpole Society for the early 1950s. They form part of the Van Der Hem Atlas (also known as the Blaeu Atlas), one of the treasures of the National Library in Vienna. The Atlas comprises views of cities across Europe and Schellinks' works appear alongside other artists. He had been employed to sketch various cities and to return these with him to the Netherlands where he completed the final work. His style is representational rather than idealised with a great deal of detail. Indeed there is so much that it has even been suggested that Schellinks was in the employ of the Dutch intelligence services to record the defences of England.[10]

Exeter in 1662 was a prosperous place with the cloth trade making the city one of the leading urban centres in the county: some seventeen years had passed since the devastating sieges of the civil war and Exeter was adapting to life under Charles II. Perhaps it was a prevailing sense of embarrassment or shame that led the City Chamber to present the newly-crowned king with the rich gift of a silver salt; this extraordinary item remains one of the chief exhibits to be seen in the Tower of London. The effects of the recent war are still visible in Schellinks' drawings and the local divisions evident with the depiction of a quarter of the body of a local man executed for treason still hanging from Rougemont Castle.

This view is taken from the northeast, at a position located somewhere in what is now known as Pennsylvania, with Haldon Hill bereft of buildings. The Longbrook Valley has a few isolated cottages. The three most prominent features from left to right are the church of St Sidwell, the Cathedral (with its remaining tower) and Rougemont Castle with the city walls. St Sidwell's church is shown towering over the suburb that had been devastated during the civil war and was then being rebuilt. To the right can be seen the medieval East Gate (demolished in 1784) and the building to its left is possibly the (old) London Inn (taken down in 1933).

Schellinks placed the cathedral to appear as if it hung over the city walls probably in order to give the building a greater impact. The lines of wall running down from the castle may well be the remains of fortifications built during the Civil War. The building seen to the right of the cathedral may be Rougemont Tower. Schellinks noted with numerals the cathedral, Rougemont Castle, the church of St Mary Major (to the immediate right of the cathedral) and the body of a man hanging from the far right of the castle walls. He noted that this was `a quarter of a constable, hanged upon the evidence of two false witnesses, who was cut down half alive, sat up, and

holding tight his wound with both hands shouted Oh, what are you doing? etc.' In his journal Schellinks wrote that the remaining quarters were on the city gates and that he later saw the man's head on Plymouth's Guildhall. The constable had been accused of making derogatory remarks about the king.[12] The bare character of the slopes of Northernhay was due to the destruction of the trees during the Civil War.

Schellinks was very sociable while in Exeter; he wandered through the streets to see the sites, walked the city walls and met local people. He spent one night at the New Inn in High Street and was afterwards the guest of a merchant in the parish of St Mary Major.[13] During this time he managed to make a drawing of Exe Bridge, a view of the city from Exwick and another from what would later be known as Pennsylvania.

The second view is taken from Exwick. Schellinks indicated with numerals the castle, cathedral, the church of St Mary Major (that was demolished two hundred years later), the river Exe and the medieval bridge that was partly taken down in the 1770s. Once again Schellinks noted the body of the constable on the walls of Rougemont. He wrote in his journal that Exeter 'lies on a small hill, gradually rising to the top and is surrounded by strong walls and dry ditches, the circumference being 1½ miles. Its suburbs stretch out far all round, it has a fine bridge over the river, and a quay, where ships of 20 tons come in from down river.'[14] The steepness of the Longbrook Valley is accentuated but the North Gate is lost amidst the general buildings. The identification of landmarks is difficult because of a distortion in relative distances, which Schellinks used in other urban drawings. Also, Schellinks confused the church of St Mary Major with what was probably St Olave. The medieval bridge is shown in some detail with the church of St Edmund on the eastern side. Churches most likely depicted include those of St Mary Steps, All-Hallows-on-the-Walls (demolished in the 1770s) and St John (taken down in stages in the nineteenth and early twentieth centuries).

2. The sketchbook of Henry Ellis, 1790-1858

Including pen and ink sketches redrawn by George Townsend, comprising Portview Cottage in Livery Dole, 263 High Street, 199-200 High Street, a cottage in Palace Gate and Grovelands in St Leonard's as well as photographs of family portraits.

Henry Ellis, an Exeter merchant wrote eight journals to recount his life from 1790 through to the middle of the nineteenth century. He thought that future generations would question why and Ellis noted in his first page 'wonder not to thyself, gentle reader, shouldst thou by chance get a glance at these pages, what motive could possibly have induced an obscure individual to write this delectable history of himself'. He explained further that they were to provide amusement for his latter years because old men are prone to recalling the adventures of their youth.

The journals provide a unique view into the home and work life of a prosperous Exeter merchant in the first part of the nineteenth century. Ellis began his working life as a 'watch and clock maker' but in 1848 he was appointed a Royal Silversmith. He had been born on 3 December 1790 in Liverydole, the son of a malster. He married Mary White in 1815 and then, after her death in 1844, married Mary Cooke Snell in 1850. Ellis served his apprenticeship in Tiverton and Bideford and returned to Exeter in 1813. He lived in three houses in the city. In 1814 he resided at 263 High Street, the following year he was at 246 High Street but a year later he moved to 199 High Street. In 1828 Ellis moved once again, to 200 High Street, next door to the Turk's Head. His final move was in 1850 when he rented Grovelands in the parish of St Leonard's. Ellis died on 18 July 1871 at the age of 80.[15]

Included in his memoirs are a series of pen and ink drawings, all of which were probably by George Townsend but based on Ellis' own sketches. Ellis also included a number of copies of family portraits. His own, sometimes lengthy, descriptions are included with each illustration.

4. 'My portrait', c.1858. Ellis was then about 68 years old.

5. Drawing of Mary Ellis wearing a cap styled after Mary, Queen of Scots. Ellis wrote that he had suggested she wore a cap because he was 'a little apprehensive perhaps lest the exhibitions of her glossy ringlets might cause her to be taken for une femme demarie'.

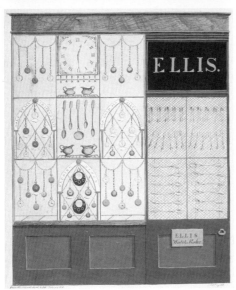

6. Photograph by Mr James of a portrait of Mary Ellis, 1833. Ellis wrote that his wife was initially unwilling to have herself photographed. He also wrote `Dearest Mary although now arrived at the meridian of life was still in the bloom of matronly beauty, and while grown stout and the mother of so large a family, her face still retained its `Madonna like' expression of calm cheerful benignity'.

7. Portrait of Mary C. Ellis `photographed by Angel, coloured by Tremlett', c.1855. The second Mrs Ellis (Mary Cooke Snell) was born in Chawleigh and raised in nearby Chulmleigh. She was an acquaintance of the first Mrs Ellis and they first met in Torrington years before either knew Henry Ellis. She later moved to Exeter and helped run a dress makers and milliners. Henry Ellis asked her to marry him six years after the death of the first Mrs Ellis and he quoted Samuel Johnson in claiming a second marriage was a compliment to the first wife. They married in Ringmore near Teignmouth on 15 August 1850. The wedding, he wrote, was quiet `as best befitting our age and inclinations'.[16] A dozen years later Mr Angel was still perfecting his method of colouring photographs.[17]

8. Photograph of a painting entitled `Home' by Mr Mogford, 1846. From left to right, Lucy A., Frederick William, Emily, William H., Mary and Henry, Mary W., Henry S., Eliza J. and Elizabeth W. The original picture was exhibited at the British Institution in 1847. The Athenaeum noted it as `a careful and well arranged study of portraits drawn with great care and painted with much refinement'. Mogford's portraits were described in 1854 as having `a lifelike intellectuality of expression'.[18]

9. Tinted photograph of Henry Ellis' daughter Eliza and stepdaughter Eliza, 1858.

10. Henry Ellis' shop window at 199 High Street, 1828.

11. Drawing entitled 'Portview Cottage, Liverydole'. Ellis' parents met in this cottage: when a young woman his mother, Elizabeth Bickford, lived in the house with her aunt Escott who rented out a room the master of Henry Ellis' father. They married in 1784. The house stood near the Livery Dole Almshouses at the south-west junction of what is now Barrack Road and Magdalene Road. See Illustration 51.

12. Drawing entitled 'The Beaufettel'. Ellis noted that the room 'bore an air of neatness, comfort and respectability beyond that of many in my father's rank of life' and that it was only used on Sundays and holidays. Above the fireplace was a map of England made by his elder sister in 1796. In the room was a three-cornered cupboard, called a beautfettel, in which his parents kept their valuables. It was lined with rose coloured paper and the edges of the shelves were gilt. Among the items kept inside were two large china bowls, four china tea cups (without handles) and saucers, silver spoons and a cream ewer, silver tongs, a punch ladle and a large silver tankard which had been given to Mrs Ellis by her uncle on her marriage.

13. Drawing of Ellis' father's residence at Palace Gate by George Townsend, 1813. Ellis wrote that 'on the ground floor adjoining the door was the counting house (the entrance to which was from the warehouse contiguous) and over the courtyard with the large entrance gates, the drawing room formerly occupied by my father's employer'. See Illustration 50.

14. Drawing entitled 'cottage in the court behind and new residence Number 246 High Street as described in the last volume, page 369. Here was our dormitory', 1815. Ellis wrote that 'the back part of the house is open and airy. There is a pump in the yard, and a supply of soft water, with a little garden plot, which I may have the use of. The two lodging rooms are detached from the shop, for my part of a little cottage, whose front is adorned with shrubs and flowers. Of this Mrs J[acobs] reserves to herself the parlour only. There is also an outhouse, and little room over which might serve for a servant or apprentice. A short distance back through a passage leads to the sleeping apartments, this however as we should be in the former the greatest part of the day, I hope will not be considered a great disadvantage'. The front building was later known as the Apothecaries Hall. See Illustration 50.

15. Drawing entitled 'my house and shop Number 199 High Street', 1816. The shop had been the premises of Benjamin Bowring, a fellow watchmaker and silversmith, who had disagreed with his fellow Dissenters, notably over the installation of an organ at George's Meeting House, and had migrated to St John's, Newfoundland. Ellis noted that the front was 'old and heavy'. It opened on 4 January 1816. See Illustration 50.

16. Drawing entitled '200 High Street', 1828. Ellis wrote that the house was rebuilt in 1789 and that one of the previous occupants remembered standing on the scaffolding watching the arrival of George III that year. Mr Richard Hart, a druggist, opened the building. Ellis renovated the shop front and travelled first to Plymouth, and subsequently to London, to see the most modern styles in jewellers' windows and shops.

17. Drawing entitled 'sketch of the exterior', 1836. Ellis noted that the door 'opened into a narrow court covered with lead, here were our casks for soft water, at first we had only one, which I remember from the circumstances of one of our servants springing at the top to look in, and pulling the cask with its contents over her! This deluging the passage and the kitchen; which operation was accustomed with the usual amount of screaming'. The shop's blinds were kept under the kitchen windows.

18. Drawing entitled `Stairwell', 1839. Ellis' renovations included rebuilding the stairs and removing the back window. He decorated the hall with marble paper in blocks and varnished the paper.

19. Drawing entitled `new dining room, court and fountain' by George Townsend, 1841. This was `the hanging garden'. Ellis noted `in the court and on the lead flats above, when not inclined for a morning's ramble, I attended to my gardening operation and birds, generally keeping one or two larks, a blackbird and thrush'. He decided not to have an aviary as he began to think it was cruel. The fountain cost £5 15s 2d and at first Ellis filled the basin with gold and silver fish but he noted that they kept leaping out onto the courtyard. He replaced them with minnows. On the walls of the courtyard he planted ivy and Virginia Creeper. After Ellis moved to Grovelands he admitted the difficulties he had gardening in his former home where it was nearly all shade: he said the plants were, in effect, `brought there to die'.

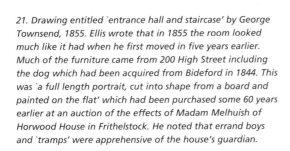

20. Drawing entitled 'Grovelands, Mount Radford', 1850, now known as 58 St Leonard's Road – located at the western end of the road. In 1851 it was known as Number One, Groveland Villas. That year the Ellis household included two female servants.[19] Henry Ellis moved in May 1850 and paid a rental of £45 per year to the owner, Mr Pridham.[20] See Illustrations 50 and 53.

21. Drawing entitled 'entrance hall and staircase' by George Townsend, 1855. Ellis wrote that in 1855 the room looked much like it had when he first moved in five years earlier. Much of the furniture came from 200 High Street including the dog which had been acquired from Bideford in 1844. This was 'a full length portrait, cut into shape from a board and painted on the flat' which had been purchased some 60 years earlier at an auction of the effects of Madam Melhuish of Horwood House in Frithelstock. He noted that errand boys and 'tramps' were apprehensive of the house's guardian.

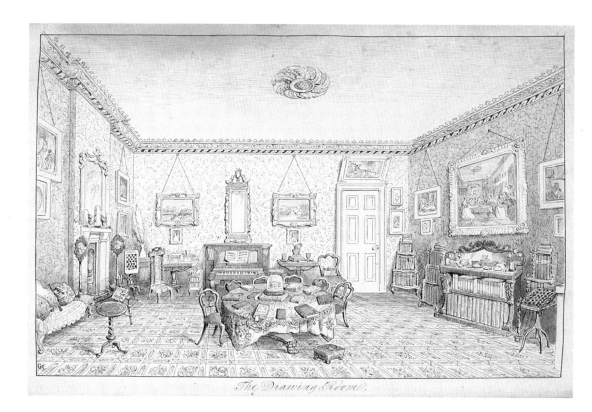

The Drawing Room.

22. Drawing entitled `the drawing room' by George Townsend, 1855. Ellis noted that the family portrait hung on the right and that in the room were two views of North Wales by C. F. Williams.

THE PARLOUR.
Our usual sitting Room.

23. Drawing entitled `the parlour our usual sitting room' by George Townsend, 1854. He noted that he and his wife, along with her niece and his two daughters, were all pictured engaged in their accustomed occupations.

THE GARDEN,
as seen from the Parlour:-

"One of these neat & quiet nooks
That into a garden looks."
The Wish.

24. Drawing entitled 'The garden as seen from the parlour' by George Townsend, 1850. The view includes the cathedral to the left. Ellis noted that the garden was bereft of attention when he moved in and that there were only old fruit trees, shrubs, cabbages, potatoes and that he also inherited a great amount of slugs, snails and weeds. On digging the ground he discovered that the ground was full of rags, bones, stones, broken bottles and crockery. He constructed the bower, erected the iron wire arches for climbers and planted the privet hedge with the inverted arches.

3. Exeter in the 1820s

The sketchbook of John Harris comprising the North Gate, the Cathedral, St Nicholas' Priory, the Guildhall, and various caricatures.

Caricatures
25. `A black beggar Mr White'.
Who this individual was is
uncertain.
26. An unidentified woman.

27. `B. W. Johnson'. Johnson was a surgeon and apothecary who lived in Bradninch Place.[21]
28. `Benjamin Honeycomb Walker Esquire, Senior Alderman and Magistrate of the city, 1824 Father of the city'. Walker was Steward of the city in 1777, Receiver in 1781, Sheriff in 1782, a member of the Common Council in 1778 and Mayor in 1784.[22]

29. `Bachapin, chief'. These two drawings may have been made of people exhibited for public view. Exhibitions of `curiosities' were common at this time in Exeter as elsewhere including in 1815 Madame Tussaud's collection of wax figures and in 1845 General Tom Thumb.[23] In October 1823 the `Wild Indian Venus' was on public show in the Swan Tavern (on the western corner of what is now Queen Street with High Street) for several weeks. This woman was from South America and her name was given as Botucudos. It was claimed in one local newspaper that local people should `gratify themselves with a sight of this extraordinary woman of the savage tribe'.[24] Another journalist wrote that she was `a being, once little better than a savage beast, almost christianised, and reconciled to a situation so widely different from the natural ferocity and ignorance of her tribe'.[25]
30. `Massisan daughter of Bachapin, chief'

Included within the holdings of the Devon Record Office is a small volume entitled `Fordland Sketches &c J. H. 1823'. It provides unusual images of Exeter people and places at a time in which few other sketchbooks survive. The book was the property of John Harris, probably the surgeon and apothecary who lived in 3 Higher Southernhay Place from 1828.[26] He had married in 1822[27] and was the city's Receiver in 1819, Mayor in 1822 and Sheriff in 1827.[28] His book comprises a series of mainly pen and ink sketches of places and people drawn in or near Exeter in 1823 and 1824. In addition to the Exeter sketches reproduced here, there are also views of the theatre in Bedford Street, the church of St Mary Major and Broadgate.[29] See Introduction, Illustration 10.

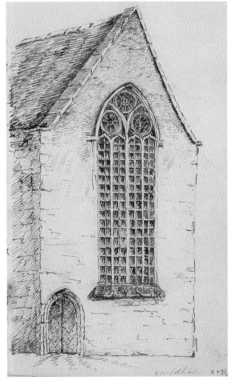

Views
31. `North Gate Xon Aug 27 from the archives of the Chamber'. Harris' drawing of the North Gate was made from a vignette in the city's great map book, then probably still kept in the Guildhall and now in the Devon Record Office. He could not then have drawn the gate given it was demolished 58 years before in 1769. See Illustrations 2 & 50.
32. Drawing entitled `Cathedral from South', looking into Cathedral Close from Southernhay.
33. `Mint Exon April 1824'. The west front of the priory of St Nicholas is seen with slightly different windows from those that were restored in 1915. `Mint' refers to the priory being situated to the lane known as The Mint.
34. `Guildhall Exon'. The view is of the back of the Guildhall on Waterbeer Street. See Illustrations Introduction 6 & 50, 251-4.

4. Victorian celebrations of the 5th of November

These seven drawings by George Townsend help illustrate one of the city's most popular events of the Victorian period: 'Young' Exeter's celebrations of the 5th of November in Cathedral Yard were once the leading occasion in the county even though, or because of, the notoriety of the rowdiness. Great bonfires were often lit in front of the cathedral's West Front and tar barrels rolled through the Yard. The bonfire was enormous. In 1881 ten tons of railway sleepers were made into a hollow square which was filled with oil and tar barrels. A further six tons of moots (the stumps and roots of trees) and seams of faggot wood were piled around it.[30] In 1892 Beatrix Potter thought those taking part were 'notorious rabble' but significant portion of the city took part each year.[31] Then, as now, firecrackers were let off days in advance and guys were brought about the city for contributions. One of the appeals was:

> Please to remember the fifth of November.
> Up with the ladder, down with the rope,
> Please to give a penny to burn the old pope.

In 1877 one local man remembered the celebrations with fondness but he was a passionate supporter of it. There were sharp divisions in the city over the event and on several occasions mayors tried to ban it: for example, in

1853 the authorities sponsored an alternative event in a field near Paris Street but after watching the fireworks a crowd moved on to Cathedral Yard. They first burnt a shed in New North Road to draw the city's few policemen away from the cathedral. They then brought in their own wood for the bonfire. The official concerns were partly over the risk of fire to the city: lit tar barrels were occasionally brought through the surrounding streets.[32] In 1852 it was claimed that the reason for stopping the event was because it caused two deaths the previous year[33] but the following year it was questioned whether the actual pressure to stop the celebrations lay with pro-Catholic clergy in the Church of England.[34] In 1867 the city tried to stop the celebrations once again in Cathedral Yard (on the grounds of objections by the

35-41. Seven drawings by George Townsend, some undated, comprising 'Exeter Guys', 'The Cardinal of Westminster', 'His Holiness the Pope', 'Interior of Bonfire Cathedral Yard, Exeter November 5 1875', 'Building the Bonfire, Exeter, November 5 1880', 'Exeter 5th November, Cathedral Yard' and 'Building the Bonfire, 6 November 1865' at Broadgate looking towards High Street.

residents) but general discontent over the price of bread and meat turned patriotic celebrations into a riot. The militia was called out, armed with bayonets, 170 special constables were on hand armed with staves and 200 soldiers were brought in from Plymouth. Nevertheless, more than 68 shops, many of them bakers and butchers, had their windows broken and many were ransacked.[35] It was not until the late 1880s that the city's enthusiasm waned: that year it was transferred to the Cyclist Carnival held in October. By 1893 there was only a small bonfire lit to celebrate the fifth of November in Cathedral Yard and shortly afterwards the celebrations ceased altogether.[36]

In some years processions through the streets brought hundreds in costume to Cathedral Yard. Meeting points were varied including the Buller's Arms in St Thomas, St Anne's Chapel at the end of Sidwell Street and at the Turk's Head.[37] In the procession in 1877 the boys wore white jackets and trousers, southwester hats and high boots; there was a crescent on their arms as a badge. Costumes included Roman soldiers, 'gay cavaliers with ruffles and plumed hats, clowns, harlequins, 'savages in war paint and feathers' and the Prince of Darkness with his horns and tails.[38] In some years a band accompanied the boys and it played 'Auld Lang Syne' and 'God Save the Queen'.[39]

The event was often more concerned with contemporary politics than with the events of 1605. In 1875 it was said that half of those attending had little knowledge of the original events of the fifth of November and in 1861 that the night was merely an 'annual amusement for the boys'.[40] Effigies were burnt of various figures, some of whom were foreign figures and occasionally, as in 1849, local people: in that year a cleric and his daughter were carried in effigy through the streets before being thrown onto the bonfire.[41] In 1880 a bill was passed banning the use of effigies.[42]

Damage occasionally happened to private property, for instance in 1819 five rockets were thrown through the window of one Cathedral Yard resident and caused damage to his drawing room carpet[43] but there was greater hurt caused to individuals taking part or observing. For example, in 1875 nine local people suffered burns. And in 1881 there were fifteen injuries.[44] The event was often derided in the local newspapers: in one year it was said to be 'rough, barbaric and uncivilised lawlessness'[45] but public enthusiasm maintained it as one of Exeter's major occasions until nearly three hundred years after the original events of 5 November.

5. A map by an 'invalid' of Exeter, 1839

42. The sections of the map are shown as they were stitched together. The fragility of the paper has made it impossible to flatten the map for photographing.

Included in the holdings of the Devon Record Office is an unnoticed manuscript map of the city with the title 'Walks in Exeter and its neighbourhood by an invalid from September 1838 to June 1839'. It is unlikely that a similar map was done of any other place outside Devon. At the top right-hand corner of this map is stated 'Note: As the annexed has been written without the aid of mathematical instruments, accuracy cannot be expected:

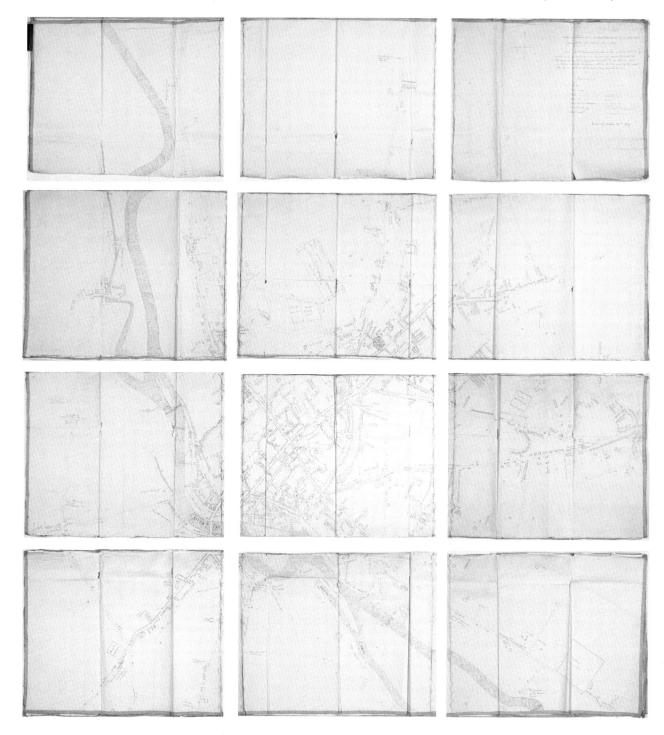

the ground has been passed over by the author on his crutches and the bearings taken by the cast of the eye. The parts omitted here have not been walked on.' The map is very early Victorian, with the date given as 22 October 1839, and it was signed from Exmouth. It would have been an incredible feat to complete this map on crutches, an accomplishment that is attested by the nine months it took. The map was drawn on twelve separate pieces of paper that were later stitched together and measures nearly four and one half feet by five feet. The

individual sheets have been reproduced in the following pages. The map maker noted most of the names of the streets and was particularly interested in new developments: he identified recently constructed terraces as well as prominent cottages and villas. He also noted Mile End Buildings on Topsham Road as well as the one mile point on Stoke Hill and that on Exwick Road.

43. The top left-hand corner of the map shows how little developed Cowley Bridge Road was. Duryard House and Great Duryard (since the 1930s known as the University of Exeter's Thomas Hall) are shown as rectangular buildings. 'Halfway House' was presumably demolished to make way for the railway only a few years later. The map-maker evidently did not walk further up the western side of the river Exe to Exwick Weir.

44. The map-maker made it as far as the top of Pennsylvania. Pennsylvania Park can be distinguished near the top as well as some of the prominent villas such as Portland Lodge and Moor View Cottage. Cobham (see Illustrations 89 to 94) was not yet built in the large field above Pennsylvania Park.

45. The top right-hand corner of the map includes the brief description of the map along with a compass point and the map-maker's symbols for roads, 'foot roads' (foot paths), water, churches, viaducts, viaducts and bridges, buildings and the city wall. Note there is no scale. He depicts the northern end of St Sidwell's parish including what is now Sylvan Road and Stoke Hill to the far right.

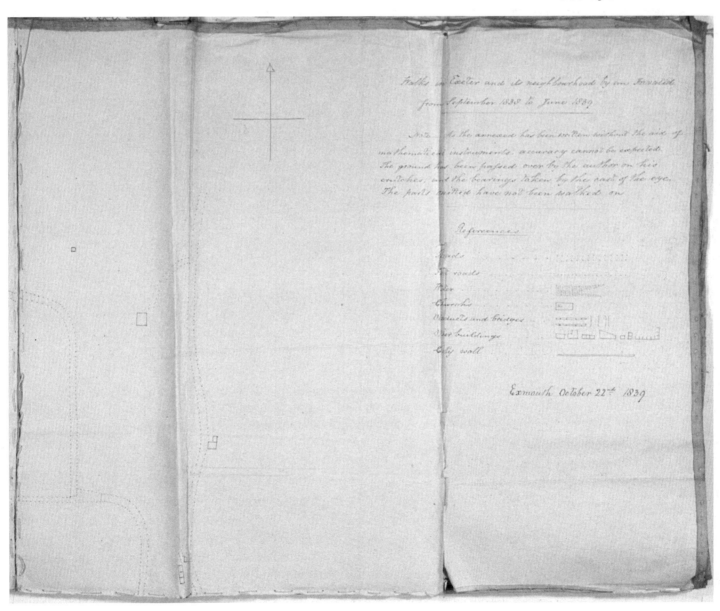

46. On the left is the village of Exwick with the mill noted. The right-hand side shows part of the parish of St David's. Only five years later the railway was brought through the valley on the eastern side of the river. St David's hill is on the bottom of the map with the parish church noted with a cross. Little Silver can be seen across from the church with Bystock Terrace in the corner. The road marked 'Elm Field' with its gate is New North Road with the Imperial Hotel shown as a large rectangular building. Peep Lane is seen leading down towards the river.

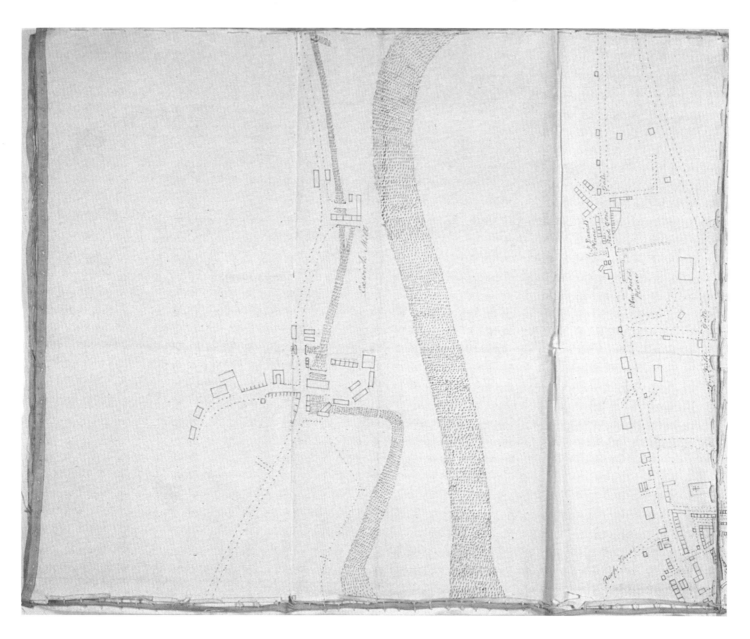

47. The county gaol and the barracks dominates what was a part of Exeter just being developed. The railway through the Longbrook Valley to Central Station was not carved out until 1860. The line of New North Road can be seen leading from the end of High Street just out of the map with the stables for the New London Inn later the site of the Theatre Royal. Longbrook Street, with the Black Horse prominently shown, leads up towards Hill Court and Hoopern Place (now Pennsylvania Crescent). Other new developments shown are Victoria Terrace and Devonshire Place off Union Road. The greatest concentration of buildings to be seen is around Sidwell Street, largely rebuilt after the Civil War.

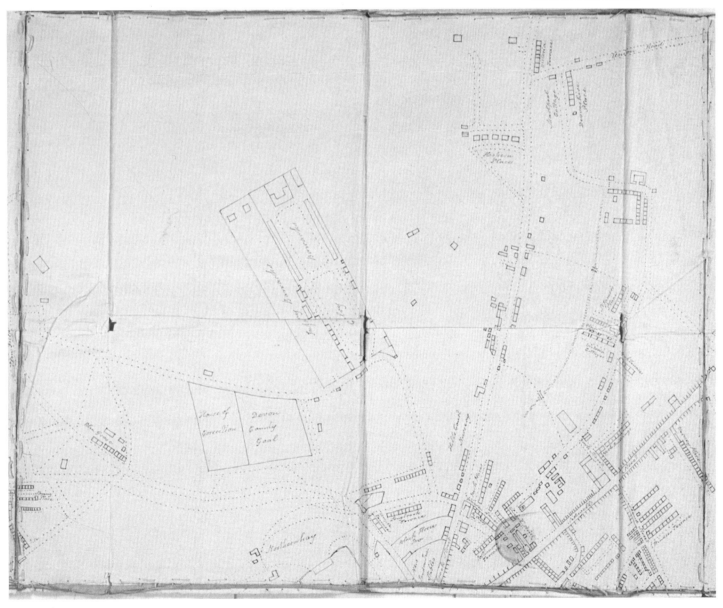

48. This section is dominated by the junction of Sidwell Street, Old Tiverton Road and Blackboy Road. The map maker identified recent developments such as Saluatory Place (now Belmont Road), Grosvenor Place, Coburg Place, Wellington Place, Hampton Buildings, Hopkins Buildings, Clarence Place, Rose Mount Terrace, St James Terrace and Clifton Terrace. Union Road can be seen at the top left running to its junction with Old Tiverton Road and Mount Pleasant Road. St James' church is also noted.

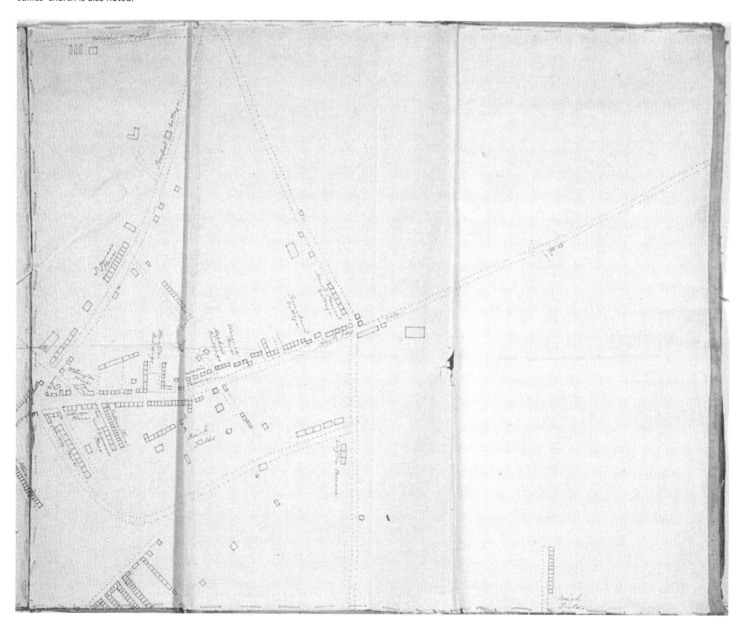

49. The map maker walked as far
as the end of Okehampton Road.
On the bottom right can be seen
Okehampton Place. The eastern
side of the river is more developed
including the cattle market along
the Bonhay and the series of leats
running off the river. The
eighteenth-century bridge (then
still relatively new) crosses the
river leading up New Bridge Street
to Fore Street. The line of what
became Bonhay Road can be
imagined along the river.

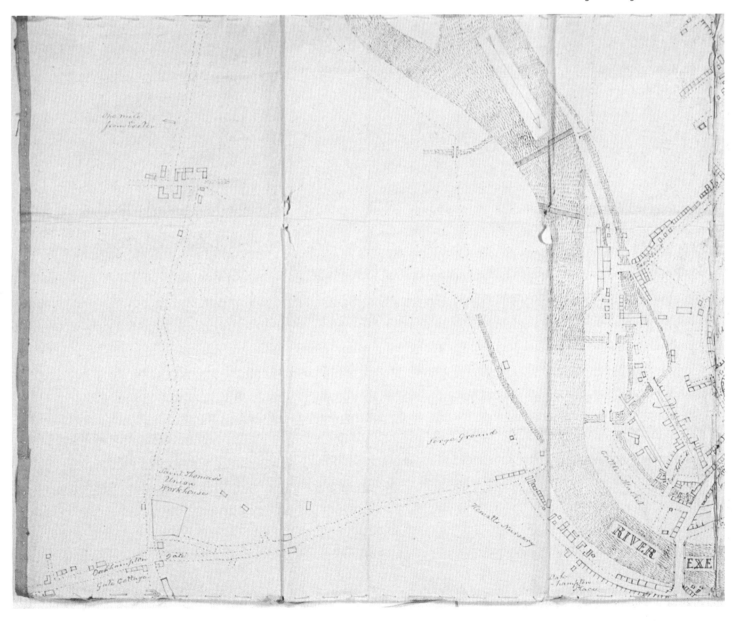

50. The Carfax (the junction of Fore and High Streets with North and South Streets) is at the middle of the left of the map with the cathedral seen to its right. At the bottom left is the line of the river with quay and the Customs House marked. Edmund Street with its church and row of houses can be seen (see Illustrations 67-71). St Leonard's parish is at the bottom right hand corner with Magdalene Street and Road leading off from the end of South Street. Between it and the cathedral are the newly built developments of Southernhay and Dix's Field. Bedford's Circus is also noted. Other recent buildings to be seen are Higher Market (along as yet unnamed Queen Street) and Lower Market at the top of Fore Street. The Iron Bridge, which was built four years earlier in 1835 to link St David's Hill and North Street, is shown.

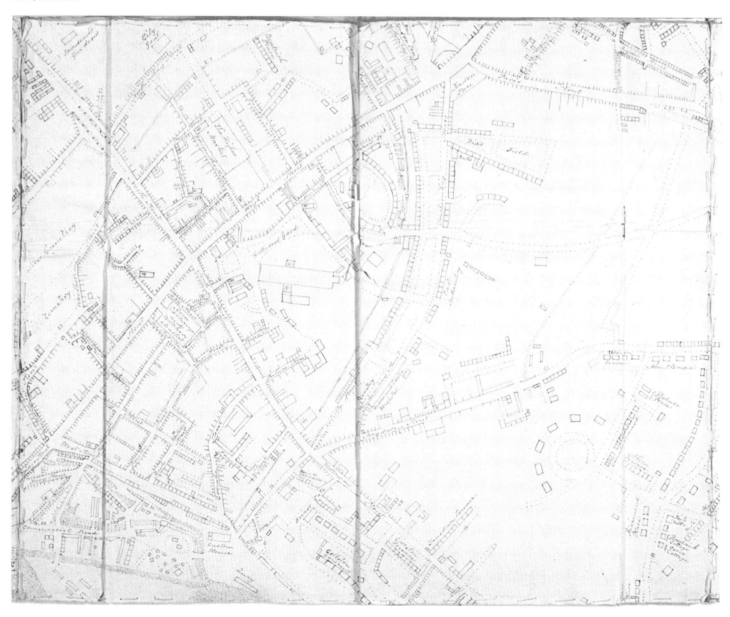

51. Near the centre of the map is the junction of Magdalene Road, Heavitree Road, Polsloe Road and Fore Street. In its centre are the Livery Dole almshouses. Baring Crescent can be seen to its left and the other prominent building is the city's late seventeenth-century Work House. The field in the bottom right hand corner is where the Royal Devon & Exeter Hospital was later sited.

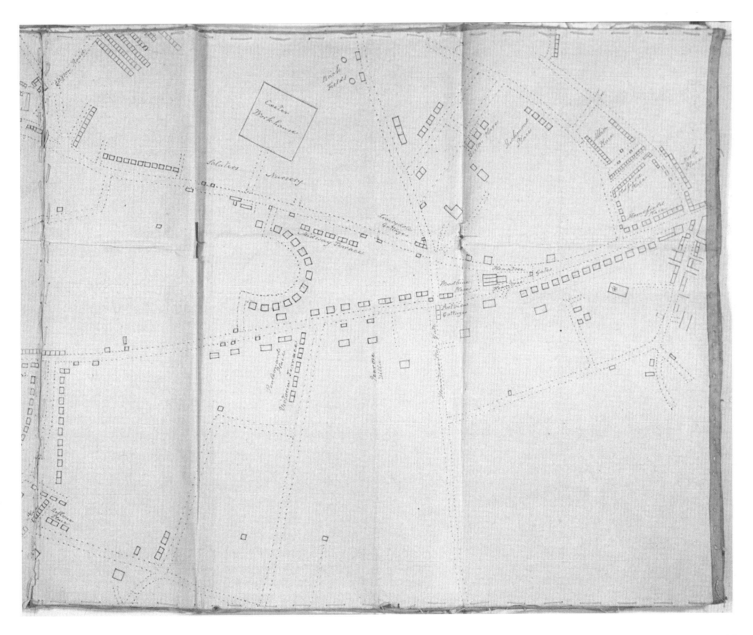

52. Cowick Street and the junction with Dunsford Road, Buddle Lane and Barton Road dominate the map. The eighteenth-century St Thomas Lunatic Asylum (later replaced by the Wonford Home for the Insane) is prominently shown at the crossroads and among the buildings noted on Cowick Street is the parish church. Alphington Road lies to the right with a string of cottages. The locations of three nurseries are indicated.

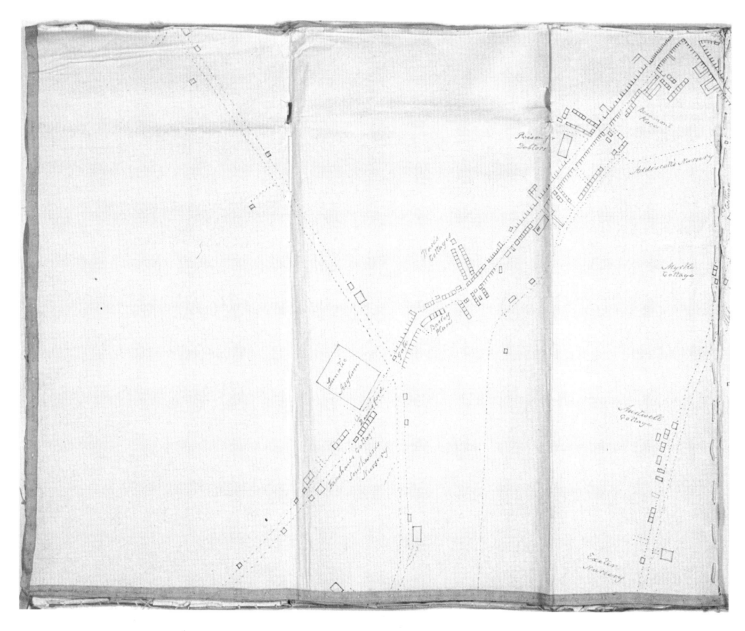

53. A map of mostly St Thomas with the river and part of St Leonard's to the right. The Basin, prominently shown, had only been built nine years previously and the canal is seen leading down to Topsham. Hampden Place and the road to Alphington is shown near the top left hand corner.

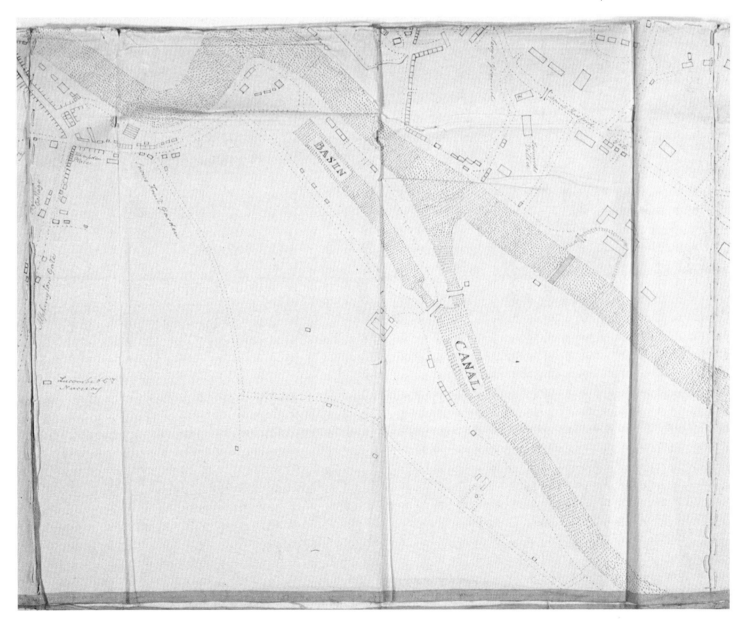

54. This map is dominated by Topsham Road which runs from Exeter on the left. The Artillery Barracks (now known as Wyvern Barracks) is prominently shown and the area where the Royal Devon & Exeter Hospital is now located is represented by open fields. Eleven years later the Royal Agricultural Society exhibition was held here.[46] One of the Veitch nurseries was located here and several villas are named. St James' Weir can be seen at the end of the river. The map maker may have visited Quick's Tea Rooms, a popular destination for Exonians walking along the river.

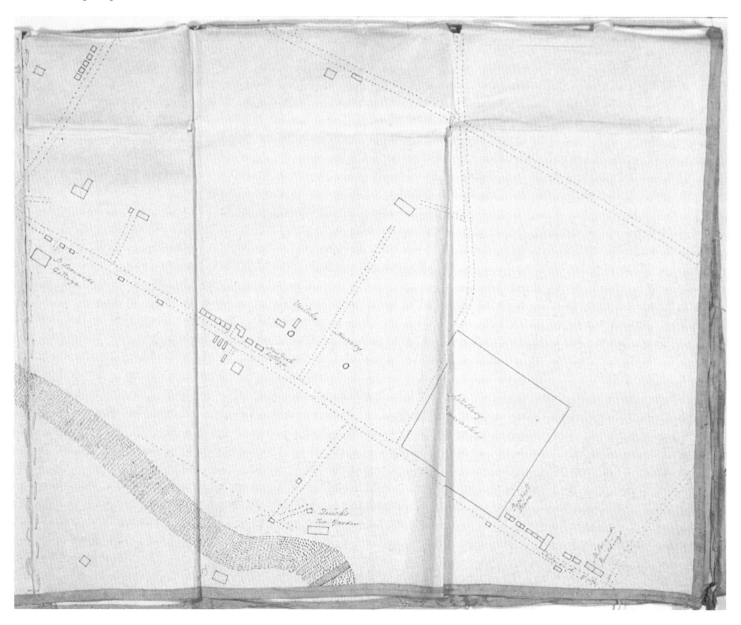

6. Buildings

Dix's Field in about 1840, Exeter Gaol in 1863, Broadgate in 1825, South Street in about 1834, Devon & Exeter Subscription Rooms in about 1860, row of houses on Exe Bridge in 1883, Abbot's Lodge in the 1870s and Larkbeare Mansion in 1889, Southernhay in about 1820, Mol's Coffee House in about 1834, Bystock Square in 1865 and Cobham in the mid to late nineteenth century

a. Dix's Field in about 1840

This is an unusual picture of one of Exeter's grand developments of the early nineteenth century. In 1796 John Dix planned to develop buildings on land which had been owned by his father, William Spicer Dix, a cloth merchant, for some twenty years. The site had a house, at least one garden and bowling green. Part of the land comprised a garden known as the Sicaccary.[47] The site was actually developed by Mathew Nosworthy, an Exeter builder.[48] He lived in Number Two.[49] Most of the buildings were destroyed during the second world war with the exception of Numbers Seven to Nine and two buildings at the southern end of the west range.

55. Drawing attributed to E. Jeffery and entitled 'Dixs', mid nineteenth century. The painting was made after 1828 as that year the iron gates had recently been erected.[50] The painting was part of Thomas Shapter's collection. See Illustrations 50 & 226.

In 1823 Number Five was described as 'newly built'[51] but the two rows of brick buildings were probably built as early as 1808. Number One was known as 'the Bow Window House'.[52] In 1851 the twenty-eight buildings were occupied by a variety of people including a magistrate, retired naval officer, schoolmaster, physician, accountant, barrister and several 'fund-holders' (people living off investments in public funds). Only eight of the heads of households were born in Exeter and the remainder came from Bath, Dorset, Windsor, Surrey, Cambridge, London, Ireland, Southampton and other parts of Devon.[53]

56-7. Photographs of Numbers 7 to 9, April 1969, which escaped the destruction of the second world war but were demolished in 1969 to make way for the Civic Centre.

b. Exeter Gaol in 1863

In 1819 the city's new gaol opened on the corner of Queen Street with Northernhay Street. It was needed because of the demolition of the prison at the end of South Street. The new building only lasted 57 years: in 1876 it was demolished and shortly afterwards the Rougemont Hotel was constructed. The drawing was made in 1863 when the building was made redundant by the construction of the new prison on New North Road.

On 13 June 1854 an anonymous writer described the prison in an article in The Western Luminary. The report was part of a series that investigated conditions for the poorer people of Exeter following the recent bread riots.[54] He noted that there were then 38 inmates of whom 4 were debtors and the remainder, including 9 females, were there for felonies, misdemeanours and other crimes. He wrote that 'in the county gaol a man gets up from his bed in silence, walks in silence, goes to chapel in silence, sits there in silence, is locked in silence, everywhere a death-like, desolating silence about him. In the city gaol there is no silence. The building outside looks something like a prison, but inside, all is domesticity – all is cheerful, except for the treadmill. The prisoner gets up with companions, breakfasts with companions, walks with companions, works with companions, laughs with companions, goes to church with companions, retires to bed with companions, everywhere he companionises, and is companionised'.

Of the treadmill he wrote 'this machine is capable of holding 16 persons, it is divided into 2 parts, one side for felons, the other for misdemeants. The former are attired in parti-coloured costume, the latter in plain grey. When we visited the prison there were 6 prisoners on the machine, and there they were with their backs towards the light, their faces towards the well-trod steps which they for ever clamber… All was blank, this work is regulated by means of what the officer called the 'beaters' which, when let down, impeded the motion of the wheel, and required more effort on the part of the prisoners to move it . . .'

He also wrote 'the sleeping apartments appeared exceedingly cheerful and clean, most of them

58. Sketch by George Townsend, 17 September 1863.[55]

commanding very pleasant views. We were informed that several prisoners slept together in one room, there being no sufficient accommodation for them otherwise. The Refractory Cell is a small room at the top of the house. When a prisoner misbehaves himself, he is shut up in this cell for a period not exceeding 3 days, the window being darkened during the whole of that time, while the offender is kept upon dry bread and cold water – his allowance per diem being one quart of water and one lb of bread. This discipline is generally found very effective, and the 'dose' is seldom repeated.'

59. Undated and un-attributed watercolour of prisoners being led from Rougemont Castle back to the gaol along Northernhay. One local man later remembered how they were brought eight at a time in chains and wearing heavy shackles. Four javelin men guarded them carrying spear-headed long staffs.[56]

c. Broadgate in 1825

These four views show one of the city's most substantial medieval buildings. The Broad Gate was demolished in 1825 because it was too narrow to allow coaches to safely pass through en route to the Hotel (shortly afterwards known as the Royal Clarence). There had been some controversy in pulling down this ancient gate, which stood between the Cathedral Yard and High Street, but as with all the other gates, the notion of progress won.[57] The four views show it in varying detail. Some of the paintings may have been prompted by the demolition of the gate. Smale's, on the eastern side of the gate, was a confectioners run by the Misses Smale by at least 1816.[58]

60. View by John Gendall, by 1825. The City Bank had been established in 1786.[59]

61. A second view of the
Broadgate which is also by John
Gendall, by 1825. There are slight
differences in the two images
including of the window near the
top of the gate. This once formed
part of Thomas Shapter's
collection.

62. This anonymous painting has also survived which shows a more extensive view.[60] It is entitled 'The Mayor, Chamber and Incorporated Trades of Exeter, going in procession to the Cathedral on the King's Birthday' and, unless it is a retrospective work, also must have been painted before 1825.

63. A second view, also by the
same painter, survives which
shows Broadgate in a similar way.

d. South Street in about 1834

This depiction of South Street, looking down Bell Hill (from the top of South Street which was also known as Cook Row), shows it just as the city's Improvement Commissioners were widening the street and removing impediments to traffic. The new Conduit, only erected a generation before, was taken down and removed to a site nearer to what became the Lower Market. Part of the range of buildings of the Vicar's Choral is shown behind the conduit. Many of the buildings shown were cut back from the street to increase the width for traffic.

64. Watercolour of South Street by George Townsend, c.1834.

e. Devon & Exeter Subscription Rooms, c.1860

The building was known as the Royal Public Rooms as well as the Royal Subscription Rooms, the Devon & Exeter Public Rooms and the Exeter Subscription Rooms. It was situated in London Inn Square near Northernhay Place and appears to have opened twice in 1820. Joseph Congdon, also the proprietor of the Hotel, some seven years later renamed the Royal Clarence, shortly afterwards became the owner and sold the building in 1839.[61] By 1870 it was owned by W. W. Hooper but occupied by Thomas Gardner. Gardner later purchased the building.[62] There were also Assembly Rooms at the

grave and gay mingle in the entertainment but the gay predominating most decidedly. The ballad singing is much admired, but the great attraction of those clever minstrels is the grotesque and the humorous, in which they excel. The queer melodies and energetic acting elicit peals of hearty laughter'.[66] After the death of John Gendall in 1865 an exhibition of his work was held in the Royal Public Rooms.[67] In 1908 the building became The Hippodrome, a High Class Music Hall', and accommodated some 1,080 patrons.[68] It was sold in 1925[69] and in 1931 reopened as The Plaza cinema.[70] This building was destroyed in the bombing of the city in 1942.

New London Inn and at the Hotel in Cathedral Yard.[63] The building was home to the Devon & Exeter Horticultural Society from its inception in 1829[64] and hosted many of the city's visiting entertainments including in 1865 Mr D'Arc's exhibition of wax work figures, which included the Chamber of Horrors featuring a dozen murderers,[65] and in 1867 there was Harry Clifton, the 'well-known buffo singer'. Two years later 'the slave troupe' appeared: it was said of them that 'the

THE SUBSCRIPTION ROOMS, A NEW LONDON INN, EXETER.

65. Anonymous watercolour, no date given but probably mid-nineteenth century. The painting was owned by Thomas Shapter who noted it as 'exhibition of paintings, subscription rooms'. See Illustration 215.

The first opening was prompted by a suspicious fire in March at the theatre in Bedford Street. It destroyed that building. The cause of the fire was not found but some questions were raised about a faulty chimney while others questioned the installation of a gas chandelier in the recent refurbishment. On 18 March, only a few weeks later, the manager of what was described as the 'new' Subscription Rooms announced in the local press that the theatre's productions would take place in his building. An unusual event which took place in April reveals that the building was still unfinished: three men took advantage of a ladder being casually left against the building in order to watch 'The Falls of the Clyde' possibly through the glass dome which is illustrated here. The ladder's unfortunate fall caused the death of a woman who happened to be walking by. In the local press the building was still described as new and it may have been that it was not expected to open until later that year.[71] Plays continued to be performed there for several months but on 17 October the first event of its own making happened with a series of concerts and a ball. The building had been erected by public subscription and had a ballroom which was 80 feet in length and 40 feet in breadth. The ceiling was 40 feet high.

66. Steel line engraving of the Subscription Rooms and London Inn Square, 1830.

f. Row of houses on Exeter Bridge, c.1883

The views of the row of houses on Exe Bridge were taken from New Bridge Street and show Cuckingstool Mill Leat leading to the bridge and church of St Edmund. In 1885 James Crocker thought it 'the most picturesque peep to be found in the city of Exeter'. But he also regarded the buildings as 'the black abodes of sin and shame' and wrote 'the houses in question gave shelter to a numerous community of probably a somewhat mixed character, till the local authority intervened and levelled all to the ground'.[72]

The houses were built by Jonas Bampfylde sometime in the late seventeenth or early eighteenth centuries on the medieval bridge when it was still in operation. They replaced earlier buildings. The area had been devastated during the sieges of the civil war. They were owned by the city and in the early eighteenth century the buildings were divided into different tenancies. In 1823 the five properties were measured as being (from left to right)

67-8. Two drawings of the properties, 1755 and 1823, from leases. The church shown is the earlier building which was reconstructed in 1834.

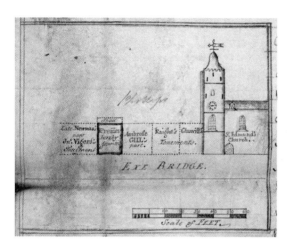

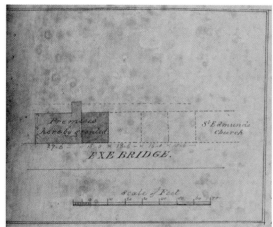

69. Drawing by James Crocker, 1879, which show the south fronts of the row of buildings and which can be compared with the views taken from the north.[73]

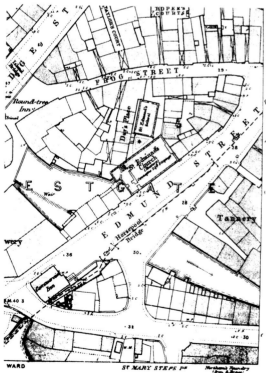

Map 1 shows Edmund Street in 1877.

fifteen feet, sixteen feet, eighteen feet, sixteen feet and twenty-seven feet six inches long. The last building was seventeen feet and four inches in breadth. The wooden porches overlooking the water were known as galleries.[74] The city authorities attempted to improve Edmund Street in the early 1880s.[75] In 1883 the adults of the street included a wood turner, laundress, sawyer, rag sorter, public lodging housekeeper, dyer, seaman, peddler, agricultural labourer, general labourer, stay-maker, moulder in iron and general dealer as well as three shoemakers, five hawkers and three paupers. Only eleven were born in Exeter.[76] In 1908 one writer[77] thought that the row had been demolished in 1883 but the process was already underway; there were 15 properties on the bridge listed through the 1870s but that year they fell to only six.[78] The houses against the church were actually pulled down in 1881 and nothing remains of them but images.[79]

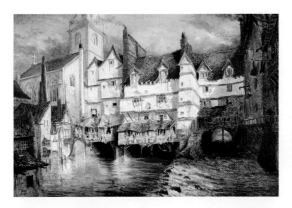

Four views of the bridge and its houses.

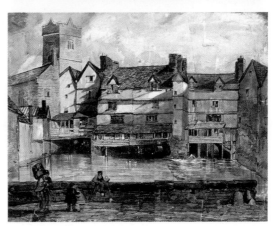

70. Watercolour attributed to Robert Medley Fulford entitled 'old houses on old Exe bridge and St Edmund church recently pulled down', 1883.

71. Anonymous watercolour, no date given.

72-3. Two watercolours by George Pycroft, no date given. Pycroft was a resident of Kenton.

g. Abbot's Lodge in the 1870s

The Exeter residence of the abbots of Buckfast Abbey was located behind Numbers Ten and Eleven in Cathedral Close. The building was constructed of Heavitree stone and was a medieval building, presumably reconstructed in the early seventeenth century. It was destroyed by the Nazi bombing of the city in the second world war.

74. Watercolour attributed to Edward Ashworth, entitled 'Residence of Mr Dawson, the Close, Exeter', c.1870s.

The Rolle family acquired the building at the dissolution of the monasteries and Cosmos III, Grand Duke of Tuscany, visited in 1669. The Rolles kept it until 1737 and it passed through several owners into the middle of the nineteenth century (Reverend Thomas Heskett in 1737 and then to his nephew Edward Chute, followed by Joseph Traine, James Rodd in 1775, Henry James in 1822, the Dean and Chapter in 1847 and the Ecclesiastical Commissioners in 1862). From 1861 to 1878 William Dawson, a civil engineer and land surveyor, was the tenant. The Reverend John Hellins followed him and afterwards the female members of the Hellins family ran a Kinder Garten school there until 1908.[80]

75. A drawing by James Crocker, 1885, which provides similar details.

76. A postcard printed by Thomas Burnett Worth, late nineteenth century.

h. Larkbeare Mansion, 1889

In 1889 the sixteenth-century Larkbeare Mansion in Holloway Street was largely demolished in order to build houses in what became Roberts Road and to widen Holloway Street. Six acres of land were developed to erect 239 'working men's dwellings'. Each house cost £31 to build.[81] Edward Ashworth, the Exeter-based architect who lived in Dix's Field, wrote on the history of the building and painted these three watercolours.

The largely Georgian front disguised the building's medieval origins. John Baring, the Exeter cloth merchant, bought the property in 1737 but the family remained there only until 1770 when they moved to nearby Mount Radford. The house passed through several owners until Mr George Diggines who was the last owner. The house had already been occupied by several different individuals and in 1889 Oliver Kingdon lived in the remaining part of the building. In the 1970s the house, now 38 Holloway Street, was faced with demolition but financial assistance from the Devon Historic Buildings Trust resulted in its renovation in 1979.[82] The building is now numbered 38 Holloway Street.

77. First of three watercolours by Edward Ashworth that is entitled 'Larkbeare House', 1889. The view looks back up Holloway Street towards the centre of the city with Lansdowne Terrace behind.

78. Watercolour entitled
'Larkbear House north front'.

79. Watercolour entitled 'Larkbear House Front to the street'. The view is looking south towards Topsham Road and Countess Wear. R. Hodge, located at 35 Holloway Street, was a dairyman.[83]

i. Southernhay in about 1820

An anonymous depiction of Southernhay, painted by 1825, that shows the complex of buildings in an unfinished state. This was one of the grand Georgian developments of Exeter along with Bedford Circus, Dix's Field and Pennsylvania Park. The suburb of St Leonard's was its continuation. Plans were made by the city in the 1770s to turn the open ground of Southernhay into homes for the wealthy. The top end had been the site for fairs and visiting attractions. The length of the green from Dix's Field to the Barnfield was occasionally used for the horse fair.[84] By the late 1790s the first houses had been built but many were re-mortgaged by the city in 1829 to pay for the extension to the canal and for the new basin.[85] By 1830 Southernhay had become the favoured place for Exeter people to promenade on Sunday evenings. Local residents were said to resent the noise.[86] Immediately to the left of the painting (out of view) is the site of what is now the United Reform Church, which was not built until 1868, but in 1821 it was occupied by the Public Baths.[87]

80. An undated and anonymous view of Southernhay that was once in the collection of Thomas Shapter, early nineteenth century. He noted that on the left it was the 'site of Chichester Place'. The view is looking south. Numbers 23 to 24 Southernhay East, the first buildings seen on the far left of the picture, were built about then. In the empty space to their left was erected Chichester Place (later known as Chichester Terrace),[88] a stucco terrace with a long portico with Greek Doric columns, in about 1825. In 1825 one of the houses, which had just been completed, comprised two parlours, a drawing room, six bedrooms, two kitchens, gardens and offices.[89] The next row of buildings, Numbers 25 to 27, were probably built in the late eighteenth century. Dean Clarke House in the middle distance with its cupola, opened as Devon & Exeter Hospital in 1742. On the right is Southernhay West and halfway along is the corner with Bedford Street. The entire terrace to the far right of the picture was destroyed during the second world war and replaced by Broadwalk House in 1974.[90]

j. Mol's Coffee House in about 1834

A series of images of one of the city's most prominent buildings which has had a history more interesting than the tales popularly told about it. In 1834 John Gendall, one of Exeter's most accomplished artists, leased what was described in 1949 as 'the most sketched of all Exeter buildings' (see Illustration 86). Gendall ran the building as a studio[91] and until recently it has continued to serve that purpose. It has been one of the city's most familiar buildings, partly because of its prominent position in Cathedral Close, but the last serious research was done in 1915[92] with the result that its history has been murky at best with several misleading stories told for some 120 years. Its actual history is much more interesting.

The building was originally part of the Annuellers' College,[93] or Annuellers' House,[94] named after the chantry priests who lived there until the late 1540s, and it extended as a single range of buildings to include Numbers 1-5 in the Close. The properties were sublet into different ownership after the Reformation with the result that the building was reconstructed at various times.[95] It is assumed that Mol's Coffee House (Number One) was rebuilt in 1596 because that date is on the coat of arms situated at the top of the building. This is a Victorian replacement, of about 1885, of a pediment with the carved arms of Queen Elizabeth together with her initials and the date 1596, that had been removed by 1806.[96] Internal building evidence confirms that the building may well have been reconstructed in the 1590s. The misleading feature is the Dutch gable which was added in about 1879.[97] The insertion of the gable and coat of arms were the work of Thomas Burnett Worth, who ran an art gallery in the building from 1873 until 1922 and who was also responsible for linking the building with Elizabethan heroes.

Some parts of the established history of Mol's are accurate: by the early 1800s it was an establishment that catered to gentlemen and run by subscription. One local man later remembered that in the 1820s it was a 'club for the county and city gentlemen'. A main attraction was that the national newspapers were brought direct from the London coaches. Seats were sited at the entrance and used for political and other gossip by men who were said in 1806 to be of 'the first distinction'.[98] One of the sketches of W. B. Tucker, whose caricatures feature in this book, is of a country squire at Mol's and is dated 1820. See Illustration 85.

But much of Mol's popular history is murky and some parts a mixture of half-truths and fantasy. Like other buildings that were open to the public, Mol's rented out its rooms for local meetings. For example, in the 1740s the committee of the Devon and Exeter Hospital met

there before the Southernhay hospital was finished.[99] Most likely other groups were there as well. This aspect of its history may have contributed to a story, unfortunately still repeated today,[100] that the building was used by Elizabeth's 'admirals'. It is even suggested that the meetings included strategy meetings against the Armada.[101] If these men, variously named as Sir Francis Drake, Sir John Hawkins, Sir Humphrey Gilbert and Sir Walter Raleigh, were at Mol's it would have been very newsworthy in 1596: in the autumn of 1595 Drake and Hawkins sailed for the Caribbean and died a few months later, Gilbert drowned thirteen years previously and in 1596 Raleigh was too involved in plans for the Orinoco or Cadiz to be in Exeter.[102] Moreover, in 1596 any discussions regarding the Armada would have been reminiscences rather than strategic meetings given the Spanish navy had been defeated eight years previously. Strangely, Exeter's thirst for a Drake association also has him frequenting a public inn near Mol's[103] but there is no evidence that Drake ever visited this inn, Mol's or even Exeter. We owe this fantasy to Worth: in the late nineteenth century he invented the tale about the 'sea dogs'. He fed this information to James Crocker[104] and Worth repeated it in postcards and in his own city guide. He claimed that, because of the arms on the building, 'the house was used as a club under royal authority for the nobility, naval and military commanders, and statesmen directly associated with the government of the realm'. It was, he wrote, 'only feasible to suggest that this old oak room . . . was the meeting room of the

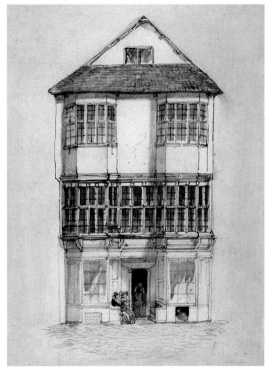

81. Pen and pencil drawing attributed to John Gendall, early to mid-nineteenth century, titled 'Moll's Coffee House afterwards Gendall's shop'. It was probably made just as the building was ending its period as a coffee house and about to have a longer one as an art studio: following the move of the coffee house to Castle Street, John Gendall, the local artist, occupied the building as a studio from 1835 until his death in 1865, after which Henry Hodge ran his 'bookbinders, stationers and gilders' there. Mr Worth then occupied it as a studio from 1873 to 1922. This view shows the building before the Dutch gable that was added in the 1870s. The drawing includes several people in the seats described by James Cossins and it comes from the collection of Thomas Shapter.

82. Second view, by Karl Wood, 19 April 1934. There was a second coffee house run by a woman named Moll. Moll King famously established her business near Covent Garden in London only three years or so after Mol's Coffee House in Exeter can be traced as being in operation. The two were very different: whereas the London business was a late-hours affair associated with prostitution, that in Cathedral Close has been credited with being highly respectable. It is unlikely that, given its location the coffee house shared a similar clientele of debauched gentlemen and their paid escorts until the early hours of the morning.[122] No doubt at least a few Exeter men were familiar with both businesses and possibly shared a wry smile over their differences. This may have been why the second proprietor was acknowledged as running the coffee house 'for many years . . . with great reputation'.[123] Other Exeter coffee houses had reputations for disorderly behaviour, including the West Gate Coffee House that, in 1854, was said on one occasion to have attracted 'a hundred women of bad character and others'.[124] There has never been any suggestion that Mol's was a similar establishment although in 1830 it relocated to what had previously been the centre of prostitution in Exeter. In the early 1700s Castle Street was, according to Andrew Brice, 'as infamous (formerly) for drabbing etc. as was ever the Surbura of ancient Rome, or are Drury Lane of London or Damnation Alley (as tis nicknamed) in Plymouth'.[125]

83-4. The two sides of a token for Brocas' coffee house, 1670. Achier Brocas married in the cathedral in 1656[126] and by 1660 lived in the parish of St Mary Major but there is no suggestion that he was connected to Mol's.[127] There could be a connection with the Turk's Head Inn that existed by the end of the seventeenth century.[128]

gallant captains . . .' and that they 'more than probable met in this same room for conference and debate'. He printed on the envelopes to his postcard series that Mol's was 'the old clubhouse of Raleigh and Drake'. Worth's reasons to encourage popular interest ('no visitor or tourist should pass through Exeter without paying a visit to this interesting relic of over 300 years') was to promote his own gallery in the building.[105] Some writers have expressed their suspicions about the myth[106] but many did not comment perhaps because in Exeter it was realised it was merely for visitors. Lately however many writers have accepted it without any discrimination.

Curiously, Worth was on the right track. Documents in the Exeter Cathedral Archives point to an unsuspected history of the building which correlates with the Elizabethan coat of arms. A new lease was granted by the cathedral authorities a few days before Christmas in 1595 to John Dyer. He was renewing his lease of 1585 and it seems too unlikely a coincidence that the coat of arms is dated the following year, 1596, when, it seems likely, the building was rebuilt. More intriguing is Dyer's professional activities: he had the status of a yeoman but in November 1588 Dyer was involved in negotiations with the government over the payment for the city's contribution of ships against the Armada.[107] His maritime interest is highly significant given a reference in a later lease, of 1661, which recounts the then recent history of the building. By that date the property had been converted into a shop: Edmond Thomas, an apothecary,[108] had divided it 'with doors, shelves, boards and other necessary things' for the use of an apothecary. The following year it was a shoe shop and by 1715 it housed a haberdasher.[109] However, before 1660 it served as the city's Customs House.

This most likely happened during Dyer's tenure which only lasted eleven years.[110] Dyer, in the last few days of 1595, planned the renovation of the building which presumably included hoisting the Royal Coat of Arms the following year to indicate the building had an official government function. It appears as though only the ground floor was rented as the Customs House.[111] It was not the city's customs house for long: The work of the customs officials had moved before the Restoration to another location, possibly Topsham,[112] and then in 1680 the city built its new Customs House on the quay.[113] Worth enlarged the history of the building, feeling a need to associate it with some of the period's leading figures, but the building did have a maritime role and indirectly an association with the Armada.

Whereas the story of a 'sea dogs' association can be seen to have been fiction, the identity of Mol remains the murkiest part of its history. It was first claimed 'from the accounts that can be gathered' nearly two hundred years ago, in 1806, that the coffee house was named after an Italian who was its first proprietor.[114] In 1886 James Crocker, a local architect, repeated that Mol was 'an Italian who doubtless found his way to Exeter during the palmy days of the woollen trade'.[115] At about the same time Worth wrote that the Italian Mol opened the coffee house during the Commonwealth.[116] Some writers have been suspicious of the Italian link; in 1927 Beatrix Cresswell wrote 'nothing is known of the reputed proprietor Mol who, in spite of his name, is said to have been an Italian'.[117] In 1940 W. G. Hoskins thought he connected the name of Thomas Mol with the property in 1595 but noted that he left shortly afterwards.[118] However, Hoskins placed Mol in a neighbouring parish and not the one in which Mol's Coffee House is situated. Neither the evidence of Hoskins or Jenkins can be identified[119] although it is possible that either was right.

Clearly the building was not an Elizabethan coffee house given they were not popular, in London or elsewhere, until two generations later. Exeter's first recorded coffee house was in 1670. A token survives for that date with the name Achier Brocas with a Turk's head on one side and a coffee pot on the other (see Illustrations 83 & 84). Worth's theory of the 1650s is more plausible than the 1590s and it is possible, though unlikely, that he had access to documents that have not survived.

There is another possible explanation for the identification of Mol. In the 1720s there were a number of other coffee houses in Exeter including Lewis Jones' in High Street,[120] Will's near the Globe Tavern[121] and 'Dick's Coffee House' in St Peter's Churchyard. In Exeter it may have been only men that ran the earliest coffee houses

85. Drawing by W. B. Tucker entitled 'The Country Squire, Mol's Coffee House about 1820'. One Exeter writer described another member of the club: Charles Sanders, a local banker, wore 'a wide brim hat, Newmarket cut coat, drab waistcoat, breeches and gaiters, and a neat white necktie. He would stand outside, with his hands in his pockets, the right one ready to be withdrawn to grasp a friend, his other hand with a coin in it ready for any poor or deserving person passing by.'[145]

86. Drawing by Harold Murray, 1949, entitled 'The most sketched of all Exeter's buildings – old Moll's Coffee House in the Close. St Martin's on the left.'

(in Taunton it was Graham's Coffee House)[129] but later women joined them as owners or proprietors.[130] It is probably significant that Mol's only had women in charge. The business seems to have begun in 1726:[131] the earliest confirmed year is derived from an advertisement in Brice's Weekly Journal in that December which gives the name Mol's[132] and in June of that year Mary Wildy was noted as having leased the building.[133] In 1824 it was claimed that Mol's had been in operation for 'upwards of a century past' which would confirm its origins to, at least, the 1720s. A lease of 1823 referred to Mol's having been formerly run by one Margaret Wildy:[134] undoubtedly she was related to the afore-mentioned Mary Wildy.[135] The naming of the coffee house could have originated with the first Wildy, Mary. It is unlikely to have been the Thomas Mol of 1596 or the 1650s, nor another Thomas Mol who in 1472 lived on the west corner of St Martin's Lane and the High Street,[136] but it is more probable that the establishment derived its name from Mol (or Mollie) being a common abbreviation of Mary. Margaret Wildy may well have kept the name as a family business.

Mol's was run by at least seven women during its history of just over one hundred years: Mary Wildy was followed by Margaret 'Wildier' who was at Mol's from the 1750s until 1787.[137] She had been there possibly as early as 1752.[138] No doubt these two women were related. Afterwards it was kept by Mrs Vinnicombe (1787 to 1789), Mary Murch (1789 to 1792), Miss Sarah Hurd (1793 to 1817), Mrs Mary Commins (1817 to 1832) and Mary Ann Crosse (1833 to 1837/8).[139] Great changes took place with the last two women. It was Mrs Commins who in 1830 relocated the business to the bottom of Castle Street.[140] She retained the name and

announced in local newspapers that she had moved to 253 High Street, the building at the western corner with Castle Street that was later the Adelphi Hotel. Coincidentally, this was the date at which W. Tucker, possibly the man responsible for a series of local caricatures, including the of a country squire at Mol's, gave up the lease on the building (see below, Illustrations 104-82). Until 1829 Tucker had run his business as a carver and gilder there.[141]

There were the final few years of Mol's Coffee House: James Cossins, a local man, noted in his memoirs that the 'club' closed that year. He could not remember why this had happened.[142] Commins' niece, Mary Ann Crosse, tried to continue Mol's Coffee House but in 1838 she was listed in the local directory as only having billiard rooms in Castle Street and Mol's Coffee House appears to have closed that year. The end of Mol's in Cathedral Close may have been hastened by competition for books and newspapers. Henry Ellis ran his Subscription Library nearby in High Street in 1819 and there was at least one other in the city, the Subscription Rooms were opened at Eastgate early in 1820 and, more importantly, the Devon & Exeter Institution opened only six doors away in 1814; not only did the Institution have newspapers like Mol's,[143] but it also offered books and better facilities. There was also the Public Select Library in High Street which opened in 1807.[144] These establishments both sought to appeal to city and country gentlemen.

The building has had a much more interesting history than the legends ascribed to it: in five hundred years it has been home to chantry priests, the city's Elizabethan Customs House, a Georgian coffee house run only by women for a full century and finally, a centre of art in the city for more than another hundred years.

87. Postcard by Worth of Mol's Coffee House, late nineteenth century.

k. Bystock Square in 1865.

This is a rare depiction of Bystock Square, part of the Victorian expansion of the city but not an area that attracted artists. The watercolour was taken from Number Ten, situated at the northern end of Bystock Terrace, known in 1865 as 'the Diggins'. The terrace was built in the 1840s following the creation of Queen Street in the mid 1830s.[146] The view looks towards the northern end of Queen Street where the Clock Tower is now sited.

88. Watercolour entitled 'view from ye Diggins, 10 Bystock Terrace', March 1865. There are illegible initials of the artist.

I. Cobham in the late to mid nineteenth century

Five views survive of Cobham, an unusual and largely unknown house between Rosebarn (formerly known as Rowe's Barn) Avenue and Pennsylvania Park. It was built in 1854 and three years later a plan was drawn of the house and gardens.[147] Cobham was built in a curious style that could be described as colonial cottage orné. It was sited on a slight rise with its garden falling below and dramatic views looking south towards the estuary. In the 1870s and 1880s Cobham was listed as being in Mary Pole Head and by 1890 in Mary Bow Lane.[148] The house was built for Dr Thomas Shapter, one of Exeter's most illustrious figures of the nineteenth century. He owned the house until 1882.[149] Shapter bought the land from the Feoffees of the parish of St Sidwell but public objections were made which appeared in the local newspapers and were investigated by the Charity Commissioners. It was claimed that Shapter acquired the land at too low a price but the sale went ahead. The land had been a field known as Whipping Field; it is unclear why it, located at the furthest end of the parish, was given this name but possibly it was connected with the beating of the bounds of St Sidwell's.[150] Shapter was born in Gibraltar in 1809 and died nearly a hundred years later in 1902 in Earl's Court. He was Exeter's mayor in 1848 but his chief contribution lay through his work at the Dispensary and his book on the history of the cholera epidemic in 1832. He later retired to Surrey and died largely forgotten in Exeter[151] but in 1883 Shapter was still remembered: it was pointed out in the local press that year that he was the only member of the pre-reformed city chamber of 1833 still living.[152] Shapter appears to have also lived at 21 Barnfield Crescent: in 1881, when he was aged 72, he was listed as retired and resident at Cobham unlike the census returns for 1861 and 1871. He was there with a housekeeper, gardener and cook.[153] Two years later, in 1883, the house was purchased by Charles Edwin Ware, a civil engineer and

architect who had moved from Sunnyside Villa in Howell Lane.[154] Over the next twenty years Cobham was occupied by a number of individuals for short periods of time: Ware was there between 1883 and 1886 as well as again in the early 1900s, in the meanwhile he leased it to W. E. Colebrooke in 1890 and to Lieut. Col. W. R. Purchas by 1895. John Edward Daw was in residence by 1916.[155]

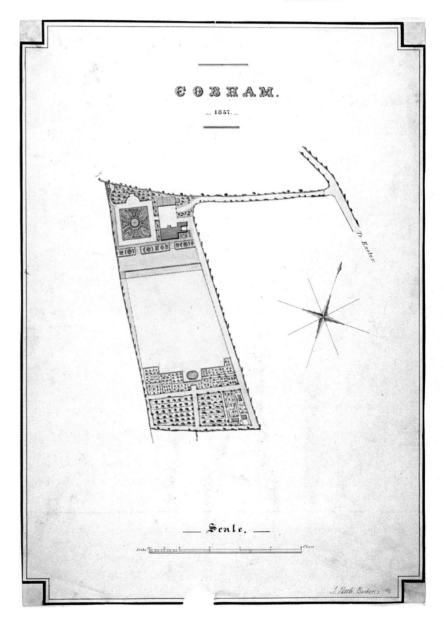

89. Plan of the house and grounds by J. Pattle Becker, 1857. 'Italianate' parterres were one of the features of the garden. See Illustration 44.

*90. Anonymous and untitled view
of Cobham, late nineteenth century.*

91. Untitled painting by F. Richardson, 1879. There are differences in the plantings shown here with more shrubs and herbaceous plants. Italian Cypress or possibly Incense Cedars were planted.

*92-3. Two paintings of the southern
end of the garden with views
looking towards the Exe estuary,
the bottom view is by A. Shelly,
1893.*

94. Undated painting of the parterre, attributed to John Gendall, located at the northern end of the garden near the house.

7. The river Exe in the nineteenth century

The following views of the river Exe show aspects of its commercial importance as well as its picturesque qualities. When the railway arrived in 1844 the river was still the city's main commerical thoroughfare but the level of traffic had already diminished.

95. A view of Exeter from the north west attributed to John Gendall, between 1816 and 1844. The painting was made before the railway arrived in 1844 and after the building of the 'pepper pot' church of St David's church of 1816 seen on the far left. There is considerable damage to the bottom, including to the figure and cows, as well as to parts of the city. See Illustrations 2, 43 & 46.

96. Watercolour attributed to John Gendall of the city from what was known as Shooting Marsh in St Thomas, by 1820. The South Gate, demolished in 1820, can be seen to the right of the cathedral. The building to the far right may be Colleton Crescent. The eighteenth-century bridge is on the far left and the building on the far right was 'Gray's'.[156] Charles Tozer's map of the city, made in 1792, shows it within its grounds.[157]

97. Untitled watercolour by John Gendall of the quay, early nineteenth century. The view is taken looking at the southern end of the quay. The prominent tower to the left of the centre of the skyline is most likely that of the church of St John on Fore Street. Colleton Crescent, shown to the left of the cathedral, was built between 1802 and 1814.[158]

98. An anonymous drawing of the quay from the south east in about 1860. The buildings to the right were known as Sheldon's and William's.[159] Rocque's map of 1744 shows lime kilns further to the right.

99. Watercolour attributed to John Gendall of the southern end of the quay, nineteenth century.

100. Watercolour entitled 'Coal Quay Bridge, with old buildings at the end of Coombe Street, since removed' by Emmanuel Jeffery, 1827. It is also noted 'wash from nature'.

101. Watercolour attributed to John
Gendall, mid-nineteenth century.
The cliffs of Collabear are on the
left and the 'mill on the exe' can be
seen to the right.

102-103. Two anonymous drawings of the Bonhay, no date given, where Bonhay Road now runs. The north-west corner of the city walls is shown with Snayle Tower, Bonhay Mills and the mill leats.

104. This self-portrait is entitled 'W. B. Tucker as Deputy Marshall of the Field at the Eglinton Tournament, 1839' and 'Day costume of a Deputy Marshall of the Eglinton Tournament, 1839'. It is difficult to identify this individual: a William Best Tucker was baptised at Devonport in 1829 and a William Tucker was baptised in Exeter on 2 August 1835. Unfortunately no artist, with that name can be identified in the 1860s. There were earlier Tuckers: W. W. Tucker ran the Devon and Exeter Gallery in 1825[161] and was a 'carver and gilder' at 253 High Street in 1828.[162] In the 1830s there was also Edwin Wallace, also a carver and gilder as well as a herald painter and, for a short while in the early 1830s,[163] W. B. and A. Tucker were also carvers and gilders at 5 High Street. But W. B. Tucker disappeared from Exeter after the 1830s. However, in the 1860s and 1870s there was an artist resident in Exeter with that surname: Frederick Wallace Tucker lived at Number 18, The Mint, from the late 1820s until his death at 64 in March 1876. He was listed in the 1861 census as an 'artist and teacher of painting and drawing'. His obituary noted he was known as Fred Tucker and ainted Devon scenery which were 'small but gems in their way'.[164] Tucker was baptised in Holy Trinity on 4 Sept. 1811 and his house was the family home. It seems implausible that these two were not connected given the death of Frederick Tucker coincides with the last caricature. Curiously, one drawing is of a young woman with the name Mary and coincidentally Frederick Tucker shared his home with his housekeeper, Maria Cummings, and her daughter Mary.[165] The caricature is of a young woman with whom he was personally familiar; he refers to her as Mary. Another is of an Abbess; Frederick Tucker's near neighbours were the Sisters of Mercy.

105. Tucker also drew the military men who were camped at Exeter in July 1873.

106. Undated view of crowd, with weighing machine.

8. Exeter people in the 1860s and 1870s: the caricatures of W. B. Tucker

Included in the holdings of the Westcountry Studies Library is a small bound volume of 83 caricatures of Exeter people drawn and painted between 1865 and 1875. These images are signed 'WBT' and the book has been attributed to one William Tucker.[160]

The caricatures are unusual in that there is no other collection similar for Exeter and although the drawings are not noted as being Exeter people, it is clear that this is a collection of people the artist knew in the city. The images are divided into two main groups with captions headed men the artist knew or women that he saw in the street. There are a few others, some of which are untitled. Many of them have a further caption and a few are in local dialect. Tucker drew eccentrics, people with deformities or pronounced body features, individuals who exhibited unusual styles of dress or fashions, and attractive young women. Not all are pleasant; some have particularly caustic descriptions, notably a West African

schoolgirl ('the fairest of the fair'), an older woman ('the miserable remains of an Exeter beauty'), and a Jewish woman ('Porky'), and several others poke fun at the expense of the individuals ('the new haycock style'). It may have been that these drawings, along with their captions, were meant to amuse a small circle of friends

107-110. Four portraits all headed 'Men I have known' and numbered one to four and dated, 1873, 1872, 1870 and 1873. Number Two is unusual among Tucker's drawings for its perspective and Number Four is presumably an Exeter fish seller.

111-114. Four further drawings in his 'Men I have known' series.

Number 5 is titled 'My excellent Papa' and is undated. Also see Illustrations 123 and 124.

Number 6 is entitled 'An Eccentric sketched from life' and is undated. Also see Illustration 114 and 122.

Number 7 is entitled 'Prince of Abyssinia sketched at St David's Station' and is undated. He appears to be wearing a veil. This was probably Dejatch Alamaeo, the son of King Theodore. In 1868 the young prince had been sent to England to be educated.[166] Presumably Tucker was aware that he would be travelling by rail and arrived there to draw him. Local people already knew of the Abyssinians because of Britain's military campaign there in 1867 and at least one local newspaper ran an editorial about the 'Christian savage' King Theodore.[167] They would have been intrigued by the contrast in the appearance of the young prince with the descriptions of his people in the popular press.

Number 8 is entitled 'The Shop Fuddler', 1871. A fuddler is one who tipples. Also see Illustrations 112 and 122.

with whom the artist was acquainted. Certainly some of the captions have lost their meanings over time. Tucker included in his book some other drawings including sketches of men brought to Exeter for military manoeuvres on Dartmoor in 1873, of the cathedral at night and of Donarth's Comet of 1858. There are two retrospective drawings: besides his self portrait of 1839 there is a drawing of a squire at Mol's Coffee House in 1820 (see Illustration 85). Most of his drawings show that he initially made a pencil sketch. They were made on slips of paper later placed in a bound book most likely by another individual. The original captions are reproduced in full with each picture.

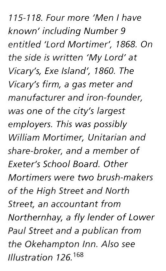

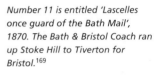

115-118. Four more 'Men I have known' including Number 9 entitled 'Lord Mortimer', 1868. On the side is written 'My Lord' at Vicary's, Exe Island', 1860. The Vicary's firm, a gas meter and manufacturer and iron-founder, was one of the city's largest employers. This was possibly William Mortimer, Unitarian and share-broker, and a member of Exeter's School Board. Other Mortimers were two brush-makers of the High Street and North Street, an accountant from Northernhay, a fly lender of Lower Paul Street and a publican from the Okehampton Inn. Also see Illustration 126.[168]

Number 11 is entitled 'Lascelles once guard of the Bath Mail', 1870. The Bath & Bristol Coach ran up Stoke Hill to Tiverton for Bristol.[169]

Number 12 is entitled 'The Church Militant returning from Wimbledon', 1870. In pencil 'Reverend Willm Brown'. Brown was the rector of Whitestone and presumably he is pictured carrying his tents home from a church rally on Wimbledon Common. Also see Illustration 122.

Number 13 is 'Mr Bold', 1870.

119-122. Four more in his 'Men I have known' include Number 14 entitled 'To sit in the sun and talk of bygone days', 1871.

Number 15 is entitled 'Railway G[illegible] Sir', 1870.

Number 16 is entitled 'Long Charlie', 1866.

Number 17, the title is illegible but could be 'Dormer & Pill', undated. In 1874 there was a Joseph Dormer residing in Rack Street who was an axle tree maker.[170]

123. Men I have known Number 18, 'Burton? Sir! Mine Host'. Also see following illustration and 111.

124. An untitled view of the same individual. Also see Illustration 111.

125. 'Dr R–'s £1 – 0 – 0'

126. Untitled. Also see Illustration 114.

127-130. Four drawings entitled 'Women I have seen'. Number 1 is titled 'Miserable weather' and 'returning home from the cattle show', 1872. This is one of several images of women walking in the rain with an umbrella.

Number 2 is entitled 'The Night' and 'The Crisis', undated.

Number 3 is entitled 'Pincher! Pincher! You Naughty Pincher!', undated

Number 4 is entitled 'An Unpretending style of hair', 1872.

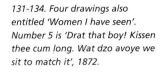

131-134. Four drawings also entitled 'Women I have seen'. Number 5 is 'Drat that boy! Kissen thee cum long. Wat dzo avoye we sit to match it', 1872.

Number 6 is entitled 'The Stepper', 1872.

Number 7 is untitled and undated.

Number 8 is entitled 'Lovely Abbess'. She may have been one of the Sisters of Mercy, possibly Julia Toll, the head of the group of ten, who were resident in The Mint.[171]

89

135-8. Four more 'Women I have seen' drawings. Number 9 is entitled 'An Blarney', 1869.

Number 10 is entitled 'The Cathedral Ghost', 1869.

Number 11 is entitled 'Miss Clink', undated.

Number 12 is of 'The New Alphington Ponies', 1872. The 'Alphington Ponies' were two eccentric sisters, the Misses Dunsfords, who returned to Exeter after having lived in Torquay. See above, pages 12-13 and Illustration 140.

139-142. Four further drawings in the 'Women I have seen' series.

Number 12 [sic] is entitled 'Porky', 1870. In pencil 'Solomon's'. The subject may have been the daughter of M. Solomon, an optician, who lived in 6 High Street.[172] The reference to 'Porky' is probably twofold. See also Illustration 161.

Number 13 is entitled 'The Queen Bends', 1870. See also Illustration 138.

Number 14 is entitled 'Miss – daughter of an English merchant in West Africa sent to England to be educated. The fairest of the fair', 1871. It is not certain whether this young woman was at a school in Exeter or another part of the country. There were several schools for girls in the city at the time but this individual has not yet been identified.

Number 14 [sic] is entitled 'The Giraffe', 1865.

143. The final drawing in the 'Women I have seen' series, numbered 15 and entitled 'My best bonnet'.

144. Drawing entitled 'Mary's Sunday Out. I wonder if that Roger chap 'es a looking after me'.

145-6. A pair of images entitled 'A day's difference The School Girl' and 'A day's difference The Nursemaid'.

147-50. *Four untitled and undated drawings.*

151-4. *Four more untitled drawings,*
1870.

155-6. Two untitled drawings.

157-8. Two drawings of the same woman entitled 'The streamers waving in the wind', 1870, and 'Hogarth's Lines of Beauty'. The latter is a reference to William Hogarth's use of a curved line in a self-portrait of the 1740s and on the title page of his The Analysis of Beauty that was printed in 1753. It is unclear what Tucker understood by his reference but Hogarth illustrated in his book a number of dancers' legs in which these lines are seen. In Tucker's own drawing the young woman is shown buffeted by a strong wind which reveals the lines not only of her legs but also of the small of her back.[173]

159. Drawing entitled 'A fishwoman of the period', no date.

160. Drawing entitled 'Lucky I thought of my Zumberreller', 1870.

161. 'A daughter of Israel', 1871. She was possibly the daughter of a member of Exeter's Jewish community with the surname Israel. See Illustration 139.

162. Drawing entitled 'The Gentle Ophelia, Miss Glazen'

163. Drawing entitled 'The miserable remains of an Exeter beauty', no date.

164. An untitled drawing.

165. Undated drawing entitled 'A reminiscence of a charming face'.

166. 'Caroline', 1870.

167. Drawing entitled 'Prodigious! The new haycock style', 1870.

168. Drawing entitled 'A Savan, Mr Golding', 1873. It is uncertain in what capacity Mr Golding was a man of learning. 'English tokens' is also written which could refer to the list of tokens added at the end of the book, possibly by another hand.

169-170. Two untitled and undated drawings of two women.

171. Drawing entitled 'Pantomime', 1876. Miss Minnie Barrier played the Fairy Dewdrop in 'The Babes in the Wood' at the Theatre Royal in 1875-6. See Illustration 248.

172. Drawing entitled 'infant prodigies', 'Children in the Wood', no date given. These were presumably the child actors in the pantomime of 1875 to 1876.

173-4. Two drawings entitled 'Mace bearer, Exeter' and 'The Sword Bearer, Exeter', both undated. See Illustrations 253-4.

175-8. Four drawings entitled 'Hats!', 1871. Tucker appeared to have been particularly interested in the fashions of young women.

179-182. Four drawings in a different style, all undated and unsigned, possibly not by Tucker.

9. Exeter in 1949: the drawings of Harold Murray

183. Drawing entitled 'A familiar police warning in 1949 – but time did more damage than young vandals'.

Murray was a journalist who lived for a few years at The Glendale Commercial Hotel, 8 St David's Hill.[174] He first came to Exeter in 1946 when the city's redevelopment plans were on public show (he thought the majority of locals were of the opinion that the scheme was 'Very nice, but we shan't live to see it'.) and subsequently stayed. Murray had worked as a journalist on the *Sunday Pictorial*, *Great Thoughts* and *The Christian Age* but his first long article went back to 1901 when he covered the funeral of Queen Victoria.[175] His first book was published shortly afterwards: *The Letters of a Ridiculous Optimist* appeared in 1905. By the mid 1940s he had written some twenty-five books,[176] this includes *End of the World?* which was printed in Exeter.

Murray was obviously enthusiastic about Exeter and left a collection of drawings which he entitled 'amateur snaps of Exeter and District in 1949' and also 'A collection of rough drawings mostly made in the street,

184. A drawing of an Exeter eccentric.

1949'. One of them was drawn in March 1948. The year 1949 was an interesting time to record the city given that it was adapting to life after the blitz but anticipating the great redevelopment. Interestingly, he was not familiar with Exeter before the bombing, which he referred to as 'that dread avalanche of hell', but keenly felt the loss of the city.

Murray made his drawings on miscellaneous slips of paper and then pasted them into a book. He indicated on some of the drawings that he drew them on the spot.

Some are reminiscent of L. S. Lowry. Murray often displays a touch of humour as well as affection for his adopted city. There are a few sketches of eccentrics, and he seemed fond of drawing a dark-haired woman in a red dress, but he seemed mostly interested in how the city had adapted after the devastation of the war. For instance, he noted in the following poem, as well as depicted in many of his drawings, that signs were erected along High Street to indicate where buildings and their businesses once stood. Although not as clinical as black

& white photography, the personal character and freshness of his coloured drawings gives the destruction of the city a great impact. Murray's own captions are given in inverted commas and in some places additional text has been supplied afterwards.

185. 'Panoramic view of the High Street, 1949, from back of Telephone Exchange.'
'New Road now being made here.'

186-7. 'Two rough drawings showing Lloyd's Bank corner before a new road was begun in 1949… Blitzed High Street, with ruins of Burton's establishment on the left.'

188. 'The last pleasure fair held in the High Street'

189. 'A view from Northernhay Gardens. The building top left is the Odeon Cinema'.

The following poem was, according to Murray, his attempt 'to picture a stricken but forward-looking city'.[177]

Exeter in 1946

Wounded at heart, the fine old city stands,
Still torn and scarred like any battlefield;
Yet undismayed, as one who stoutly braved
Many a shock, and many an angry storm.
Landmarks once prized have disappeared from view
Gone in a night; crude signboards mark the spot.
Like gravestones, showing where the shell has laid
Since that dread avalanche of hell . . .
To dark antique shops touring visitors come,
Explore, and say 'Gee, that is vurry cute!'
Stoop, entering Raleigh's favourite inn.
Give old Moll's coffee house a hasty call,
Discover Roman well in bookman's crowded store.
Learn history in the venerable Mint.
The famous Guildhall's much-prized portico
Still proudly juts out in the narrow street,
Thence, on occasion, civic fathers wend
Their solemn way to the Cathedral Church
With all the colour, pomp and circumstance
That no blitz ever could eradicate.
Within the fane, is silent spaciousness,
Yet everywhere the enemy has struck . . .
These lovely arches echo, as of yore,
The pure, sweet voices of the choir boys
Where praise has sounded night a thousand years.
From the once brilliant Minstrels' Gallery
Carols are sweetly sung at Christmastide.
Quite undisturbed, the Astronomical Clock
Slowly proclaims th' inexorable march of Time.
Beneath is seen a stout old oaken door
In which, some centuries ago, was made,
By solemn order of the Bishop, a small hole
For the convenience of the Cathedral cat!
High above all, the noble Norman towers
Calmly survey the modern vandal's work,
Piles of red stone from ancient, hallowed shrines,
Havoc quite clearly irreplaceable . . .
The Exe still peacefully flows on to the sea,
The tide of life is not one moment stayed.
The pride of Glorious Devon is intact,
In old age has its visions, and its Hope.

190. 'All that was left of St Lawrence, High Street, when workmen began demolishing in July 1949. Many of the graves were very old. They were removed to a place of safety. St Lawrence dated back to the 13th century.' The only reminder of the church is a plaque on the wall.

191. 'The ice cream seller in front of Messrs Burton's premises in High Street.'

192. 'Nearly opposite, the old St Stephen's Bow.'

193. 'From the Cathedral Close. This rough sketch is put in to show how South Street, the blitzed market, obelisk and waste ground (mostly used as a cark park) looked in 1949. The church is St Olaves in Fore Street.' The Lower Market, built in the late 1830s, was destroyed by the bombing in the 1940s and replaced by the current St George's Market in 1960.

194. 'The blitzed site in the street, near North Street and South Street, which was the subject of much controversy in 1949 owing to the use of it by visiting traders, who paid no fees (they were banished during the Industries Trade, 1949).' The view is of the north side of the top of Fore Street across from St George's Market.

195. 'The Old Mint Methodist
Church'. The church was taken
down and replaced by the current
building in 1969-70.[178]

196-7. 'Part of the blitzed [Lower]
market is shown in these sketches.
It was opposite the site shown on
the left.'

198. 'The Market, Queen Street'

199. 'Goldsmith Street' looking towards High Street. Goldsmith Street is hardly recognisable. It was redeveloped as part of the Guildhall Shopping Centre in the 1970s.

200. 'In the market' at Higher Market on Queen Street.

201. 'Civic Hall platform (before the Hall was renovated)'.

202. The market.

203. The Civic Hall was situated on the northern side of Higher Market on Paul Street and was a popular venue for events in the city.

204. 'Quaint old shop in Paul Street (demolished December 1949).' Paul Street was subsequently cleared of its old buildings and now must vie for the title of the ugliest street in Exeter. Just as Queen Street is Exeter's best example of a Victorian street, this is now completely a legacy of 1970s and 1980s design.

205. 'The gloomy entrance to St Thomas Station.'

206. `Entrance Hall, Central Station' on Queen Street.

207. Northernhay Gardens

208. 'Paul Street where there were new bus parks in 1949. Information Bureau at the corner.' The church of All Hallows on the Walls can be seen in the distance but nearly every building has been demolished with the notable exception of what was the Crown & Sceptre public house at the bottom of North Street (now known as the City Gate).

209. 'The Rougemont Hotel.' This is Exeter's grand railway hotel of the nineteenth century which opened in 1879. In its first seven months it had 4,175 visitors and made a profit of just over £94.[179] On 28 January 1949 the mayor of the city gave a speech in which he said 'there are big days ahead for Exeter. I know there is not much to show now. But a start has been made – a start in building out of the ashes, and the heaps of rubbish a city which will eventually show that those who have planned have done wisely and well. Exeter of the future will exceed in glory and splendour anything of the past'. See Illustration 58.

210. 'The congested entrance to the temporary General Post Office.' The Post Office was then sited in Queen Street.

211. 'A sketch made in Northernhay Garden'.

212. 'Sidwell Street, from St Anne's and the Fountain. Odeon Cinema is on the right.' The fountain is still situated at the beginning of Black Boy Road.

213-214. *'Part of a panoramic view of the blitzed Sidwell Street, from St Sidwell's ruined church. In spite of opposition the little radio station store seen above retained its position during the war and afterwards.'*

215. 'Hereabouts six or seven roads conveyed in 1949, a plan was produced for the formation of a new square and sunken garden. Sidwell Street in the centre, the Savoy Cinema on the left. On the blitzed site in the foreground the Plaza Cinema used to stand.' See Illustration 65.

216. 'The first of the temporary shops built at Eastgate facing the High Street. A pretty garden was made by the city wall.'

217. *'Impression of Industries Fair, Sidwell Street, 1949.' The fair was held in September.*

218. *'Ruins of St Sidwells, which had a fine tower. A temporary church was erected in 1949'. See Illustrations 1 & 32.*

219. 'A new view of Cathedral from South Street.'

220. 'Motor cars before the West Front were almost too modern, but very profitable.'

221. 'In July 1949 the once busy
Bedford Circus was cut up in the
preparations for the new road. And
at this spot Princess Elizabeth later
unveiled a tablet commemorating
the event.'

222. 'Sunset view of Bedford Circus
as it was early in 1949.'

223. 'This rough sketch shows how
in 1949 the work of making the new
Exeter was begun at Bedford Circus
with preparations for a new road
into the High Street.' The first work
at Bedford Street began in early
January.[180]

117

224. 'Southernhay from Eastgate, had a melancholy appearance in 1949. On the right is part of the old city wall.' See Illustration 84.

225. 'The Devon & General Hospital'. The mid-eighteenth century building in Southernhay was subsequently replaced by the building of the new hospital in Wonford. See Illustration 80.

226. 'What Dix's Field looked like in 1949. The ruined Congregational Church at the corner, where later a small garden of remembrance was made.' See Illustration 55.

227. 'Municipal offices in Southernhay.' See Illustration 80.

228. 'Bridge near Cathedral'

229. 'Congregational Church, Southernhay (formerly Methodist)'. The church suffered heavy damage during the war. See Illustration 80.

230. 'A sketch on the spot during the big tannery fire in July 1949, West Quarter, opposite St Edmund's.' Tremlett's was located at 19 Commercial Road and in Edmund Street.

231. 'Site of West Gate and Old House, now demolished.' On this site was placed 'The House that Moved' in 1961.

232. 'The old Penniless bench' outside the church of St Mary Steps. The original bench was taken away in 1757. It acquired its name from the 'idle and disorderly' people it attracted.[181]

233. 'The old Tudor House.' The 'Tudor' House is thought to have been built in the mid to late seventeenth century.[182]

234. 'Old water mill at Cricklepit in the West Quarter'.

235. 'St Mary Steps. Matthew the Miller clock.'

236. *'Fore Street, near Exe Bridge'*

237. *'One of Exeter's curious canals, West Quarter.' A view of one of the city's ancient leats.*

238. *No further caption was made of Prospect Steps which lead down to the quay.*

239. 'The ferry' between the quay and the western bank of the river. See Illustrations 97 to 100.

240. 'Industrial Quarter down by the river.' This was drawn in March 1948.

241. 'The Public Swimming Bath [in Heavitree Road], from the Café.'

242. 'In the High Street (still queuing for papers in 1949).' The Express & Echo was located at 226 High Street between Queen and Gandy Streets.

243. 'Pennsylvania, Cricket Ground' located on Prince of Wales Road.

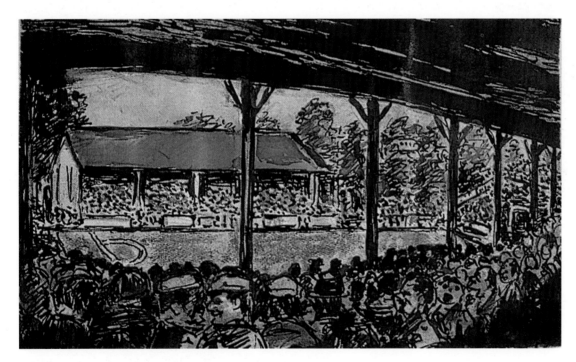

244. 'St James Park, football yard' on St James Road, home of the Grecians.

245. 'Part of the front of the University buildings in Gandy Street, half hidden by surrounding buildings'. The University of Exeter (then the University College of the South West) was then located partly in what is now the Arts Centre.

246. 'Bury Meadow', the public park on New North Road, which was used during the cholera epidemic of 1832.

247. 'A Sunday evening religious service at Northernhay (prison in background)'

248. 'The Theatre Royal (twice burned down).' The theatre survived the bombing of the city in the 1940s only to be demolished in 1962. On the evening of 9 February 1949 an eighty-one year old woman visited the theatre for the first time since it was rebuilt. She was last there more than seventy-five years before in the previous building which was destroyed by fire in 1887. Her father had been a fire fighter.[183] See Illustrations 171 & 172.

249. 'The Central Library. Gutted in 1942 and the temporary landing department (redecorated 1949).' The city's library in Castle Street was a casualty of the bombing with a great number of books lost to fire. In June 1949 the city received a gift of 2,500 books, many of them classics, which began to fill the great gaps in the city's collection.[184]

250. 'The Staircase of the Public Library as it was in 1949.'

251. 'At the opening of the time-honoured Lammas Fair a stuffed white glove was hoisted on the Guildhall in accordance with ancient custom'. The opening ceremony was on 19 July. See Introduction Illustration 6 and Illustrations 34 and 251.

252. 'Houses in Waterbeer Street.' The houses can still be seen, encased by the Guildhall Shopping Centre.

253-4. 'The famous cap of maintenance, carried to and deposited in the cathedral on special occasions.' More than five hundred years later, Henry VII's gift can still be seen in the Guildhall. See Illustrations 173-4.

255. 'The children loved the 18 foot giraffe in the Museum.' Gerald the Giraffe, a bull Masai, has been in the museum since 1919.

256. 'Upper Gallery, Museum.'

257. 'Visitors to Exeter in 1949 were always asking why a modern church was even built right up against the Cathedral, completely spoiling (as this sketch shows) the view. The answer was that for centuries an old parish church stood on the site. In the new Exeter plan it was suggested that St Mary Major should be removed, but it was expected to remain here for many more years while more important works were carried out.' The Victorian church was demolished twelve years later in 1971.

258. 'Old Houses in the Close' in the western side of Cathedral Yard.

259. 'Old figure of St Peter, for many years seen in High Street.' The medieval statue was moved from its position on the eastern corner of High and North Streets for safety during the second world war and returned in 1946.[185] In 1983 it was moved to the Royal Albert Memorial Museum where it can be seen today.[186] The empty niche can still be seen high above the crowds of oblivious shoppers.

260. 'Old house in Frog Street.' The house was demolished to make way for Western Way in the 1960s.

261. 'All that remains of the old St Kerian's church. It was not blitzed but was demolished fifty years ago. There is an old bell which never rings, though it is said to have come loose and sounded once during the war.' The church stood on the eastern side of North Street.

262. 'A snap in Woolworth's.' There were two branches of Woolworth's in Exeter in 1949; one was located in Sidwell Street and the other between High Street and Waterbeer Street.

263. *'An impression of the Iron Bridge as seen from North Street (up St David's Hill towards St David's Station). The bridge, which is not able to bear very heavy traffic, cost £3,500. The lower road takes one under the bridge into Exe Street.'* See also Introduction, Illustration 8.

264. *'House in Bartholomew Terrace'* near Bartholomew Yard.

265. *'All Hallow's, in 1949 used as a factory.'* The church of All Hallows on the Walls was built in Bartholomew Yard, the Victorian replacement cemetery for the city, but it was demolished a year later in 1950.

266. *'St Michael's spire, a fine landmark, from the Iron Bridge.'* The tower has been a prominent part of the city's skyline since the late 1860s when the chapel of ease was built.[187]

Notes

1. Todd Gray, *Lost Exeter: Five centuries of Change* (Exeter, 2002), 22.
2. Westcountry Studies Library (afterwards WSL), Exeter listed buildings survey.
3. *Exeter Flying Post* (afterwards *EFP*), 6 1 1825.
4. *The Western Times* (afterwards *WT*), 4 2 1949.
5. Sabine Baring-Gould, *Devonshire Characters and Strange Events* (1926), 16-17.
6. *The Alfred*, 4 11 1823.
7. Four illustrations from his memoirs were published in 1978. This includes two of the portraits of Henry and Mary Ellis: Clive N. Ponsford, *Time in Exeter* (Exeter, 1978).
8. *Exeter Plymouth and Gazette* (afterwards *EPG*), 3 11 1865.
9. Todd Gray, *Exeter Engraved* (Exeter, 2000), II, 11.
10. P. H. Hulton, 'Drawings of England in the seventeenth century by Willem Schellinks, Jacob Essens and Lambert Doomer' (Walpole Society, 1954-6, vol. 35, part one), xix.
11. See Gray, *Exeter Unveiled*, 2.
12. Exwood and Lehmann, *Schellinks*, 112.
13. Maurice Exwood & H. L. Lehmann, *The Journal of William Schellinks' Travels in England, 1661-1663*, (Camden fifth series, vol. 1, 1993), 112; W. G. Hoskins (ed.), *Exeter in the Seventeenth Century: Tax and Rate Assessments, 1602-1699* (Devon & Cornwall Record Society, NS, vol. 2, 1955), 53.
14. Exwood and Lehmann, *Schellinks*, 111.
15. Ellis wrote full details of his life in the eight journals. For a synopsis see Clive N. Ponsford, *Time In Exeter* (Exeter, 1978), 126-48.
16. Devon Record Office (afterwards DRO), 76/20/8, pages 2-3, 7.
17. *EPG*, 15 11 1867.
18. *EPG*, 2 9 1854.
19. Census for St Leonard's parish, 1851.
20. DRO, 76/20/8, page 7.
21. *Exeter Pocket Book*, 1823.
22. *EFP*, 26 9 1777, 28 9 1781, 4 10 1782, 21 9 1778, 30 9 1784.
23. *EFP*, 4 5 1815, 6 2 1845.
24. *EFP*, 20 10 1823.
25. *The Alfred*, 28 10 1823.
26. *Besley's Exeter Book*, 1829; *EFP*, 11 12 1828.
27. *EFP*, 1 2 1810.
28. *EFP*, 30 9 1819, 26 9 1822, 4 10 1827.
29. Gray, *Lost Exeter*, 68, 44, 48.
30. *EFP*, 9 11 1881.
31. Todd Gray, *Exeter: The Travellers Tales* (Exeter, 2000), 158.
32. James Cossins, *Reminiscences of Exeter fifty years since* (Exeter, 1877), 66-8.
33. *EFP*, 11 11 1852.
34. *EFP*, 10 11 1853.
35. *Exeter and Plymouth Gazette*, 8 11 1867.
36. *EFP*, 30 9 1893, 6 11 1897; *Devon Weekly Times*, 6 11 1896.
37. *EFP*, 8 11 1876, 10 11 1880, 7 11 1877.
38. *EFP*, 7 11 1877.
39. *EFP*, 9 11 1881.
40. *EFP*, 10 11 1875, 6 11 1861.
41. *EFP*, 8 11 1849.
42. *EFP*, 10 11 1880.
43. *EPG*, 13 11 1819.
44. *EFP*, 10 11 1875, 9 11 1881.
45. *EFP*, 10 11 1875.
46. Gray, *Exeter Engraved*, I, 200-204.
47. DRO, 53/6, box 88; 74/3/341; D7/282/16-21; D5/73/1.
48. W. G. Hoskins, *Devon* (1954), 139.
49. WSL, 1851 census.
50. *Beasley's Exeter Pocket Guide*, 1828.
51. *EFP*, 6 5 1822, 2 12 1822, 25 9 1823.
52. DRO, D7/498/1.
53. WSL, census, St Sidwell's parish, 1851.
54. For the other reports see Todd Gray, *The Victorian Under Class of Exeter* (Exeter, 2001).
55. WSL, p&d 04979.
56. Cossins, *Reminiscences*, 59.
57. Gray, *Lost Exeter*, 48-9.
58. *Exeter Pocket Book*, 1816.
59. Robert Newton, *Eighteenth Century Exeter* (Exeter, 1984), 67.
60. DRO, 68/28.
61. *Beasley's Exeter Pocket Guide*, 1828; *Woolmer's Exeter and Plymouth Gazette*, 15-22 6 1839; Newton, *Eighteenth Century Exeter*, 144.
62. DRO, city rates, St David's parish, 1870.
63. *EFP*, 16 12 1819.
64. John Caldwell, 'A Provincial Horticultural Society', *Devonshire Association Transactions*, 1960, XCII, 104-6.
65. *EPG*, 17 2 1865.
66. *EPG*, 18 4 1867; *WT*, 26 2 1869.
67. *EPG*, 3 11 1865.
68. *Devon & Exeter Gazette*, 15 11 1925.
69. W. G. Hoskins, *Two Thousand Years in Exeter* (Exeter, 1960) 121.
70. Stuart Smith, *The Cinemas and Theatres of Exeter* (Wakefield, 1994), 9.
71. *EPG*, 29 4 1820, 18 4 1820.
72. James Crocker, *Sketches of Old Exeter* (London, 1886), plate V.
73. DRO, D5/104/1-5; D2/276.
74. DRO, ECA 9/6, bk/515.
75. WSL, census, St Edmond's parish, 1881.
76. George Townsend and W. R. Best, *Sketches of Bygone Exeter* (Exeter, 1908). For other drawings see Gray, *Lost Exeter*, 4-5.
77. DRO, city rates, St Edmund's parish, 1870, 1878-83, 1890.
78. *EFP*, 25 1 1882.
79. Crocker, *Sketches*, plate v.
80. Ethel Lega-Weekes, *Some Studies in the Topography of the Cathedral Close, Exeter* (Exeter, 1915), 142-6.
81. Daniel Radford, 'Working men's dwellings' (*DAT*, XXII, 1890), 140.
82. Edward Ashworth, 'Larkbear House', *Notes & Gleanings*, volume 2, p.109; Gilbert Venn, *Discovering Exeter: 2 St Leonard's* (Exeter, 1982), 17; DRO, St Leonard's rates, 1888-90.

83. *Exeter Pocket Journal*, 1889.
84. Cossins, *Reminiscences*, 53.
85. Newton, *Eighteenth Century Exeter*, 124-6; DRO, D5/133/1.
86. Cossins, *Reminiscences*, 57, 62.
87. Gray, *Exeter Engraved*, I, 98.
88. One resident of Chichester Place was concerned that renumbering of Southernhay in 1878 threatened the continuation of the place name: DRO, ECA 9/5, Streets Committee Minute Book , 1881-4, page 9.
89. *EFP*, 20 10 1825.
90. Bridget Cherry and Nikolaus Pevsner, *Devon* (1989), 431.
91. DRO, 55/6/40/1.
92. Lega-Weekes, *Cathedral Close Exeter*, 65.
93. Exeter Cathedral Archives, 3932, see rates for 1676, 1679, 1686, for Dr Bidgood.
94. It was still remembered as the Annuellers' House in the early 1800s: DRO, 55/6/40/2.
95. The range of buildings was acquired by Richard Weston, a London gentleman, in 1549 (ECA, 60001/1/1), then the lease was transferred to John Ridgeway of Torre in 1550 (6001/1/2-3). In 1585 John Dyer acquired the lease and renewed it in 1595 (6001/1/4-5), in 1607 Christopher Mainwaring took the lease and renewed it in 1624 (6001/1/6-9). In 1641 it was taken by John Baldwyn and it passed to his executrix Ann Short, and her husband John, by 1661 (6001/1/12, 6002/12/4). John Short assigned the lease to his sister Dorothy in 1665 and surrendered the lease three years later (6001/1/13-14). From 1668 to 1682 it was leased by John Bidgood (6001/15-19) and by 1699 he had died and the lease passed to Edmund Drewe, George Snell, John Cholwich, John Snell and Nicholas Oliver (6001/1/20). Their lease then passed to another John Bidgood in 1708 (6001/1/21-2). For a short while it passed to Robert Prowse, an Exeter merchant, (6001/1/23-5) before being acquired by William Clare, Abel Moyle and Robert Pearce sometime before 1716 (6002/8/5). They renewed their lease (6001/1/35) and by 1716 Ann Worth had taken the property (6002/8/5 & 6001/1/35). She surrendered that lease in 1726 (6001/1/30-1). By this date Worth had sublet part of the range, namely Number One, to Mrs Wilday who began Mol's Coffee House. Two plans exist for the late eighteenth century (6001/3/7a & 6001/3/15). See DRO, 55/6/40/1-2 for abstracts of title to the property from the late eighteenth century until the 1830s.
96. A. Jenkins, *Civil and Ecclesiastical History of the City of Exeter* (Exeter, 1806), 314.
97. James Crocker published a drawing of the building, with the new coat of arms, with the date 1879. In 1886 he noted that the new coats of arms were a 'modern innovation' which were redone 'in the past few months': Crocker, *Sketches*, plate 26. See also Lega-Weekes, *Some studies*, 64.
98. Cossins, *Reminiscences*, 41-2; Jenkins, *Exeter*, 314.
99. Hoskins, *Exeter*, 89.
100. Hazel Harvey, *Exeter Past* (Chichster, 1996), 37 and most recently, *Express & Echo*, 11 3 2003.
101. Maurice H. Bradley, *Railway Modeller*, January 1981, page 9; *Express & Echo*, 22 7 1982.
102. See Agnes Latham and Joyce Youings (eds), *The Letters of Sir Walter Raleigh* (Exeter, 1999), 135-53.
103. Above the door is proudly written 'Next to mine own shippe, I love most that old ship in Exon. A tavern in St Martin's Lane'.
104. Crocker, *Sketches*, plate xxvi.
105. *Worth's Exeter Guide Book* (Exeter, c.1890), 78-90; A copy of the postcard is in the Devon & Exeter Institution postcard collection. On the postcard of Mol's he wrote 'Mol's Coffee House, Exeter, dated 1580. Now Worth's Art Gallery. Containing the old Club Room where Raleigh, Drake, Gilbert and other Armada heroes formerly met'.
106. *Exeter Now and Then* (Exeter, 1945), 21.
107. Report on the Records of the City of Exeter (Historical Manuscripts Commission, 1916), 64.
108. ECA, 6001/1/3-5 & 6001/1/12. Dyer's original lease is dated 9 10 1585.
109. ECA, 6002/12/4 & 6002/8/5.
110. ECA, 6001/1/5, lease of Christopher Mainwaring, 26 12 1607.
111. ECA, 6002/12/4.
112. Personal communication with Richard Parker.
113. Pevsner and Cherry, *Devon*, 426.
114. Jenkins, *Exeter*, 314.
115. Crocker, *Sketches*, 26.
116. Worth, *Exeter*, 80.
117. Beatrix Cresswell, *Rambles in Old Exeter* (Exeter, 1927), 63.
118. W. G. H., 'Mol's Coffee House', *Devon & Cornwall Notes & Queries*, volume 21, page 25.
119. Hoskins noted an entry in a rate for St Martin's parish on 23 September 1595 but the building is within the Close. Interestingly, a collection of rates for that month does not include Mol in St Martin's parish or in the city: Margery M. Rowe (ed.), *Tudor Exeter* (Devon & Cornwall Record Society, 1977, New Series 22), 73-7.
120. *The Post Master or the Loyal Mercury*, 21 6 1723.
121. *The Post Master or the Loyal Mercury*, 19 3 1725.
122. Helen Berry, 'Rethinking Politeness in Eighteenth-Century England: Moll King's Coffee House and the Significance of Flash Talk' (*Transactions of the Royal Historical Society*, 6th series, 2001), 65-82. I am grateful to Mrs Audrey Erskine for drawing my attention to this article.
123. *EFP*, 6 12 1787.
124. *EPG*, 23 9 1854.
125. Andrew Brice, *The Mobiad* (Exeter, 1770), 50.
126. Devon & Cornwall Record Society Library, marriage register of Exeter Cathedral, 23 12 1656.
127. Hoskins, *Exeter in the seventeenth century*, 13, 16, 56, 57.
128. Hoskins, *Exeter in the seventeenth century*, 115.
129. *The Post Master or the Loyal Mercury*, 12 3 1725.
130. In 1797 Emmanuel Grigg opened a coffee house in Exeter in 1797, Owen MacDonald ran the City Coffee House in 1814 and in Plymouth the Navy and Army Coffee House and Tavern was opened by Sarah Kingswell in 1779: *EFP*, 12 1797, 13 10 1814, 2 7 1779.
131. ECA, 3564, pages 458-9. See also 6002/8/5 and 6001/1/30-1.
132. *Brice's Weekly Journal*, 30 12 1726.
133. ECA, 6001/1/30-1. Ann Worth surrendered a lease from 1716 on 20 June 1726.
134. DRO, 55/6/40/2.
135. DRO, ECA/159b, 1732 rate for The Close.
136. DRO, DD50198. I am grateful to Tony Collings for this reference.
137. *EFP*, 6 12 1787.
138. ECA, 6001/3/7a.

139. See *EFP*, 24 11 1777, 2 11 1781, 6 12 1787, 5 11 1789, 8 11 1810, 22 5 1817, 16 9 1819, 30 3 1820, 2 12 1824, 22 2 1827, 6 8 1829, 18 10 1832.
140. Curiously, in 1827 one Mrs Andrews, who had run the King John's Tavern on South Street, advertised she was taking over the business but it appears this did not happen: *EFP*, 22 2 1827.
141. DRO, D7/409/17-27.
142. Cossins, *Reminiscences*, 42, 52.
143. By 1820 the Institution offered local papers: *EFP*, 10 8 1820.
144. Newton, *Victorian Exeter*, 14.
145. Cossins, *Reminiscences*, 41-2.
146. *EFP*, 12 8 1847. See also 28 5 1883.
147. DRO, St Sidwell rates, 1853 & 1854. Only the fields are shown on the tithe map of 1842: DRO, St Sidwell tithe map.
148. DRO, city rates, 1880, 1890.
149. DRO, city rates, 1880, 1881.
150. *EPG*, 8 4 1854, 26 11 1853 and *WT*, 1 4 1854.
151. Robert Newton, *Victorian Exeter, 1837-1914* (Leicester, 1968), 174.
152. *EFP*, 31 1 1883.
153. WSL, census returns, St Sidwell parish, 1851, 1861, 1871.
154. DRO, voters' list, 1881.
155. *Exeter Pocket Journal*, 1884-5, 1889, 1895, 1905, 1906, 1916; DRO, city rates, 1880, 1890.
156. See WSL, p&d06886.
157. WSL, map collection. See endpapers in Gray, *Exeter Engraved*, I & II.
158. Pevsner and Cherry, *Devon*, 425-6.
159. See WSL, p&d 06889.
160. Two topographical drawings have survived: WSL, p&d08622 & 08621.
161. *EFP*, 11 June 1825.
162. *Exeter Pocket Journal*, 1828.
163. *Exeter Pocket Journal*, 1830, 1832.
164. *EFP*, 19 3 1876.
165. Census records show the three lived together from 1841 to 1871. Tucker's housekeeper was eighteen years his junior.
166. *The Illustrated London News*, 1868 (2), 52.
167. *Exeter and Plymouth Gazette*, 2 8 1867.
168. *Exeter Pocket Books*, 1868, 1869.
169. Cossins, *Reminiscences*, 24.
170. *Mortimer's Handbook and Directory for Exeter* (1874).
171. WSL, census 1871, St Olave's parish.
172. *West of England and Exeter Pocket Journal*, 1867.
173. I am grateful to Charlie Page for these references.
174. He was last noted in the Exeter Voters' List in 1953: WSL, Voters' Lists.
175. Harold Murray, *Kaleidoscope: an old journalist's snapshots* (1946), 96.
176. These included *Press, Pulpit and Pew*, *Sixty years an Evangelist*, *Boys of Sancotes*, and *True Soldiers*.
177. Murray, *Kaleidoscope: an old journalist's snapshots*, 97.
178. Cherry and Pevsner, *Devon*, 397.
179. *EFP*, 25 2 1880.
180. *WT*, 14 1 1949.
181. William Harding, 'An account of some of the ancient ecclesiastical edifices of Exeter', *TEDAS*, IV, 1853, 111.
182. Cherry and Pevsner, *Devon*, 424.
183. *WT*, 4 2 1949.
184. *WT*, 3 6 1949.
185. DRO, ECA 12/15, 11 3 1946.
186. Gray, *Lost Exeter*, 18-19.
187. Cherry and Pevsner, *Devon*, 393.